≋ OMNIGENDER

OMNIGENDER

a trans-religious approach

VIRGINIA RAMEY MOLLENKOTT

THE
PILGRIM
PRESS

Cleveland, Ohio

This book is dedicated with love
to my immediate family:
Suzannah
Paul and Barbara
Miranda, Sarina,
and the third grandchild due in April 2001.
Starting with them, I seek to
enact love
toward God, Her world, and
all the creatures in it.

The Pilgrim Press, Cleveland, Ohio 44115
www.pilgrimpress.com
Copyright © 2001 Virginia Ramey Mollenkott.

Grateful acknowledgment for permission to reprint from the following: Thorkild
Jacobsen, *The Treasures of Darkness: A History of Mesopotamian Religion* (New Haven:
Yale University Press, 1976). Copyright © 1976 Yale University Press. • William O.
Beeman, "What Are You? Male, Merm, Herm, Ferm, or Female?" *Baltimore Sun*, 17
March 1996. • Roz Kaveny, "Talking Transgender Politics," *Reclaiming Genders:
Transsexual Grammars at the Fin de Siècle*, ed. Kate More and Stephen Whittle (New
York: Cassell, 1999). Copyright © 1999 Cassell.

Printed in the United States of America on acid-free paper

06   05   04   03   02   01   5   4   3   2   1

Library of Congress Cataloging-in-Publication Data

Mollenkott, Virginia R.
      Omnigender : a trans-religious approach / Virginia Ramey Mollenkott.
      p.   cm.
      Includes bibliographical references.
      ISBN 0-8298-1422-1 (alk. paper)
      1.Transvestism—Religious aspects—Christianity   2. Transvestism—Religious
aspects—Comparative studies.   3. Transsexualism—Religious aspect—Christianity.   4. Transsexualism—Religious aspects—Comparative studies.   I. Title.

BR115.T76 M65   2001
261.8'3576—dc21   2001021114

≋ Contents

≋ Preface

AS A CHILD AND YOUNG WOMAN, I was taught that if I wanted to please God and humanity, my place was secondary and my role supportive. There was no question that the binary gender paradigm of two opposite sexes was the proper context—indeed, the only context—within which to think and live ethically. Even when I was arguing that the Bible supports male-female equality in the 1977 edition of my *Women, Men, and the Bible* (Nashville: Abingdon, 1977), I was unable to lift myself free of the confines of gender duality. There, and in my book about biblical imagery of God as female, *The Divine Feminine* (New York: Crossroad, 1983), I argued that human language about God needs feminine as well as masculine analogies because God, being spirit, is neither masculine nor feminine and *every human being is both.* That latter phrase, and also my encouragement of nature analogies for God, pointed toward liberation from the cognitive prison of *either-or*, a male versus female dualism. However, a gender paradigm shift had certainly not occurred to me. This book is my attempt to move beyond the binary gender construct in order to set forth a new gender paradigm, which seeks to include and offer liberation to everyone who has been oppressed by the old model.

Thanks to a remark by Mary McClintock Fulkerson[1] of Duke Divinity School, I began to think that perhaps the baptismal for-

---

1. Mary McClintock Fulkerson, "Gender—Being It or Doing It? The Church, Homosexuality, and the Politics of Identity," *Que(e)rying Religion: A Critical Anthology*, ed. Gary David Comstock and Susan E. Henking (New York: Continuum, 1997), 189, 199.

mula recorded in Galatians 3:28 could and should be taken literally: in Christ "no male and female." Previously, I had taken "no
male and female" to mean only that the social and political advantages of being male in patriarchal cultures were to be shared equitably with females within the New Creation. But Professor Fulkerson
jarred me into realizing that all the people whose bodily experience
is marginalized or erased by gender and orientational dualities would
be represented if only the statement were interpreted literally.

It's worth noticing that the three statements in Galatians 3:28
about the New Creation's transcendence of race/ethnicity, class, and
gender are not precisely parallel in the Greek text. This lack of
parallelism is reflected in the *New Revised Standard Version* translation: "There is no longer Jew or Greek, there is no longer slave or
free, there is no longer male and female; for all of you are one in
Christ Jesus." If there is any meaning to be found in that grammatical shift from *or* to *and*, what might it be? Does it reflect a belief that
women and men are so necessary to one another that *or* cannot be
spoken, because without either there could be no humankind, a
fact Paul emphasized in 1 Corinthians 11:11–12? And does it point
toward a time when instead of separate gender obligations, both
physical maleness-femaleness and masculine-feminine social roles
will be recognized as a continuum on which individuals may locate
themselves comfortably and without fear of reprisal? At any rate, I
concur with Professor Fulkerson that "it is time to read Galatians
3:28 with a new literalness, admitting that we are all performing
our sex/gender."

Stone Butch Blues, Leslie Feinberg's novel about working-class
lesbians, describes the feelings of some masculine women who were
forced to wear dresses to gain admission to the funeral of one of
their closest friends. They felt great consternation because these
"butches" sensed that they looked totally out of place in dresses.
They felt foolish, unattractive, inappropriate, and humiliated, but
they did what they had to do in order to pay last respects to one of
their own. That scene brought floods of memories back to me, memories of years of being forced to wear clothes that did not match my
sense of myself. For the first time, I understood experientially something about what it means to be transgendered.

I can now acknowledge that to the degree I feel myself to be a masculine woman, I am transgendered. *Not* transsexual. I feel myself to be female all right, but masculine at the same time, so that dresses and skirts feel rather ridiculous—and this despite the fact that as a child I was not allowed to wear overalls, shorts, or pants. I played with the boys a great deal, and I defended my older brother with my fists, but always I was wearing a skirt. One of the greatest benefits of coming out publicly as lesbian was that I could go through my closets and give away all my dresses and skirts except for a few Gertrude Stein-ish floor-length skirts that somehow seemed less of an affront to my nature.

Sometimes I wonder why it took Leslie Feinberg's novel to stimulate my awareness that the binary gender construct had been oppressing me all my life. But then, that's the function of a paradigm: It provides the frame of reference within which we think, live, move, and have our being—until some event or pressure forces a gap that opens the way to larger, more liberated thoughts.

Stone Butch Blues was the catalyst that released my energy to study transgender issues. I wanted to find out what they might teach me about myself, society, and "normal" genderedness. I read the novel in 1996 and since then have been talking with transgendered people and reading everything I could concerning transgender, intersexual, and transsexual experience. Of course, these three years of study have taken place against the background of my longtime and ongoing commitment to lesbian, gay, and bisexual liberation. I published a book with Letha Dawson Scanzoni entitled *Is the Homosexual My Neighbor? A Positive Christian Response* (San Francisco: Harper & Row, 1978), which was revised and vastly expanded in 1994. *Sensuous Spirituality: Out from Fundamentalism* (New York: Crossroad, 1992) discusses my lesbianism and some of my spiritual practices. So this current book is an extension, a logical outgrowth of a trajectory I have been traveling all my life.

What I have learned from my most recent studies is that gender normality is a myth as long as it is forced to locate itself within a binary paradigm that fits very few members of the human race. I am not the only person who limited, shrank, and truncated aspects of myself in an attempt to fit that paradigm. Millions have done the same; and some have killed themselves or been murdered because of their inability to pass gender muster. Many transgender youngsters have run away from home or been evicted by their parents, have lived on the streets and been used by predatory adults, and have become HIV positive. Others have been institutionalized for no other reason than their inability to satisfy society's gender expectations.

So much pain. So much waste of human potential. It cannot continue!

What society has constructed, society can also deconstruct and reconstruct. The goal is worthwhile: to learn from the facts of human sexuality and genderedness and to develop attitudes that match those facts and, thus, alleviate human pain. Although I have written books arguing the human equality of females and males and homosexuals and heterosexuals, I now understand that no matter how liberationist the context may be, as long as these terms are handled in a binary fashion, they continue to reinforce the dominant gender paradigm. This book is my attempt to break out of a system that has worked only by silencing the outcries of millions and to move instead toward a new, omnigender paradigm.

In researching and writing this book, I am grateful to all the people who have helped me find resources, have told me about their own lives, have written concerning sex and gender issues, and have encouraged me in my work. Prominent among them have been Timothy G. Staveteig, publisher at the Pilgrim Press, and my supportive and efficient editor, George R. Graham. Especially, I am grateful to Letha Dawson Scanzoni for her word processing and indexing assistance, and to Debra Lynn Morrison for our good years together and for the expert financial planning that made my retirement comfortable enough that I could be free to do this work.

Above all, I am grateful to Suzannah Tilton for the loving companionship she has provided for my senior years, for her cograndparenting our delightful grandchildren, and for her willingness to participate in a holy relationship.

CHAPTER ONE

≋ *The Gender Crisis*

WESTERN SOCIETY IS currently involved in a crisis of gender definition. Throughout all the centuries of heteropatriarchy, the concept of two opposite sexes has served as a boundary to hold in place the established patterns of power. The binary gender construct has dictated that real males must be naturally drawn to those attitudes, behaviors, and roles any given society considers "masculine," including sexual attraction to females only. And real females must be naturally drawn to those attitudes, behaviors, and roles any given society considers "feminine," including sexual attraction to males only. Any person who deviates from these standards is a gender transgressor, outside the pale of genuine humanity, undeserving of full human consideration. The binary gender construct is assumed to be The Way Things Ought to Be—the order of creation, the will of God, unchangeable and beyond question.

So what's wrong with the time-honored concept that men are men and women are women and *viva la difference*? Plenty.

In the first place, the binary gender construct ignores or contradicts factual reality. Many heterosexual men are *not* drawn to "masculine" attitudes, behaviors, and roles; and many heterosexual women are *not* drawn to "feminine" behaviors, attitudes, and roles. Bisexual and homosexual women and men are *not* attracted exclusively to the "opposite" sex. As many as four percent of all births are intersexual—babies with indeterminate genitals or with both male and female genitals, sometimes internal and difficult to discover.[1]

---

1. Martine Aliana Rothblatt, *The Apartheid of Sex: A Manifesto on the Freedom of Gender* (New York: Crown, 1995), 9.

Some people with apparently normal male bodies sense themselves to be female; some people with female bodies sense themselves to be male; and these people are willing to cross-dress permanently and use hormonal and /or surgical means to become or "pass" as the gender they feel themselves to be. Some people sense that they are heterosexual but "two-spirited" or "bigendered," so they cross-dress periodically in order to express all aspects of their nature. And some "two-spirited" people are homosexual or bisexual. Some people look like "normal" males or females but are chromosomally different from the statistical norm of XX for females and XY for males. Differences in hormone levels and in how the cells of some newborns have re-sisted or responded to hormones prenatally can also be factors in what is often called gender ambiguity. Because common speech of-ten confuses *biological* categories with gender-*assignment*, gender-*identity*, and gender-*expression*, enormous diversity is possible. I do not doubt that there are people who would read through this para-graph and still not find an adequate description of themselves; for their sake, I will add a category of "otherwise." In the face of so much diversity, it is no wonder that the binary gender paradigm is in the process of collapse.

In the second place, societies vary radically in their understand-ings of what constitutes "masculinity" and "femininity" (that is, in their gender *roles*). As I pointed out in *Women, Men, and the Bible*, one multicultural study found that in 12 societies, men carry the heavy burdens, but in 57 societies, women do; in 158 societies, women do the cooking, but in 5 societies, men do; in 95 societies, the making and repairing of clothes is women's work; but in 12 so-cieties, men do it; in 14 societies, women build the houses, but in 86 societies men do the building.[2] And anthropologist Margaret

---

2. See discussion in Virginia Mollenkott, *Women, Men, and the Bible*, rev. ed. (New York: Crossroad, 1988), 62. The study cited was reported by Roy G. D'Andrade, "Sex Differences and Cultural Institutions," in *The Development of Sex Differences*, ed. Eleanor Maccoby (Stanford, Calif.: Stanford University Press, 1966), 174–204. In *The Myths of Gender* (New York: Basic Books, 1992),

Mead reported finding that in one New Guinea tribe, the ideal temperament for both males and females was gentleness; in a second tribe, it was aggressiveness; and in a third tribe, the ideal for males was dependence and affectionate sensitivity, while the ideal for females was aggressive dominance.[3] Such variations are enough to prove that there is no universally uniform innate "masculinity" and "femininity" and, therefore, that those concepts neither follow any universal natural law nor constitute the will of God.

In the third place, the social construction of gender has not been even-handed about the assignment of roles and rewards. We westerners tend to think hierarchically, and when there are dualities we prefer one over the other: thin rather than fat, young rather than old, light rather than dark, heterosexual rather than homosexual. Gender is no exception. Although most of our contemporaries might deny preferring boys to girls, males to females, the traditional assignment of males to the more powerful roles of the public sphere and females to the more supportive roles of the private sphere has brought with it a host of inequities. Money, prestige, influence, and honor are accorded to those who function publicly; but domestic work is hardly respected as work, let alone financially rewarded. No one could possibly cram into one book the tremendous research documenting gender injustice. But such injustice renders urgent the need for a new gender pluralism, a nonhierarchical omnigender paradigm.

Anne Fausto-Sterling comments that "the division of labor by sex embodies a seeming contradiction: it is a human universal but it has no universal meaning. Instead each culture has its own particular division of labor by sex . . . and attaches to it its own set of interpretations. . . . It seems then that we can extract meaning only by examining that division in a particular social setting. . . . [T]here is no single undisputed claim about universal behavior (sexual or otherwise). The notion of a naked human essence is meaningless because human behavior acquires significance only in a particular social context" (198).

3. Margaret Mead, *Sex and Temperament in Three Primitive Societies* (New York: Morrow Quill, 1935).

But Isn't Our Society Sufficiently Aware of Gender Issues?

Many people may assume that in combination, the women's movement and the movement for gay, lesbian, and bisexual civil rights have already accomplished all the gender-related consciousness raising that is necessary. Three recent sources should be sufficient to prove otherwise: first, a 1999 handbook for girls published worldwide by Pocket Books; second, a current entry from a Christian Web site on the Internet; and third, a 1997 theology of sexuality.

The 1999 handbook is called *Deal with It! A Whole New Approach to Your Body, Brain, and Life as a Gurl* by Esther Drill, Heather McDonald, and Rebecca Odes. In many ways, this book is a marvelous gift to teen and pre-teen girls: It speaks straightforwardly about everything from the basics of nutrition to drugs to beliefs to money. But in the sections about girls' (and boys') body parts, there is no mention of the fact that some babies are born intersexual (hermaphroditic); the treatment of sexuality is inclusive about bisexuality, homosexuality, preserving virginity, birth control, pregnancy, how to avoid AIDS, and other hot topics, but says not one word about transsexuality; the pages about defining oneself say nothing about transgender identities; the pages on homophobia fail to mention its most virulent aspect—genderphobia or transphobia; the pages on family life deal well with conflicts but never mention the conflicts of and about intersexual or transgender children or even conflicts over gender roles. The one page concerning Gay Rights mentions nothing about transgender rights, the most threatened of all, so far not even included in the pending Employment Non-Discrimination Act. The section on "being yourself and fitting in" contains just one Web site complaint about being called "tomboy"(because of basketball skills) and nothing about androgynous or "masculine" behaviors or clothing. And no resources are listed that serve specifically transgender youth, who more than any others are in danger for their lives. The authors might reply that their target readers are "normal" girls, and I admit that their book is chock-full of information I'd love to have had when I was twelve or thirteen. But it would be a lonely and perhaps frightening experience to read this book as a consciously transgender girl—left out from even a source as inclusive as this one. The ignoring of transgender issues causes *Deal with It!* to seem to support the binary gender construct.

The Christian Internet Web site belongs to the Intersex Support Group International (ISGI) at <http://www.isgi.org>. Their manifesto expresses faith in "our Creator and Lord, Jesus Christ" and declares that "the many consequences of fallen nature, including the conditions now designated as intersexual, are the damaged result of what was God's perfect creation." Yet the manifesto later contradicts this declaration by claiming that "We know that God made no mistake when He made us. We are His unique creation."

The ISGI has the laudable goals of providing a counseling network "for the physical, mental, and spiritual wellbeing of intersexuals and their families" and praying for "persons around the earth who daily must battle against a world which made no place for those with congenital physical/sexual/self identities, real babies, real children, real adults whose physical bodies simply do not conform to female or male." But apparently ISGI leadership does not realize the drastic disrespect involved in classifying intersexuals as the damaged results of human sinfulness. I profoundly believe the ISGI is right to say that God made no mistake by creating intersexuals. Therefore, their condition represents God's perfect will for them and for our culture; in no way are they "damaged goods." They are here to walk the path of their eternal Selves and to teach the rest of us some important lessons.

The theology of sexuality is L. J. Tessier's *Dancing after the Whirlwind: Feminist Reflections on Sex, Denial, and Spiritual Transformation* (Boston: Beacon Press, 1997). Although this work is inclusive of heterosexual, bisexual, and homosexual identities, there is not a word about intersexuals, transsexuals, or transgenderists—not even in the section on Hindu eroticism, where Tessier acknowledges that "each human body contains both male and female elements" and that these, through sexo-yogic practice, might "unite into the nondual state of Absolute Reality" (83). The word *gender* to Tessier apparently refers simply to male versus female, so that even in recognizing the "union of male and female" as the earliest symbol for "the union of all forces," she sees that union exclusively as sexual intercourse. Thus, she misses the opportunity to affirm the people among us whose identity is literally both male and female and therefore powerfully symbolic of ultimate, nondualistic reality. Although *Dancing after the Whirlwind* is an excellent exploration of how denying sexuality harms spiritual identity, it too winds up supporting the binary concept of "opposite" sexes.

Such support is particularly unfortunate in an author able to understand that "the relationship between sexuality and spirituality is transformed when creation is understood as an act of the One in copulation with Itself. . . . In this cosmogonic vision, creation comes about from the self-expression (which is also the divine union) of primordial male and female forces—from this conjunction (*purusa* and *prokrit*) all things arise" (81). I think of the intensely sexual imagery of God's creation of the world in the great Puritan epic *Paradise Lost*, and of John Milton, its 17th century author, who understood his own creativity to be stemming from the androgynous holy Muse who impregnated him nightly through his ear. That same Milton was not ashamed to tell his third wife that at Christ's College, Cambridge, his classmates had sometimes called him "Our Lady of Christ's."[4] How much healthier his omnigender vision than the current simplistic opposition of male and female!

So however much gender-related consciousness raising has already occurred, it is far from enough. If people are ever going to be free to embody and enact the precise gender-blend they sense themselves to be, they need to be aware of the range of human possibilities—as Milton demonstrated and as I have attempted to present in this book.

Gender as a Social Construct

In order to clarify the meaning of the social construction of gender, it is necessary to do a little repeating: Namely, that many, if not most, people assume that attraction to appropriate gender roles, appearances, presentations, and sexual desires follow naturally upon

---

4. Mollenkott, "Some Implications of Milton's Androgynous Muse," *Bucknell Review* 24 (spring 1978): 27–36.

possession of a penis or a vagina at birth. Normal boys are born with a masculine essence that leads them naturally toward a preference for whatever our society considers properly masculine toys and eventually toward "masculine" gender roles, gender presentations, and the heterosexual orientation. Normal girls naturally develop in a "feminine" direction that is the perfect complement to the male of the species. These are *essentialist* assumptions based on the idea that there are such things as universal and eternal "masculinity" and "femininity," not only embodied in real people within space and time but also existing on some other more abstract spiritual level, like that of Platonic ideas.

By contrast, a *construct* is a useful fiction developed in order to summarize masses of facts or to formulate theories that explain a configuration of facts. When historians write about the "mood" of a certain nation at a certain time, they are engaging in a *construct*. There is nothing in objective reality to correspond to the historians' precise naming of the mood, and in order to achieve that common denominator they may be slightly distorting the attitudes and behaviors of millions of people. Nevertheless, the abstraction may be a useful one for understanding that certain place and time; it may even provide a central unifying theme for an entire treatise.

By logical extension, then, a *social construct* is a useful fiction that is devised to aid in analyzing and understanding certain sets of social phenomena.[5] But like any other construct, a social construct can outlive its usefulness if the exceptions begin to outweigh the advantages achieved from the central abstraction. In this book, I am opposing the essentialist notion that assumes an eternal polarization between female and male, femininity and masculinity. I am instead asserting that *male = masculine, female = feminine,* and *normal = heterosexual* form a bipolar social construct that has seemed accurate only because so many were intimidated into making silent efforts to conform to it. This binary gender construct has outrun its usefulness because of the massive damage it is doing to real human lives.

---

5. See Alan Bullock and Oliver Stallybrass, *The Harper Dictionary of Modern Thought* (New York: Harper & Row, 1977), 578, 133, and 213–14.

Within modern thought, especially within gender studies, there has been a great deal of conflict between *essentialists* and social *constructionists*. Is it possible, for instance, to call a person *homosexual* if she or he lived prior to the medical model that first designated that term a little more than a century ago? I think Lillian Faderman has gotten the answer right in her 1999 book *To Believe in Women: What Lesbians Have Done for America* (New York: Houghton Mifflin, 1999). The answer is that she has in practice come down somewhere between pure essentialism and constructionism. If a woman chose to live all or most of her life outside of heterosexual marriage, made her home with another woman with whom she shared romance, drew her energy from other women, and worked to better the lot of womankind, Faderman is content to call her *lesbian* whether or not she would have known or accepted the term. But at the same time, Faderman constantly emphasizes the enormous impact of the medical model that constructed "healthy femininity" in such a way as to stigmatize unmarried and/or assertive women, oppose women's rights, and discourage women from seeking higher education. In other words, Faderman demonstrates that it is possible to situate oneself as neither totally essentialist nor totally constructionist. Like many other binaries, this one is too simplistic.

People who dislike my proposal of an omnigender social construct will no doubt do so out of loyalty to the idea that there really is an essential feminine and masculine binary that is either God's will or nature's perpetual norm or both. Ironically, they will cling to this essentialist gender construct by denying that gender *is* socially constructed in any way. And I wonder to what degree such people understand what social constructs are and the way they work. It was, for instance, a social construct propagated by Hitler that made heterosexual blond-haired blue-eyed "Aryan" people normative and others disposable. Yet that social construct was powerful enough to cause otherwise decent people either to commit or condone acts of unspeakable brutality.

For another instance, in the early twentieth century, Wilhelm Stekel helped popularize an invented category, *frigidity*, to construct the notion that women who will not/do not reach orgasm exclusively through vaginal penetration are unnatural women who refuse to take their rightful place as submissive and conquered individuals. Since the majority of women do not climax through penetration alone, myriads of women were humiliated and myriads of marriages disrupted by this erroneous social construct.[6] Closely related was the Victorian idea that good religious women are free from passion, as opposed to the carnality of men.[7] *That* social construct sent many worried women to their doctors, some of whom performed clitorectomies in order to help the women in their attempt to make their experience conform to the false abstraction!

For yet another illustration, Serena Nanda points out that in India, an impotent male is understood to be a eunuch, a third sex, a third gender. Sexual and reproductive capacity are so important in defining who is man and who is woman that a man who dresses and acts like a woman is still a man; but if and when his genitals are removed, he becomes neither man nor woman but third gender. Hinduism, Jainism, and other Indian religions have long upheld this social construct. But in Brazil, the construct is very different: Men who penetrate women or other men are defined as men, whereas men who permit themselves to be penetrated are women.[8]

In American and British gender studies, it has been largely transsexual experience that has caused many "gendered and heterosexist social constructs [to] collapse like cardboard seawalls against the ocean of [peoples'] transsexual reality."[9] For instance, when Jamison Green was a woman, she was part of lesbian culture, and people who subscribe to gender polarity understood her to be disobeying the immutable laws of God and nature by loving other women. But when Jamison Green had transitioned through sex reassignment surgery, he became a heterosexual man. Is he now an embodiment

---

6. Lisa Isherwood, "Body Politics: A Theological Issue?" in *Religion and Sexuality*, ed. Michael A. Hayes, Wendy Porter, and David Townes (Sheffield, England: Sheffield Academic Press, 1998), 355–56.

7. Reay Tannahill, *Sex in History* (New York: Stein & Day, 1982), 352.

8. Serena Nanda, *Neither Man nor Woman: The Hijras of India* (Belmont, Calif.: Wadsworth, 1999), 141.

9. Jamison Green, "Look! No, Don't! The Visibility Dilemma for Transsexual Men," in *Reclaiming Genders: Transsexual Grammars at the* Fin de Siècle, ed. Kate More and Stephen Whittle (New York: Cassell, 1999), 128.

of an immutable and eternal masculine essence? Of course not; his/her own history disproves that. Should Green be permitted the privileges of heterosexual marriage? Yes. He has earned them, and every human being has the right to an honorable partnership. But since Mr. Green used to be Ms. Green, wouldn't his marriage undercut the binary construct's insistence that marriage must remain available only to one man and one woman? Yes. Jamison Green's existence, and that of thousands like him, asks society to move toward acceptance of the gender diversity of humankind.

Transsexual experience also demonstrates the sense in which sex and even bodies can be said to be socially constructed. If, for instance, a pre-operative transsexual woman feels herself to be a man, she will be able to achieve sexual orgasm chiefly through "imaginary participation" in a body part she does not actually possess. For many transsexuals, there is such a "radical discontinuity between sexual pleasures and bodily parts"[10] that a mental deconstruction and reconstruction of their own body becomes necessary. But to a lesser degree, bodily reconfiguration frequently occurs within our human perceptions. Consider for instance the change that comes over people as they progress from acquaintance into friendship and from friendship into passionate love. The growth of desire for another person can seem to transform even the configuration of their faces and bodies. What at first seemed ugly or misshapen, too large or too small, can come to seem positively beautiful.

Anyone who is not able to appear to be a normal male or female—any obviously transgender person—is the best illustration of the ways in which gender and bodies are social constructs. Here, as in so many other areas of life, the exceptions unmask the norm for what it is.

I once had a dear friend, long since deceased, who had been heterosexually married for most of her life. In her youth she had been given hormones to curb tendencies toward lesbianism. Although she was female born and bred, she often looked like a flamboyant drag queen because of her extremely "feminine" makeup, clothing,

---

10. Judith Butler, *Gender Trouble: Feminism and the Subversion of Identity* (New York: Routledge, 1990), 70.

and body language. She once confided that she had been forced to learn how to perform womanhood. But so, in a sense, has every "normal" woman been forced to learn the roles and appearances of "femininity," just as every "normal" man has been forced to learn how to perform "masculinity."

By contrast, transgender people are "the exception, the strange, that gives us the clue to how the mundane and taken-for-granted world of sexual meanings is constructed." By refusing (or being unable) to perform society's expected gender roles and presentations, by falling outside of the "normal" male-female polarity, transgender people reveal that "the taken-for-granted world of sexual categorization [is] a constructed one, indeed . . . one that might well be constructed differently."[11]

Several studies of female college student experience will demonstrate the power of social constructs in the area of sexuality. In 1938, Dorothy Bromley and Florence Britten published their study of thirteen hundred college women, only four percent of whom were willing to admit to same-sex love experiences. But in a comparable study conducted in 1920 by Katherine B. Davis, over forty percent of the respondents reported they'd had "intense emotional relations" with other women; and among those born in the late nineteenth century (i.e., who were in their thirties when they responded to Davis's questions), over forty-six percent said they'd had sexual experiences to express that intense emotion. What could possibly account for a forty-two percent drop in same-sex college romance in less than two decades?

Bromley and Britten's disapproval of same-sex love might have encouraged some of their respondents to deny same-sex experiences they had actually had. But society's pathologizing of lesbianism in the late 1920s and '30s and the opprobrium heaped on unmarried women ("amazons," "intellectual tomboys," "pseudo-masculine," "mental hermaphrodites," etc.) would have been the overwhelming factor.[12] I realize that some people might consider what I've just described to be a good and positive use of a social construct to curb

---

11. Ibid., 110.
12. Faderman, *To Believe in Women*, 248–49.

lesbianism. But if church leaders believe what they teach about God's sovereignty and omnipresence and human responsibility and freedom, then such external and artificial constraints to human development are nothing short of tragic.

The Threatening Nature of the Issue

If the idea of so much fluidity seems disturbing, join the club. Recently when I had been speaking about omnigender at an interreligious seminary in New York City, a young person I had assumed was male entered the discussion by remarking, "I am a lesbian woman whom most people identify as male. And yet I feel frightened by what you are saying. From our earliest moments of life we are defined as either male or female, and I dread the confusion that would occur if people in general were not able to define one another by clear gender-markers and expectations." I could only agree with her. Until recently, I too have felt dismay when someone has called me "sir"; displaced when one of my male students told me he was inwardly female, a pre-operative transsexual; bewildered when I could not ascertain whether the person across from me was male or female.

At a Unitarian Fellowship, a heterosexually married man seemed profoundly threatened by talk of omnigender. He emphasized that because choices require great investment of time and energy, gender rules are intended to ease human life by removing choice in those areas. According to him, approving of freedom in gender would place unbearable burdens on most people. I tried to suggest to him that as an affluent heterosexual white male, he might not be in a position to judge what would feel liberating to most people, but he was having none of it.

If even people in such liberal contexts recoil from an omnigender paradigm, it is not hard to predict the reactions of more traditionalist people. Later I will discuss in depth some of the religious objections that will inevitably arise.

Despite my own occasional confusion or dismay, this book represents an attempt to heed the voices of previously silenced people and provide evidence of urgent need. My goal is to convince readers that as uncomfortable as the transition may feel at times, it is necessary. Uncertainty and temporary feelings of displacement matter only a little compared to requiring people to spend their lives being less than (or different from) what they feel themselves to be.

When fellow human fulfillment and wholeness are at stake, surely our attitudes can bear some change! This ought to be especially true among the followers of either Jesus or the prophet Isaiah. It was from Isaiah 61 that Jesus read in the synagogue at Nazareth, claiming his own ministry as the fulfillment of Isaiah's words:

> The Spirit of Our God is upon me:
> because the Most High has anointed me
> to bring Good News to those who are poor.
> God has sent me to proclaim liberty to those held captive,
> recovery of sight to those who are blind,
> and release to those in prison—
> to proclaim the year of Our God's favor.
>
> (Luke 4:18–19, *The Inclusive New Testament*)[13]

Certainly our society's binary gender construct is bad news for millions of people—a prison for some, house arrest for others, poverty of self-esteem for many, invisibility for still others, and blindness for those of us who cannot see one another's constriction and suffering.

By no means, however, do I mean to imply that sex and gender prejudice are more serious than other oppressions so that we must read the words of Jesus as metaphors concerning only these issues. On the contrary—as will be seen later in this book when I will be joining Leslie Feinberg and other activists in asking for a coalition of all the "have nots" in order to seek justice with combined strength. Releasing those held captive to literal poverty or unjust imprisonment, or to racism, disability, lack of access to education, or whatever else may be the limiting factor in their lives is the proper work of those whose souls are alive, those who value the abundant freedom envisioned by Isaiah the prophet and by Jesus the Christ.

---

13. *The Inclusive New Testament* (Brentwood, Md.: Priests for Equality, 1996) is available from Priests for Equality, P.O. Box 5243, W. Hyattsville MD 20782-0243.

Becoming Part of the Process of Change

I am aware that some of my friends will consider this book yet another of my exercises in futility, since only what is eternal is real and the concerns of the body (such as sex and gender) are merely temporary and therefore illusory from the eternal point of view. As a matter of fact, I really do derive peace from knowing that I am an eternal being who is currently having human experiences. What seems to be my material body is valuable as a vehicle of communication but not at all the solid reality it appears to be. My actual body (which Paul calls "a spiritual body" in 1 Cor. 15:44) is an extension of God's loving mind and will therefore not die when my human remains are laid to rest. I feel very blessed to have come to the realization that it is within God's eternal consciousness that my consciousness has its being (Acts 17:28). But I do not agree that these realizations entitle me to float through life with no concern for what is happening to my apparent body, the bodies of others, and the planetary body we share.

In an ultimate sense, I believe that everything is working out as it should. I also know that I am part of the process that is causing things to work out as they should! So when my soul feels moved by self-awareness to study issues of sexual orientation and the construction of gender, I know that my work is cut out for me. Knowing that I am an actor in a Divine Comedy gives me peace as I go about my work. But human suffering provides the stimulus to work, rather than to sit around focusing exclusively on my own inner peace.

Furthermore, I believe that everyone has his or her own life-path chosen for purposes of maximum spiritual growth. If a person is born transsexual, intersexual, or homosexual, for instance, then precisely those experiences are perfect for the development of that particular soul. But that fact does not indicate that I should sit back passively while bigotry exacts huge penalties from such people. Because I, as a child of God, am a manifestation of God's Self, a part of God's process, I am to do whatever I can to lighten human burdens, confident that I could not deflect any soul from its authentic path even if I tried.

I believe that eventually every created being will give heartfelt assent to the glories of the New Creation as embodied in the Christ

(Phil. 2:9–11), known in other religions by other names: the corporate Messiah, for instance, or the Buddha nature. So every one of us will eventually come home. Ultimately, for instance, things will work out well for those who were sexually and/or physically abused as children—and for those who abused them. But that does not mean that during my human experience on Planet Earth, I am intended to be complacent about child abuse. As an *eternal* being, my depths can and should remain calmly joyful; but as a *human* being, I must not only attend to my personal responsibilities (such as paying my bills) but also to my communal responsibilities (such as trying to alleviate human pain). I need dual awareness—of my connection with eternity, certainly, but also of my human and global connectedness.

Some religious traditions have always emphasized the "afterlife" to the exclusion of life here and now. The joke when I was growing up in Protestant fundamentalism was that "some folks were so heavenly-minded that they were no earthly good." Imagine my surprise to find a similar attitude cropping up among those who believe in human liberation! Certain students of *A Course in Miracles*,[14] for instance, assume that because this world and the separated ego or body-centered personality are illusory, there is no need to protect the environment and no need to work on individual psychological problems. But the whole *A Course in Miracles* is aimed precisely at removing the blockages to Love (that is, correcting the damage caused by the separated ego's misinterpretations). Therefore, we can be sure that lack of concern for our environment—the universe, the planet, and all the creatures on it, including the human creatures—is in error. We cannot help anyone by giving ultimate credence to the world that fear and alienation have projected as ultimate reality. But we *can* help by opening ourselves to a change of perception. We can ask the Holy Spirit to help us recognize and honor the sacredness of every creature.

Although I am speaking in this book about binary gender "opposite sex" attitudes as social constructions, I want to reiterate that I

---

14. This is a psycho-spiritual course in taking responsibility for our own thoughts and learning to experience oneness with our Divine Source. See *A Course in Miracles*, 2d ed. (Glen Ellen, Calif.: The Foundation for Inner Peace, 1992).

am not taking sides in the widespread debate of essentialism versus social constructionism. I consider either of these positions in their purest forms to be not only dualistic, but reductionist. Having yawned through many a debate about whether I am homosexual because of nature or nurture, I agree with Chicana Gloria Anzaldúa, who argues that when people are "queer"—gay, lesbian, bisexual, transgender, or *off-norm in any other fashion*—it is because real gods, goddesses, and/or spirits have chosen those people to embody or incarnate them.[15] Although I believe in only one Divine Source, not a multitude of gods and goddesses, I have certainly noticed that that One Source likes variety and has chosen to be incarnated in millions of diverse ways. I therefore assume that the *ultimate* reason for "queerness" does not lie in concepts constructed by society, or some eternal essence like "male" or "female" or "bigendered," but rather the fact that God has chosen to embody Himself/Herself/Itself in just this person's particularities at just this time and place. To make that statement does not rule out the freedom of human will, because God dwells within every one of Her children so that their deepest will is joined with Her will, and they are most at peace when fulfilling that one will. I am therefore in full agreement with Gloria Anzaldúa's statement that "We need to move beyond the facile dichotomy of 'essentialism' and 'constructionism' to embrace other theoretical paradigms inclusive of embodied and in-spirited knowledge."[16]

Eternity is always *here* and always *now*. And my job as an eternal being is to ask God's Wisdom for an appropriate response to what is set before me. This book is my response to an inner urging stimulated by the gender crisis *here* in the United States and *now* in the new millennium.

---

15. "Anzaldúa, Gloria," *Cassell's Encyclopedia of Queer Myth, Symbol, and Spirit,* ed. Randy P. Luncunas Conner, David Hatfield Sparks, and Mariya Sparks (New York: Cassell, 1998), 63–64.

16. Gloria Anzaldúa, foreword, *Cassell's Encyclopedia*, viii.

CHAPTER TWO

≋ Injustices of the Bi-Gender System

ＩN SEVENTEENTH-CENTURY Britain, jurist and scientific theorist Francis Bacon wrote that the human mind is like a magic mirror, full of superstitions, idols, and apparitions. Therefore, he suggested, we should become immediately suspicious when our minds fly too quickly to conclusions we deem beyond question. We should instead hang weights upon our minds to force them to move step-by-step from a broad basis of observable particular fact toward the more abstract pinnacle of theory.[1]

Similarly, contemporary Harvard science professor Stephen Jay Gould has written:

> In [the] deepest category of tribal idols, I doubt that any rule enjoys wider application, or engenders greater trouble at the same time, than our propensity for ordering nature by making dichotomous divisions into two opposite groups. . . . Thus, we start with a few basic divisions of male versus female and night versus day, and then we extend these concrete examples into greater generalities of nature versus culture . . . spirit versus matter . . . and thence (and now often

---

1. Sir Francis Bacon, "The Idols of the Mind," a section of Part One of the *Novum Organum*, 1620. Idols of the Tribe are erroneous modes of thought and feeling instinctive in the human race; Idols of the Cave are the result of individual temperament and background; Idols of the Marketplace result from the imprecise language of common speech; Idols of the Theatre stem from false systems of philosophy and erroneous demonstrations. The current binary gender construct would be an Idol of the Theatre, rooted in turn in the tendency to dichotomize (one of the Idols of the Tribe).

tragically) into ethical beliefs, anathematization, and sometimes warfare and genocide (the good versus the bad, the godly who must prevail versus the diabolical, ripe for burning).[2]

The purpose of this chapter is to describe some of the ways women, men, and children in general—from the most "feminine" or "masculine" and heterosexual to those who are otherwise—are treated unjustly within the confines of the binary gender construct. Although Stephen Jay Gould seems to take the male-female dichotomy as axiomatic, I believe that it is one of the idols of the mind that must now be questioned and laid aside.

As I write, I have recently watched the four-hour TV film concerning Joan of Arc, the profoundly spiritual fifteenth-century French girl who was deemed "ripe for burning" by the Inquisition, not only because she would not deny hearing saintly voices but also because she insisted upon wearing men's clothing.[3] In the film, Joan's father Jacques d'Arc harshly criticized Joan for not accepting the limitations of female peasant life and for behaving in a manlike fashion by leading the French army.

In 1920, Joan was canonized as a saint by the same church that in 1431 had burnt her as a heretic. And in recent years, she has become one of the patron saints of cross-dressers and the entire transgender movement.

Because I was brought up on the information that my father, Robert Franklin Ramey, was descended from Joan of Arc,[4] I have long felt

---

2. Stephen Jay Gould, "Bacon Brought Home," *Natural History* 108 (June 1999): 30.

3. See V. Sackville-West, *Saint Joan of Arc* (New York: The Literary Guild, 1936), 335. Asked by Bishop Cauchon why she had chosen men's clothing, Joan replied, "I took it of my own free will. No one constrained me to take it. I prefer to dress as a man than as a woman."

4. See Bonnelle William Rhamy, M.D., *The Remy Family in America, 1650–1942* (Fort Wayne, Ind.: n.p., 1942), 11, 162. Some of the variant spellings of the family name include Remus, Ramesis, Remi, Remy, Rheim, Ramee, Ramses, Romaine, Rainey, and Ramey. Joan lived in the village of Dom Remy; her mother was Isabel d' Ramee. The seventeenth-century Remy family members were Huguenots who fled religious persecution in France and first came to America in 1655.

a special affinity for her. Now that I realize that I myself am somewhat transgendered, and now that I find myself writing in defense of
"gender transgressors," I feel more than ever an affinity with St. Joan
of Arc, who called herself "Jehanne la Pucelle"—Joan the Virgin.[5]

Later I will return to indications that Joan was truly transgendered
and will describe other historical figures who show that the dualistic opposition of male versus female has never been a precise description of the human race. For now my point is this: The binary
gender construct has been and continues to be of life-and-death
importance to those who cannot meet society's unrealistic requirements. Joan of Arc began to wear men's clothing on the authority
of "God and His angels."[6] Is that so different from cross-dressing
because of an inner urge that arises out of the depths of one's own
authenticity? And she entered the "masculine" public sphere because she felt it her destiny to do so, just as millions of women have
entered the professional, governmental, and business spheres because that feels right to them. We have no idea of Joan's sexual
orientation because she was celibate during her nineteen years of
living, so she can serve as a good symbol of what effect the male-
female polarity has had upon heterosexual women as well as women
who are otherwise.

Gender and Social Choices

Our entire society is organized around gender roles. Females are socialized to be "feminine" (passive, dependent, and nurturant) and
then urged to pair with males, who are socialized to be "masculine"
(active, independent, and macho). It should not surprise anybody
that within such pairings, the females are subjugated and encouraged to express pseudopower harmlessly through consumerism.[7]
Thus, society in the United States depends on gender roles not only
to maintain androcentric control but also to support capitalism.

---

5. Sackville-West, *Saint Joan of Arc*, 360.

6. Ibid., 9.

7. Arlene Holp Scala, *Heterosexism in the Classroom* (unpublished Ed.D.
dissertation, Columbia Teacher's College, 1996), 319, 214.

The binary sex and gender system allows for only one set of choices: Either a person must self-define as exclusively male or female, or else admit to being mutant. Once a person has self-defined as female, social attitudes conspire to blur any distinction between her biological sex and female gender roles, which for women tend to be either in the private sphere or severely limited in the public sphere. If she refuses to conform to the limitations of "femininity," she will be labeled "controlling," "strident," and/or "lesbian." And whether or not she is actually homosexual, most women are frightened by such labels into some degree of conformity.

Boys and men are also pressured into gender conformity through name-calling, but in their case, the name-calling ("sissy," "weakling," "queen") teaches contempt for the feminine as that which is weak, dependent, or passive.[8] Thus, gender control of females is achieved by extolling "masculine" virtues but placing them beyond the reach of "real women," while gender control of men is achieved by degrading "femininity" so that no "real man" would ever want to be associated with it. Consider: Successful women are often complimented as having the minds of men or possessing manly strength, but to call a man "womanly" is a degrading insult. Women cannot win.

It should by now be obvious that homophobia and heterosexism are major supports of the binary gender construct. For the woman who wants maximum social approval, heterosexual marriage is compulsory; and within socially approved marriage, females are traditionally assigned the unpaid domestic and relational maintenance tasks, men the publicly oriented and rewarded tasks.

Even after decades of feminist and womanist activism, the cards continue to be stacked against women. The abortion controversy, for instance, is ultimately less about the value of unborn life than about keeping women in subordinate gender roles. Easy access to abortion would permit women to adopt patterns similar to those of many males: to have sex recreationally, irresponsibly, without "paying the price" of motherhood.

---

8. Ibid., 168–69.

Lesbian and somewhat transgendered as I am, I loved pregnancy and motherhood. But that was because, to the degree that a woman with heteropatriarchal socialization has freedom of choice, I *chose* to be Paul's mother. When the gynecological nurse told me my pregnancy test was positive and I responded with a joyous smile, she said grimly, "Yes, it's fine if you're prepared for it." She made me aware of all the times she had reported positive results to women or girls who had responded with outcries of pain, terror, or despair. Indeed, pregnancy and motherhood are wonderful—but only if they are freely chosen by a person with adequate health and financial and emotional support to be able to welcome the baby and give to it the love that is every child's birthright.[9] By contrast, being controlled through repeated unplanned pregnancies is a form of slavery.

Legal Inequities

Should any of my readers feel I am behind the times because women have already achieved substantial equality, I challenge them to read Deborah L. Rhode, *Speaking of Sex: The Denial of Gender Inequality* (Cambridge: Harvard University Press, 1997). Rhode teaches law and directs the Keck Center on Legal Ethics at Stanford University. In this section, I will be leaning heavily on Professor Rhode's research and insights. A married woman, Rhode has apparently won the respect of her colleagues, who elected her president of the Association of American Law Schools.

Rhode explains that two-thirds of all men and three-fourths of all male business leaders deny that women encounter unfair discrimination when they try for top positions in business, the professions, or government. Yet white males (forty percent of the population) hold ninety-five percent of senior management positions, where they command one hundred sixty times the take-home pay of the aver-

---

9. See Marge Piercy's poem, "Right to Life," in *The Moon Is Always Female* (New York: Alfred A. Knopf, 1980), 95. Everyone who is concerned about the causes of violence, and everyone who feels strongly about the abortion controversy, should read and study this brilliant, moving poem.

age worker (175).[10] White males hold ninety percent of newspaper editorships, eighty percent of the positions on *Forbes's* list of richest Americans, and eighty percent of congressional seats. In fact, eighty-five percent of all elected office holders are male, while two-thirds of poor adults are female (2). Although since the 1960s women constitute forty-five percent of attorneys, only sixteen percent of full professors in law schools are women, and only eight percent of federal judges (141).

How to explain such facts? One of my state college students, a white male confronted with similar statistics, had no trouble inter-preting the evidence: Women are simply inferior and cannot measure up to their male competition. His sexist complacency is reminiscent of the nineteenth-century "experts" who mismeasured women's brains and declared them smaller than men's and therefore inferior, or the authors of the first intelligence tests, who quickly changed the questions they had been asking when they learned that females had outscored males (26–27).

Anne Fausto-Sterling, professor of biology and medicine at Brown University, emphasizes that "there is no such thing as apo-litical science." Not only does Congress exert direct political au-thority over science by deciding which kinds of research will be supported, but scientists are consciously or unconsciously influenced by the political urgencies of their society. She charges that a very clear social vision has undergirded biological research, a vision that dictates that more women will stay at home while men will pre-dominate in business and government. If this social program continues to dominate biological research about masculinity and femininity, "the increasing slide of women into poverty may not be prevent-able."[11]

Furthermore, many studies of male-versus-female language usage tend to overlook variations such as time, culture, class, race,

---

10. As of April 24, 2000, *Time* magazine reports that the average salary of an American Chief Executive Officer is 461 times that of an American blue collar worker (25).

11. Anne Fausto-Sterling, *The Myths of Gender* (New York: Basic Books, 1992), 207.

ethnicity, age, and sexual orientation. Rhode states that "studies that take power relationships into account generally find that language styles depend less on the sex than on the social roles and status of the speakers" (38). So instead of assuming that women frequently end their sentences in questions because women are timid, we should check out the power differentials in their social context.

A 1918 trade journal on children's wear recommended as "the accepted rule" that boys be dressed in pink because pink suggests manliness and girls in blue because blue suggests delicacy (43). Although the colors of "masculinity" and "femininity" have since switched places, desirable gender characteristics have not: Girls are still supposed to be "everything nice" while boys still enjoy the freedoms associated with "snakes and snails and puppy dogs' tails." In elementary school, according to the *Wall Street Journal*, girls receive smaller allowances and are required to do more chores (142). And although in a Michigan study forty percent of schoolgirls could see advantages to being male, ninety-five percent of schoolboys could see no advantages to being female; some said they'd prefer death to being a girl (44). Alice Baumgartner's study of two thousand schoolchildren (grades 3–12) found that for girls, waking up male would increase their opportunities considerably; for boys, waking up female would be a disaster.[12]

In continuing her overview of gender inequities, Deborah Rhode points out that ninety percent of day-to-day TV sports coverage is of male events (67). The Equal Rights Amendment was first introduced into Congress in 1923 and still hasn't been passed (77). When women lack power, they are often victimized; but when they achieve power, they are vilified (90).

In adolescence, promiscuous boys are labeled "studs," while promiscuous girls are labeled "sluts"; hence, males tend not to believe a female who tells them "no" (128), and coercive sex accounts for a substantial proportion of unplanned pregnancies (212). Wives who

---

12. Cited in Winston A. Johnson, "Gender, Society, and Church" in *Gender Matters*, ed. June Steffensen Hagen (Grand Rapids, Mich.: Academie Books, 1990), 224.

are in the labor force assume at least two-thirds of domestic obligations, work longer, and have less income than men (142). Fathers
who focus on their careers are praised as "good providers"; mothers
who do the same are "selfish" (149). Pay scales for parking-lot attendants and zookeepers are higher than those for child-care attendants (147–43), so the hard evidence suggests that regardless of our
"family values" rhetoric, we value our cars and animals more than
our children. Nurses earn less than tree-trimmers; schoolteachers
earn less than state liquor store clerks (172).

Because women on welfare already have lower-than-average birth-
rates, cutting benefits cannot lower them further. And to put a welfare
child into an orphanage, as has been suggested by welfare reform-
ists, costs $40,000 a year, as opposed to an average benefit of $840 a
year for a child living with its mother (197).

Only about forty percent of single mothers receive court-awarded
assistance. And on child-support payments, divorced men are fif-
teen times more likely to default than on their car payments (128–
29). So nobody should be surprised to learn that one-fourth of pre-
school children in the United States are living in poverty.[13]

Transsexual Kate Bornstein reports that "when I left my job at
an IBM subsidiary (at which I'd been hired as a man), and took *a
more responsible* job as a woman at a similar Ford Aerospace subsidiary, I took a 30 percent pay cut." In this and other areas Bornstein
illustrates her claim that "transsexual people . . . prove the persis-
tence of male privilege over and over."[14]

As if increased female poverty were not enough, the outpouring
of violence against women is horrifying: Riane Eisler cites the United
States Senate Judiciary Committee's statement that more women
were rape victims in 1989 alone than all the Marines wounded in
all of World War II. The FBI announced that seventy-five percent
of American women can expect to be the target of at least one vio-

---

13. Riane Tennenhaus Eisler, *Sacred Pleasure: Sex, Myth, and the Politics of the
Body* (San Francisco: HarperSanFrancisco, 1996), 366.

14. Kate Bornstein, *My Gender Workbook: How to Become a Real Man, or Real
Woman, the Real You, or Something Else Entirely* (New York and London:
Routledge, 1998), 152.

lent crime.[15] Although sexual abuse (workplace harassment, rape, domestic violence, and murder) is rarely identified as "a strategy of dominance, exclusion, control, and retaliation," Deborah Rhode identifies it as precisely that: "a way to keep women in their place and out of men's" (90). The media are part of the problem: Under current movie regulations, if a man touches a woman's breast, the rating is "R"; but if he cuts off the breast with a chain saw, the rating is "PG–13" (54).

Conditions for females are even worse in many other countries. Female infanticide has long been a fact of life in China and elsewhere; and in India, one-fourth of the girls are dead by age 15 as a result of selective malnutrition, bride-burning, and other forms of violence.[16]

The Psychological Double Bind

Dana Crowley Jack writes of the double bind in which a woman finds herself as a result of living in a society where the other gender does most of the evaluating: "Society still pushes her to define herself through her relationships, but then it invalidates her wish for connection by derogating the importance of attachments."[17] As someone who suffered for decades from a serious case of codependence, I know that it is possible to be so centered in the partner that one is hardly aware of one's own needs. But at the same time, I would insist that there are worse conditions than codependence in a partnership: for example, finding satisfaction in the diminishment or suffering of one's partner, a state of affairs that is fostered by the imbalance of power in male-female relationships.

It was Joan Duncan, an outstanding therapist and human being, who finally taught me that I must respect my own needs as much as the other person's. And by that time, I was 64 years of age! When I was contemplating Buber's concept of "I-Thou" relationships, I had

---

15. Eisler, *Sacred Pleasure*, 235.
16. Ibid., 236.
17. Dana Crowley Jack, *Silencing the Self: Women and Depression* (New York: HarperPerennial, 1993), 6.

a startling realization that a healthy relationship requires a strong sense of "I" as well as a strong sense of "Thou." But like most other women, I grew up in a world where the major norms and definitions were male. Freud stated that the human ego "appears to us as something autonomous and unitary, marked off distinctly from everything else" and that the feeling of unbounded connection was infantile.[18] Yet as a girl I was taught that making connection was my purpose in life—never mind that fully mature people (i.e., men) are individuals, intrinsically separate from everyone else. So as I matured, I learned to judge myself as immature for my very adherence to the rules of the gender game. It was crazy-making, and certainly I was not the only one who felt somewhat balked at every turn.

Jack explains that "the social roles of wife and husband carry duties, obligations, and rules of relationship" that actually "drive the partners toward inequality." Yet depressed women enter into or remain in hurtful marriages because they want to "help" the man. "In their words, they see a damaged child within the grown man and want to help him heal . . . [and] they are willing to accept some hurt (some injustice) if it will help their partners learn to love."[19] Hence, it is essential for heterosexual women to violate the gender code by relating respectfully to their own selves as well as to their partners. Any healthy love relationship requires mutual justice and mutual deference.

Paradoxically, though, from my own social position as a gender transgressor, I can see that it is not just heterosexual marriages that are harmed by Freudian notions of separateness and autonomy as true human maturity (a maturity that "feminine" women are somehow supposed to avoid). Despite our apparent rejection of binary gender, or perhaps *because* of it, some lesbian women are so devoted to connection that they try to merge with their female partners in an enmeshment as severe as that of Dana Jack's heterosexual clients. Other lesbian women try to adopt for themselves the male and adult Freudian norm of separated autonomy. The "stonebutch"

---

18. As quoted by Jack, ibid., 7.
19. Ibid., 66.

model of making love to another without allowing oneself to lose control would perhaps illustrate that attempt. But I also know some very "feminine" lesbians who have developed such a horror of co-dependency that they have found it impossible to sustain a love relationship past the honeymoon period. They have insisted on their own separate autonomy to the extreme. The binary gender construct has taken many captives!

Becoming Alienated from Our Own Pain

In her book *The Beauty Myth: How Images of Beauty Are Used against Women* (New York: Doubleday, 1992), Naomi Wolf points out that weight-loss surgery, cosmetic surgery, and breast implant surgery are teaching women not to feel their own pain, not to see or feel their own bodies as human bodies. She reminds her readers of the Milgram Experiments carried out during the 1950s, when researchers put subjects in charge of administering electric shocks to people they couldn't see, but whose outcries they could hear. The subjects were told to administer an increasing level of shock each time the un-seen person gave the wrong answer to a question. Unwilling to dis-obey the "scientific authorities" who had instructed them in the rules of the experiment, the subjects continued to increase the elec-tric currents, finally pushing the button that was plainly marked "fatal." Wolf comments, "A woman learns, in the dawn of the surgi-cal age, to relate to her body as the experimental subjects related to the shock victims. Separated from it, asked not to see it or feel for it as human, she is being taught by scientific authority to do her worst" (249–50).

I do not remember precisely when I first read about the Milgram Experiments, but I do remember my distress at learning that out of respect for "scientific authority," human beings would subject oth-ers to fatal levels of electricity, ignoring cries of pain, just because the victim had uttered an incorrect response. The report caused me to do a lot of soul-searching. Would I have been willing, out of intimidation by the atmosphere of scientific objectivity and neces-sity, to push the button marked "fatal"? Remembering how often I had believed other people's statements despite my personal experience to the contrary, I feared I might have done it. And I started then and there to reconnect with my own deepest core, where all is interrelated, so that hopefully never again could I ignore outcries from behind the screen. Ask not from whom the outcries come: They come from me! And human pain, including my own, really does *matter*!

Disfigured Masculinity

Although Naomi Wolf cites the Milgram Experiments only as part of her thesis about how beauty is used to keep women subordinate, she does at one point refer to a "*global* numbing effect" (250). The global numbing is not only of women to our own pain, but inevitably to other atrocities as well. And I cannot help thinking about how boys and young men are taught to disassociate from their own pain—especially in business and athletics—since "real men don't cry."

At some period after my Milgram Experiment resolution, I was watching my little son Paul, who loved motorcycles but never cared for baseball, trying to succeed in Little League because his father had insisted. One day when I saw him standing at the plate for his at-bat, he looked tiny and alone and disconsolate. I could sense that he was forcing himself to do what he disliked to try to meet masculine requirements. I knew enough about that kind of self-alienation that I refused to be party to forcing him any longer. After the game, I told him that he'd have my support if he wanted to drop out of Little League—and he did so immediately.

As I write, the news is full of the aftermath of the massacre in Littleton, Colorado and other high school shootings—so far all of them perpetrated by males. In the case of the Littleton gun-wielding students especially, I see the results of males being socialized toward separation and domination and being encouraged to ignore their own pain and consequently the pain of others. It's the laughter that speaks to me: Those boys were *laughing* as they killed, knowing the whole time that their own self-inflicted deaths were minutes away. Talk about global numbing!

Jackson Katz, who regularly contributes to the Gender Equity Conferences at Wellesley College, has been studying the recent media images of women and men. Women are consistently shown to be thinner, more waifish, and younger than women in the real world: "Waifish women literally take up less space in the world, and hence are less threatening." But at the same time, "images of men have gotten bigger, stronger, more muscular, and more violent."

Katz thinks that these images are intended to teach males that the "real man" is "a stoic rugged individualist," so that males learn to pretend they are omnipotent and invulnerable. But, he says, such pretense is not only "emotionally stultifying"; it also gets a lot of men—and boys—killed. Poor black males and other men of color use a hypermasculine posture to try to compensate for their many disadvantages. But "white suburban middle-class males are the leading purchasers of rap music, including misogynous gangsta rap."[20] Is it entirely coincidence that a disproportionate number of the fatalities in high school shootings are female?

It is tragic for males to be trained to wear masks that shield their vulnerability, hide their humanity, and alienate them from themselves and others. I remember my own fears as I was socializing Paul: His father sometimes said I was turning Paul into a wimp, and inwardly I quailed for fear that he was right. By the time Paul reached high school, many girls had rejected feminist freedoms and had reverted to a preference for rough, tough guys. I was afraid I had socialized Paul into failure to find a partner. Now that he is a husband and father as well as a capable, gentle, and loving human being, I feel more confident about opposing the macho stereotype. But my memories will not let me forget how terrifying it is to oppose the dominant paradigm. Without the Women's Movement and my feminist colleagues, I never would have gathered the courage to do it.

According to Roger Horrocks, the message of patriarchal masculinity to men is this: "Conceal your weakness, your tears, your fear of death, your love for others. . . . Dominate others, then you

---

20. Jackson Katz, "Men, Masculinities, and the Media: Some Introductory Notes," *The Wellesley Centers for Women Research Report* (spring 1999): 16–17.

can fool everyone, especially yourself, that you feel powerful."[21] During the recent debates in the Church of England concerning the ordination of women, Oxford's Professor of Moral and Pastoral Theology opposed women's ordination with Victorian and still-powerful notions of God-given gender identities: "Maleness is associated with law, order, civilization, logos, clock time, and what Freud called the 'super ego.' Femaleness is associated with nature, instinct, biological time, feelings, eros, and what Freud called the 'id.'"[22] Here, in stark clarity, is the binary that has driven our culture into its profound gender crisis.

Wally Lamb makes a similar diagnosis in his monumental novel *I Know This Much Is True* (New York: HarperCollins, 1998). The point-of-view character, Dominick Birdsey, is coaxed into psychotherapy by a compassionate Indian psychiatrist, Dr. Patel, who also works with his schizophrenic twin brother, Thomas. Dr. Patel comments early on that "People are not like Tupperware, with their lids on securely. Nor *should* they be, although the more I work with American men, the more I see it is their perceived ideal. Which is nonsense, really, *very* unhealthy, Mr. Birdsey. Not something to aspire to at all. Never" (238).

Much later in the therapy, Dr. Patel offers another observation about male "toughness": "She saw it over and over again in her male patients, she said—it could probably qualify as an *epidemic* among American men—this stubborn reluctance to embrace our wholeness—this stoic denial that we had come from our *mothers* as well as our fathers. It was sad, really—tragic. So wasteful of human lives, as our wars and drive-by shootings kept proving to us" (608).

Interestingly enough, healing for Dominick comes about through psychological gender blending. He learns to accept as part of him-

21. Roger Horrocks, *Masculinity in Crisis: Myths, Fantasies, and Realities* (London: Macmillan, 1994), 25. As quoted by Sean Gill, "Christian Manliness Unmanned: Some Problems and Challenges in the Study of Masculinity and Religion in Nineteenth- and Twentieth-Century Western Society," in *Is There a Future for Feminist Theology?*, ed. Deborah F. Sawyer and Diane M. Collier (Sheffield, England: Sheffield Academic Press, 1999), 162.

22. As quoted by Gill, "Christian Manliness Unmanned," 172.

self the sweetness, kindness, and gentleness of Thomas, "Mama's baby-bunny," who used to enjoy secret cross-dressing and tea parties with their mother. Simultaneously, Dominick's healing comes through merging his Italian heritage with his Native American heritage: "We Wequonnoc-Italians celebrate wholeness—the roundness of things" (896).

By the end of the novel, what Dominick knows is true turns out to be threefold, and by implication strongly supportive of gender pluralism: "that love grows from the rich loam of forgiveness; that mongrels make good dogs; and that the evidence of God exists in the roundness of things" (897).

The Use of Gender Bipolarity to Reverse Progress for Women

In *To Believe in Women*, Lillian Faderman has described the ways in which the social construct of male-female polarity and complementarity was used to stem the tide of Women's Rights and restrict access to higher education and the learned professions. Commencing in the 1920s, reaching a crescendo in the '50s, with continued pressure into the '70s and beyond, women who were assertive or ambitious were stigmatized and ridiculed. I remember the only card game my family permitted us children to play during the late 1930s and '40s. It was called "Old Maid," and it implied that being an unmarried woman was a dreadful, dire disgrace. The entire social climate epitomized by that game resulted in my marrying at age twenty-one and thereby seriously impairing my professional career.

From the time in the nineteenth century that American women began to speak publicly about abolishing slavery and granting the vote to women, the binary gender construct threw its considerable weight upon them. For instance, the *St. Louis Dispatch* announced that Sojourner Truth is "the name of a man now lecturing in Kansas City." So often was Sojourner Truth accused of maleness that she once bared her breasts on the platform of an Indiana Women's Rights Convention to prove otherwise (17). Susan B. Anthony was called "a grim Old Gal with a manly air" and defended herself by arguing in 1900 that a woman who is called manly is simply a woman who is fully human (24–25).

Jane Addams, who worked tirelessly for the good of humankind, received hate mail for suggesting that women might have a role in the public sphere. One anonymous letter suggested that she purchase some criminal's "pecker and balls," since it would not be much loss to the criminal and would be her only chance to prove herself a man (117).

In the mid-nineteenth century, *The Ladies Companion* claimed that the only women who could possibly desire a higher education would be "mental hermaphrodites" or "semi-women." And *The Religious Magazine* attacked Mount Holyoke Female Seminary for creating women "expressly formed for acting a *manly* part upon the theatre of life." The effect of higher education was generally held to be a masculinizing one (178). Emily Blackwell, who earned a medical degree in 1854, was told that her professional desires were "a simple perversion of a woman's nature, a stepping out from her place in creation" (274).

None of this deterred the nineteenth century women who were determined to support one another in their careers of serving their fellow human beings. But by the beginning of the twentieth century, when the terms *homosexual* and *lesbian* gained currency and were pathologized, the pressure to succumb to heterosexual marriage and gender roles was fiercely intensified.

In the 1930s, the implication that Mount Holyoke was turning "natural women" into something akin to a "third sex" (221) caused the trustees to replace their distinguished president Mary Woolley with a mediocre male candidate, Roswell Ham, a professor who had not been able to get promoted at Yale and who proceeded to hire men as professors for female students (235). Even the influential psychologist Carl Jung stated that among women who cared about women's rights and advancement, homosexuality was prevalent (241).

A 1942 book, *Women after College*, castigated female educators for harming young women by giving them an education "designed for men," thus pretending there were not important differences between the sexes (238). Unmarried female college administrators were accused of throwing off "the normal biological inhibitions of gender," of being "pseudo-masculine" and "Amazon" and therefore dangerous to the well-being of students (245).

How well did these relentlessly gendered assaults accomplish their purpose? They were devastatingly effective. In 1920, women made up more than 30 percent of America's college professors; by 1959, only 19.4 percent. In 1900, women constituted 75 percent of the Smith College faculty; by 1966, less than 35 percent (238). In 1920, almost half of American college students were female; by the late 1930s the proportion had dropped to 40.2 percent; and by 1950, it was down to 30.2 percent (243).

I remember my dismay when as a young woman I read Ferdinand Lundberg and Marynia Farnam's *Modern Woman: The Lost Sex* (New York: Harper & Brothers, 1947), which Faderman discusses in *To Believe in Women* (313). They recommended that unmarried female teachers should be fired, because without income perhaps they would feel forced to marry. I quailed as I read the opinion of this sociologist and psychiatrist that homosexual women had distorted personalities and distorted perceptions of society. I searched myself for my personality distortions and projections. I understood my mother's "gender correctness" when she said that if there was money for only one of her children to go to college, my brother would go and not I. How could I question that, when everyone knew that careers other than marriage could never satisfy "normal women"?

By the time I was ready to begin work on my Ph.D., the percentage of Ph.D's presented to women had dropped from the 1930 high of eighteen percent to only ten percent (244). And whereas I was married, teaching full time, and caring for a baby, over half of those other female Ph.D. candidates were unmarried. It was uphill all the way for the likes of me!

And for most other women as well. Low-paid, low-prestige jobs became the rule for most of those women who had to work outside the home. In 1950, only fourteen percent of door-to-door salespeople were female; by 1960, that number had risen to sixty percent, mostly in Avon Lady kinds of roles. In 1950, females constituted forty-five percent of bank tellers; by 1960, seventy percent of them were female (314–15).

In short, "during most of the half-century between 1920 and 1970, those women who succeeded in non-traditional [public, decently paid, professional] areas were isolated, made into a minority, and 'queered' in a hostile (if sometimes ambivalent) milieu" (317). The deadly combination of the binary gender construct and compulsory heterosexuality had served to advance male privilege at the expense of women's human and civil rights.

Enough Already

In *The Beauty Myth*, Naomi Wolf writes concerning so-called cosmetic surgery, "A city of women the size of San Francisco gets cut open each year in the United States; in Britain, a village the size of Bath" (251). One risk of eyelid surgery is blindness. A nose job may destroy the ability to smell. Face-lifts cause numbness. Factory-produced breasts endanger sensual response. But "no amount of suffering or threat of disfigurement can serve as a deterrent" now that there is "the will completely to alter women" (252) in order to fit them into unrealistic heteropatriarchal (and frequently racist) ideals of beauty. As Wolf charges, these cosmetic surgeries with their infantile names ("nips," "tummy tucks") are nothing less than *human rights abuses*. "When a class of people is denied food, or forced to vomit regularly, or repeatedly cut open and stitched together to no medical purpose, we call it torture" (257). Are women less hungry, less bloody, because they have been trained to acquiesce to such torture?

Meanwhile, as we have seen, men are taught that feelings of disgust, anger, and contempt—feelings appropriate for those who dominate—are "masculine." And they are taught to feel contempt for "inferior feminine" feelings such as distress, compassion, and empathy.[23] Thus, men are split off from important aspects of their own beings. Within a binary construct that requires gender performances from behind stultifying masks, clearly everybody is the loser.

Ultimately, of course, it is the children who pay the heaviest price. Nobody has dramatized that fact more powerfully than Barbara Kingsolver in her novel about life in the Congo (Zaire), *The Poison-*

---

23. Silvan Tomkins and Donald Mosher, "Scripting the Macho Man," *The Journal of Sex Research* (1988). As quoted by Eisler, *Sacred Pleasure*, 227.

wood Bible (New York: HarperCollins, 1998). On the topic of why she did not long ago leave her domineering, inhuman, Bible-thumping missionary husband, Oleana Price explains:

> To resist occupation, whether you're a nation or merely a woman, you must understand the language of your enemy. *Conquest* and *liberation* and *democracy* and *divorce* are words that mean squat, basically, when you have hungry children and clothes to get out on the line and it looks like rain. . . . I knew Rome was burning, but I had just enough water to scrub the floor, so I did what I could (383–84).

Oleana Price's daughter, Leah, ponders the close relationship between the effect of male dominance on families and its effect on nations:

> For how many generations must we be forgiven by our children? Murdering Lamumba, keeping Mobutu in power, starting it all over again in Angola—these sound like plots between men but they are all betrayals, by men, of children. It's thirty million dollars . . . that the U.S. has now spent trying to bring down Angola's sovereignty. Every dollar of it had to come from some *person*, a man or woman (502–03).

And of course, every dollar taken ultimately deprives that person's children. As Anne Fausto-Sterling asks, "Do we care that the poorest segment of our population is comprised of women and children? All this and more is at stake as we continually redesign our concepts of masculine and feminine."[24]

That which happens to families and to governments also happens to the environment: Male dominance leads to ruthless exploitation and destruction. Conversely, respect for nature leads to respect for human diversity. Daniel T. Spencer emphasizes that "Native Ameri-

---

24. Fausto-Sterling, *The Myths of Gender*, 270. Fausto-Sterling goes on to plead that her readers grasp the fact that "the biological debate does not stand separately. It is part of the political struggle. And so are we all."

can acceptance of ambiguity and human diversity, including sexual diversity, flows from reverence and respect for nature. . . . Over-coming rigid dichotomized thinking, whether between humanity and nature, or between male and female, is basic to a liberationist ecological ethic."[25]

In *The Poisonwood Bible*, Oleana Price utters a prophecy based on her experience with her raving, megalomaniac husband: "His kind will always lose in the end . . . whether it's wife or nation they occupy, their mistake is the same: they stand still, and their stake moves underneath them" (384). To which prophecy I say, Amen! So be it! Let it happen! The fixed concept of bi-gender complementarity, with all its freight of male primacy and female subordination, has begun to collapse because its stake is moving out from underneath. And I for one will be glad to see the conclusion of the matter.

Although L. William Countryman does not exactly call for an omnigender paradigm in his study of sexual ethics in the New Tes-tament, he does recognize that changes are necessary in our gender concepts if male-female equality in marriage is ever to be achieved. He points out that "Jesus and Paul laid it down as a principle that women and men are basically equal in marriage," but then he goes on to describe what that equality must require of heterosexuals within the current paradigm:

> If the husband gives up the image of himself as sole ruler of the household, waited on by wife and children, his whim the family's law, he must also give up its spiritual equivalent—the image of him-self as the family's unique sacrificial sustainer, isolated in his moral strength and grandeur. If the wife gives up being the servant of all, with no life of her own except in responding to the needs of others, she must also give up the spiritual vision of herself as the one who gives all for others' good.

---

25. Daniel T. Spencer, *Gay and Gaia: Ethics, Ecology, and the Erotic* (Cleveland: The Pilgrim Press, 1996), 335.

He emphasizes that this "giving up" will entail "some pain and anxiety as well as some sense of liberation and joy."[26]

Since Countryman then suggests that "spouses in heterosexual marriages will have much to learn in this process from partners in stable, long-term homosexual relationships" (260), in essence he is suggesting a broadening of gender acceptability that is akin to the paradigm shift I am envisioning. I agree with him that the gospel has not yet finished transforming us, and that it does not act in such a way as to make us more respectable, conventional, predictable, and perfect. Instead, "the gospel works . . . to express the power of God's love, which rejects our rejections and breaches our best defenses and draws us out of our fortifications toward a goal that we can as yet barely imagine" (267). So it is in the spirit of the gospel that we turn now to look at the inequities wreaked upon those who may or may not be heterosexual, but certainly are not able to fit themselves into the current binary gender construct.

---

26. L. William Countryman, *Dirt, Greed, and Sex: Sexual Ethics in the New Testament and Their Implications for Today* (Philadelphia: Fortress Press, 1988), 259–60.

CHAPTER THREE

≋ *Transgender Inequities*

L ESLIE FEINBERG COMMENTS THAT "In a society in which heterosexuality and male/female dress and behavior are decreed by
law, gay, lesbian, bisexual and trans people are all gender transgressors. . . . Our histories have commingled . . . [because we are all]
guilty of the same crime: 'queerness.' Many anti-*gay* laws used over
the centuries have targeted *feminine* gay males and *masculine* lesbians. And heterosexual cross-dressers have been jailed for being gay."[1]

When I have spoken with gay, lesbian, and bisexual people of
faith about specifically transgender issues, the response has been
respectful but not enthusiastic. Apparently Feinberg has encoun-
tered similar lethargy in the more secular community, judging by
her pleas for solidarity. She refers to a 1998 poll in *The Advocate*, a
national gay magazine, in which sixty-four percent said gay and lesbian civil rights groups should make the effort to support transgender
rights, and thirteen percent weren't sure. Feinberg says "we've got
to reach that 13 percent," and I agree; but s/he does not mention

---

1. Leslie Feinberg, *Trans Liberation: Beyond Pink or Blue* (Boston: Beacon Press,
1998), 98. Feinberg's statement helps to explain why many lesbian, bisexual, gay,
and transgender people use the word *queer* concerning themselves: It identifies the
commonality of an otherwise exceedingly diverse group. At the same time, the
word *queer* is being reclaimed as something positive, similar to the way the Society
of Friends reclaimed the scornful term *Quaker*, or Wicca reclaimed a positive
meaning for *witchcraft*, or African Americans reclaimed a positive meaning for
black. Some gay men have reclaimed the pansy as a positive symbol of gay love. The
triangle as a symbol of lesbian and gay empowerment transforms the Nazi use of
triangles (pink for men, black for women) to identify homosexuals in the concen-
tration camps. Gay male adherents often call themselves Faeries or Radical Faeries,
thus reclaiming yet another term of abuse and subverting its power to injure.

the fact that the poll leaves a hefty twenty-three percent who apparently don't desire the alliance at all (50).

A more recent poll (May 25, 1999), asking whether transgender people should be part of the Gay Rights movement, brought an even more troubling response: Only forty-six percent said yes, six percent not sure, and forty-eight percent said no. Perhaps the negative shift explains the tepidness of the response when I have urged the alliance upon queer people of faith. Perhaps more faith-filled lesbians, gays, and bisexuals are more eager than others to be assimilated into the currently dominant paradigm (with the single exception of sexual orientation). If that is the case, solidarity with transgenderists might be perceived as a setback to the Cause. Or perhaps the transgender concept is still so new that people are simply confused about terminology.

Whatever the reason, any lack of solidarity bothers me because it belies the all-inclusiveness of Jesus the Christ, who according to Matthew 5:43–48 taught us to include even our worst enemies in our love and practical concern. Jesus said we ought to do that precisely because our Creator makes the sun to shine on the evil as well as the good and sends life-giving rain to the unjust as well as the just. For this reason, Jesus said, we people of faith should be whole (perfected, just, all-inclusive) as our heavenly Parent is whole (perfected, just, all-inclusive). According to Matthew 5:43–48, the very fact that we include in our love and prayers even those who persecute us constitutes the proof that we are God's children. Without that all-inclusive concern, there is no way for anyone else to know that we really do belong to God's family. Surely, if our loving concern is to extend to persecutors, bigots, and critics—as well as to our neighbor, whom we are to love as ourselves—there can be no question that our loving concern should encompass transpeople.

Who Exactly Are Transpeople?

The transgender movement is still so relatively new that trying to supply definitions is like aiming a cannon at a moving target. For starters, I quote transsexual Riki Anne Wilchins, executive director of Gender PAC, an organization devoted to "gender, affectional, and racial equality." What I have called the binary gender construct is to Wilchins "that system that punishes bodies for how they look, who they love, or how they feel—for the size or color or shape of their skin."[2] And transpeople are those who are gender-different, gender-queer, or gender-oppressed. Kate Bornstein's phrase, quoted by Wilchins, is "transgressively gendered."

At first, the term *transgender* referred only to people who had changed their gender but not their genitals—for instance, a man who uses estrogen, lives as a woman, but has no plans to undergo sex-reassignment surgery. (Now, such a person would be called a non-operative transsexual.) But gradually, the term has been extended to include intersexuals, transsexuals, cross-dressers, drag queens and kings, androgynes, and anyone else who feels "otherwise" from society's gender assumptions. Those assumptions would also define homosexuals and bisexuals as transpeople, whether or not they saw themselves that way.

For the following definitions, I am relying on *Transgender Care: Recommended Guidelines, Practical Information, and Personal Accounts* (Philadelphia: Temple University Press, 1997), written by Gianna E. Israel, a gender specialist, and Dr. Donald E. Tarver II, director of a multiservice agency for the lesbian, gay, bisexual, and transgender communities. According to these authors, *intersexual* or *hermaphrodite* individuals are "those with medically established physical or hormonal attributes of both male and female gender" (16). A *transsexual* is "a person interested in permanently changing gender through cross-gender hormones and various surgeries." A *transvestite* or *cross-dresser* is "a person interested in wearing clothing of the 'opposite' gender privately and/or socially as an opportunity to explore masculinity or femininity" (153). *Drag queens, kings,* or *performance artists* are "individuals who cross-dress for entertainment, for sex-industry purposes, to challenge social stereotypes, or for personal satisfaction" (17). A *transgenderist* or *bigenderist* is "a person interested in crossdressing and crossliving part or full time," but not

---

2. Riki Anne Wilchins, *Read My Lips: Sexual Subversion and the End of Gender* (Ithaca, N.Y.: Firebrand Books, 1997), 16–17.

in genital reassignment surgery. And an *androgyne* is "a person interested in taking on the characteristics of both or neither gender role(s), i.e., male/female or occupying a middle ground" (153).

I am aware that some transsexuals are offended by being grouped with transpeople, feeling that their unique experiences are erased by that grouping. (At a discussion of transgender politics, Kate Bornstein remarked that the word *transgender* does to *transsexual* what the word *humanism* does to *feminism*.) I am also aware that some people may feel I have not listed their gender identity in a way that feels acceptable to them and thus have kept them off the cultural map that language supplies. I can only reply that my intention is inclusive, that I have no desire to erase anyone's experience, and that I have added an "otherwise" category as evidence of my good faith.

To religious people and perhaps certain other readers, my list of transgender categories may seem to mix that which people cannot help (such as being born intersexual) and voluntarily chosen behaviors which could be interpreted as deliberate defiance (such as cross-dressing). But as Israel writes in a sample disclosure letter,[3] cross-dressing is often "necessary to [an] individual's self-integration process. Therefore it should not be misconstrued as an attempt to impersonate the opposite gender or perpetrate wrongdoing" (163).

Rather than run the risk of misjudging anybody's motives, my preference is to assume the sincerity and necessity of transgender behavior. After all, society offers no rewards for such behavior, and it often still leads to discrimination in employment, housing, and services. Why assume that any person would willfully seek out discrimination and suffering? And even if they did, wouldn't compassion be a more appropriate response than judgmentalism?

---

3. Disclosure letters are provided by gender specialists to cross-dressing individuals for use when they are stopped by law enforcement officers or are interacting with social service agencies.

On the other hand, I must also ask for the patience of readers who are extremely knowledgeable about transgenderism—perhaps from extensive personal experience. This is a book about gender justice and challenging the dominant gender construct in the search for such justice. The best I can hope to do is provide accurate general information and some suggestions about where to find more technical and thorough definitions. For my information I have relied chiefly on transpeople themselves, especially those who have thought and written extensively about gender issues.

Intersexuality

According to the best estimate of the Intersex Society of North America, "about five intersexed children have their genitals cut into in U.S. hospitals every day for cosmetic reasons, a procedure performed by accredited surgeons and covered by all major insurance plans."[4] Some operations may be necessitated by life-threatening conditions because systems of urination and defecation are situated so close to human genitals.[5] But Alice Domurat Dreger has documented the fact that Western medicine has taken pains to protect the male-female binary from the challenge of intersexuality,[6] and Suzanne J. Kessler has described how both surgery and social institutions are utilized to maintain that binary.[7] The surgeries amount to intersex genital mutilation, and it seems to me fully as horrible as the female genital mutilation that occurs in many cul-

---

4. As quoted by Wilchins, *Read My Lips*, 226. The Intersex Society of North America can be reached at P.O. Box 31791, San Francisco CA 94131; by e-mail: info@isna.org.

5. Dr. Carol A. Cobb-Nettleton, Associate Professor of Human Sexuality and Therapy at Widener University (Chester, Pennsylvania) made this point during a workshop on sexuality at the Cathedral of Hope, Dallas, Texas, on 23 October 1999.

6. Alice Domurat Dreger, *Hermaphrodites and the Medical Invention of Sex* (Cambridge: Harvard University Press, 1998). Dreger shows that in the Middle Ages in Europe, hermaphrodites were not considered pathological.

7. Suzanne J. Kessler, *Lessons from the Intersexed* (New Brunswick: Rutgers University Press, 1998).

tures.[8] For that reason, and because of what intersexuality teaches us about gender, it is important to define the most frequently occurring forms of intersexuality.

As I have been saying all along, our society conceives of sex anatomy as determining gender roles and behaviors (the binary gender construct). One of the most potent proofs that this assumption *is* a cultural construction—and an inaccurate one—is the existence of intersexual people. The fact is that "anatomic sex differentiation occurs on a male/female continuum."[9] And it seems to me that the anatomical continuum forms a good model for an omnigender paradigm in which people locate and enact the gender presentation that seems fulfilling to them at any given time, with the option of shifting along the continuum at other times, should the necessity arise. My assumption is that ethics, medicine, and theology should begin with the facts of the Creator's work, respecting that work as worthy, instead of telling people that they must adapt themselves to a humanly constructed set of abstractions. Chapters 4 and 5 will be devoted to discussing the substantial religious objections to an omnigender paradigm; but first we need to be clear about the people who are primarily impacted (not that any of us is gender-free, but that the situation is more drastic for some people than for others).

There are several dimensions to anatomical sex differentiation. The first of these, genetic sex (the organization of sex chromosomes) is anything but a sure test of true sex, since about one person in every 500 has a karyotype other than XX or XY. Sally Lehrman

---

8. Cheryl Chase, founder of the Intersex Society of North America (ISNA), and two other people wrote to the *New England Journal of Medicine* in response to an article on female "circumcision." They linked genital mutilation in Africa to surgery on intersexed children, calling both "culturally determined practices of harmful genital surgery." The letter was never printed. Nevertheless, ISNA believes that the final version of the congressional bill to ban female genital mutilation in the U.S.A. is worded in a way that could also cover surgery on intersexed infants. See Kessler, *Lessons from the Intersexed*, 80–83.

9. Intersex Society of North America, "Frequently Asked Questions," copyright © 1996, ISNA. Web site last updated May 6, 2000 <http://www.isna.org/faq.htm>. Unless otherwise indicated, this on-line document is the source of my definitions of intersexual categories.

states that "About one in 1,000 women has three X chromosomes instead of the usual two; some people have had as many as four X chromosomes—plus two Y's."[10] As recently as 1996, eight women in the Atlanta Olympic Games tested as "not women." Currently the Athletes' Commission of the International Olympics Committee has urged that sex analysis be done away with and that imposters be weeded out simply by observing their method of urination during drug testing.[11] (It is already observed to avoid the switching of specimens.) That would seem a wise suggestion, because none of the disqualified women were actually male. They simply had atypical karyotypes, and one of them gave birth to a healthy child after having been disqualified from Olympic competition as "not woman."

It seems extremely unfair to disqualify people for a genetic anomaly they may never have known about prior to being required to submit to genetic testing. As a person who does not know her own genetic makeup, I feel very uneasy about society's requiring other people to meet standards I myself might not be able to meet. When I have asked audience members to raise their hands if they know their karyotype, only one person has ever put up a hand. That means that anybody among the vast majority of us could conceivably be atypical and therefore intersexual and transgender without even knowing it—a marvelous reason for relaxing our rigid gender expectations!

It is the sex chromosomes that bring about other dimensions of anatomical sex differentiation, namely, the differentiation of the gonads into ovaries, testes, ovo-testes, or non-functioning streaks. And it is the hormones produced by the fetal gonads that determine the differentiation of the external genitalia into male, female, or intermediate (intersexual).

Contrary to popular imagination, intersexuality does not mean that there are two full sets of genitals (an impossibility), but rather that the genitals may look nearly female, nearly male, or right in

10. Sally Lehrman, "Sex Police: Measuring Penises," *Salon.Com* (on-line magazine), 5 April 1999. <http://www.salonmagazine.com/health/feature/1999/04/05/sex_police/index.html>, 2.

11. Lehrman, "Sex Police: It's All about How You Pee," *Salon.Com*, 3.

the middle (with structures that could be interpreted either way). According to transman and scholar Stephen Whittle, "Currently medicine recognizes over 70 different intersex syndromes, and one in every 200 children will be born with some sort of intersex matrix. For some this will never be discovered, whereas for others it will only be discovered when they attend a fertility treatment clinic in later life as they struggle to have their own children."[12] Obviously, I cannot here describe 70 different forms of intersexuality but will attempt to describe only the major categories.

Major Categories of Intersexuality

Androgen Insensitivity Syndrome

Androgen Insensitivity Syndrome (AIS) is one form of intersexuality, an inherited genetic defect located on the X chromosome in which the body's cells cannot respond to androgen. The condition is sometimes called *Testicular Feminization Syndrome*. The baby born with AIS has genitals of unequivocally female appearance, with undescended or partially descended testes located in the abdominal cavity. Later, she will experience breast growth but will not menstruate and will not be able to bear children because she has no womb. If the reports that Joan of Arc did not menstruate are factual, not merely misogynistic attempts to prove her saintliness, perhaps she was an AIS intersexual woman.

Partial Androgen Insensitivity Syndrome

This condition usually results in ambiguous genitals (large clitoris or small penis). It may be fairly common, and may well be the cause of infertility in some men whose genitals look typically male. Currently, the medical practice is to do corrective surgery during infancy. But the Intersex Society of North America (ISNA) calls such

---

12. Stephen Whittle, "The Becoming Man," *Reclaiming Genders: Transsexual Grammars at the* Fin de Siècle, ed. Kate More and Stephen Whittle (New York: Cassell, 1999), 24.

surgery "cosmetic" rather than "corrective" and believes it to be both harmful and unethical. Their statement seems to me beyond question: "Surgery is justified only when it is necessary for the health and well-being of the child. Surgery which is intended to make the genitals appear more male or more female should be offered, but not imposed, only when the child is old enough to make an informed decision for her/himself."[13]

Progestin Induced Virilization

Prenatal exposure to the drug progestin or other externally administered androgens can cause Progestin Induced Virilization. According to the Intersex Society, people with an XX karyotype affected in utero by such virilizing hormones may develop along a continuum ranging from "a female with a larger clitoris" to a "male with no testes." Children so born are subjected to the same surgically enforced standards as are other intersexed children. Clitoridectomies and other extensive procedures often lead to loss of erotic sensation and psychological trauma. Again, ISNA rightly opposes surgery that is "unnecessary, cosmetic . . . primarily 'cultural' in its significance [and] of no benefit to the child."

Adrenal Hyperplasia

Adrenal Hyperplasia also virilizes XX people in utero. The adrenal glands, functioning anomalously, produce a hormone that has a masculinizing effect. At puberty, a person with Congenital Adrenal Hyperplasia may experience virtually complete bodily masculinization, despite the possession of XX chromosomes. The effects are similar to those of progestin-induced virilization, and surgery can cause similar loss of erotic sensation and psychological trauma.

---

13. Intersex Society of North America, "Frequently Asked Questions: What is Partial Androgen Insensitivity Syndrome?" ISNA's Web site is updated regularly and contains the latest information on intersexuality The complete index is on the organization's home page at <http://www.isna.org>.

Klinefelter Syndrome

Instead of inheriting a single X chromosome from their mothers and a single Y from their fathers, as most men do, *Klinefelter syndrome* men inherit an extra X chromosome from either father or mother. Consequently, their chromosomal pattern could be construed as XX with an extra Y chromosome or as XY with an extra X chromosome. One medical dictionary describes people with Klinefelter's as genetically female and pragmatically male.[14] Often at puberty these people do not develop facial and body hair or deep voices and heavy muscles as strongly as their peers, and some experience breast growth. Because they produce no sperm, they are infertile. Physicians usually recommend that Klinefelter men take testosterone all their lives, but many Klinefelter members of the Intersex Society of North America do not like the effects of taking testosterone and prefer to reduce their dosage or refuse to take it at all.

According to the ISNA, many Klinefelter men are gay, some are transsexual, and nearly all experience their gender as very different from that of other males. I am privileged to have as a friend a gay male named Patrick J. Shevlin Jr. who, as a Klinefelter's person, was being poisoned by too much testosterone until a physician named John Kauderer took an interest in him and insisted that his treatment be modified. Patrick tells me that he has always felt "caught at times between masculine and feminine," feeling about seventy-five percent male and twenty-five percent female. He also feels that he lost his youthful years because in his case the Klinefelter syndrome diagnosis did not come until he was forty. He would like to see an equality of all sexualities and genders—"not special but equal." And, of course, so would I.

The Suffering of Intersexuals

Understandably, many intersexuals learn to distrust medical practitioners and consequently avoid medical care, dropping the hormone

---

14. Sally Gross, "Intersexuality and Scripture," *Theology and Sexuality* 11 (September 1999), 67.

therapy that had been prescribed for them during puberty. But ceasing to take the hormones results in extreme osteoporosis (brittle bones). Because sex hormones (principally testosterone or estrogen) are necessary for maintaining healthy bones, people without functioning gonads should maintain hormone replacement therapy all their lives.

The case of Heidi, born genetically male but with a tiny penis, demonstrates why intersexuals might want to avoid the doctors who had decided their gender fate. Born in 1961, Heidi has contemplated suicide more than once, not because she is intersexual but because of unrelenting medical attempts to make her appear "normal." When she was three months old, doctors cut open her abdomen to inspect her reproductive system. At seventeen months, they went back into her abdomen to remove her ill-formed testes. When she was five years old, her penis was removed without her prior knowledge. But as a teenager, she refused to let doctors create a vagina. She lives now as a lesbian but has never had an orgasm, since a lover's touch feels like "40-grit sandpaper." She is understandably bitter and sometimes fantasizes about hacking off the doctors' genitals. By contrast, twelve adults with intact "micropenises" reported having normal erections and orgasms. Seven of them are married or cohabiting, and one has fathered a child.[15] Angela, an intersexual who seemed to be a "normal" girl until her clitoris began to enlarge into a penis when she was twelve (in 1988) says she loved that penis and remembers the six months before surgery as being "in the pleasure garden before the fall." She regards the loss of that penis (which doctors describe as giving her a normal-looking female clitoris) as the loss of her "unique hermaproditic sexuality."

Similarly, Heidi describes the destruction of hermaproditic eroticism as genocide, not through killing people, but through taking from them that which is unique about them. To Angela, this was the theft of her "sacred sexuality."[16]

---

15. Geoffrey Cowley, "Gender Limbo," *Newsweek*, 19 May 1997, 64–67.

16. *Hermaphrodites Speak!* Videotape available from the Intersex Society of America, P.O. Box 3070, Ann Arbor MI 48106-3070. Also available through their on-line catalog at <http://www.isna.org>.

Heidi and Angela appear on a videotape, *Hermaphrodites Speak!*, made in 1996 and available from the Intersex Society of America. The videotape features 10 intersexual people at the first international gathering of intersexuals as they talk about the lies and mutilations they have suffered at the hands of the medical and psychological establishments. All agree that they would have preferred to have been left alone, "not helped so much." The one person to have "somehow avoided surgery," Hida, spoke of her good health and her love of her body. She emphasized that her only problems came from "society's need to polarize gender and the pressure to conform." Hida stressed that "the problem is not the child, but the attitudes toward the child."

It disturbs me to know that so many intersexual children are mutilated by well-meaning doctors who think surgery is necessary to prevent parents or other people from treating them like outcasts. It disturbs me that intersexuals are often brought up in secrecy that makes them feel freakish, shameful, and isolated. It disturbs me that "expert" doctors continue to make the decision that no one can be allowed to remain intersexual, instead of listening to the voices of adult intersexual people who feel they have been seriously harmed by medical intervention. It disturbs me that intersexuals should feel so abused by physicians that they would risk severe osteoporosis rather than submit themselves to medical supervision.

Morgan Holmes, who was subjected during childhood to "clitoral recession" surgery that removed most of her clitoris, writes that she would have liked to have grown up in the body she was born with. "Someone else made the decision of what and who I would always be before I even knew who and what I was."[17] The vast majority of intersex surgery involves normal little girls whose clitorises are deemed too large by doctors, often because the doctors fear the girls will grow up to be masculinized lesbians.[18] In the context of

---

17. Morgan Holmes, "Re-membering a Queer Body," *Undercurrents* (May 1994): 11–13. *Undercurrents* is published by the Faculty of Environmental Studies at York University, 4700 Kiele St., North York, Ontario, Canada M3J 1P3.

18. Wilchins, *Read My Lips*, 218.

the Golden Rule, I wonder how many surgeons would like to have been rendered sexually dysfunctional for no other purpose than to fit cosmetically into a binary male/female social construction.

I yearn for the day when sexuality might be celebrated in all of its subtle diversities, rather than feared, ridiculed, and manipulated toward an inflexible norm. In such a society, intersexual children could be raised unshamed and unashamed until such a time as they might choose either to seek medical intervention or to remain as intersexual as ever. In such a society, athletes would not be disqualified because they have genetic anomalies that give them no competitive advantage.[19] Approximately one in every five or six hundred female athletes has the Androgen Insensitivity Syndrome, which means she is genetically male, possessing both X and Y chromosomes. But since this confers no competitive advantage, it is cruel to disqualify her. Such cruelty is typical of what occurs when a culture attempts to force everyone into a single Procrustean bed of binary gender.

William O. Beeman, associate professor of anthropology at Brown University, has written that "between 3 million and 10 million Americans are neither male nor female at birth."[20] Beeman quotes Dr. Anne Fausto-Sterling's estimate that intersexual births range from one percent to four percent of all children today. Therefore, says Beeman, "there are perhaps millions of XX males and XY females living in the United States today. There are cultural males with male genitalia who are genetically female, and cultural females with female genitalia who are genetically male."

---

19. Joan Stephenson, "Medical News and Perspectives: Female Olympians' Sex Tests Outmoded," *The Journal of the American Medical Association*, 17 July 1996 <http://www.ama-assn.org/sci-pubs/journals/archive/jama/vol_276/no_3/ mn6135.htm>.

20. William O. Beeman, "What Are You? Male, Merm, Herm, Ferm, or Female?" *Baltimore Sun* (17 March 1996), Perspective Section, 1F. Used by permission. The headline refers to Dr. Anne Fausto-Sterling's tongue-in-cheek suggestion of five biological groupings. Those intersexuals with both testes and ovaries would be "herms," those with testes and some female genitals but no ovaries would be "merms," and those with ovaries and some male genitalia but no testes would be "ferms."

Beeman uses information about intersexuals to show that although legislation to grant official recognition only to marriages between "a man and a woman" is intended to block homosexual marriage, it would also "unwittingly nullify or prevent millions of supposedly heterosexual marriages." In other words, Beeman's point is that the categories of "man and woman" are not so obviously clear that they need no further explanation, and "a large number of destructive and expensive court cases will arise if such restrictive and ill-conceived marriage laws are passed."

I fully agree with Professor Beeman's conclusion that "it would seem far more reasonable to allow any two persons wishing to ratify a personal relationship to do so without having to satisfy a standard that has little relationship to reality." But as much as I favor honoring and celebrating marriages between any people who want such relational recognition, my purpose in this book is wider yet. In order to move society toward an omnigender paradigm, what I want to emphasize is Professor Beeman's statement that "a two-category male/female system can never encompass the variety of human gender construction." In short, intersexual people are the best biological evidence we have that the binary gender construct is totally inadequate and is causing terrific injustice and unnecessary suffering.

Transsexuals

Having examined some background information on intersexuality (superficial, perhaps, but better than nothing), we can more readily understand that some adults are willing to undergo complex surgery in order to shift from one socially recognized gender to another. Transsexuality is a function of the binary gender construct, because when only two alternatives exist, a person is forced to choose one and then do whatever is necessary to present herself or himself in a way that is culturally appropriate. However, the transsexual did not create and does not support the binary gender system. Instead, transsexual experience highlights the fact that the system is not natural but constructed and then maintained by laws that are gender-biased.[21]

---

21. Kate More, "Trans Theory in the U.K.," *Reclaiming Genders*, 255.

In the case of *male-to-female* transsexuals, this choosing calls for dresses, high heels, and make-up.[22] It is hard for a lesbian like me, who views high heels and skirts as a means of keeping women vulnerable, to comprehend how anyone who could have the freedom and comfort of male clothing would choose to accept such culturally devised limitations. Despite my love of women and my own identity as a woman, I find *female-to-male* transsexuality much easier to understand because of the freedoms and respect that come with "masculinity." But male-to-female transsexuality is for me excellent proof that despite the binary inequities, for some people surgery is necessary in order to fulfill their internal sense of gender and their erotic choices.

Speaking from her own experience as a transsexual person, Riki Anne Wilchins in *Read My Lips* quotes Alice Walker's wonderful statement that "no person is your friend (or kin) who demands your silence, or denies your right to grow and be perceived as fully blossomed as you were intended. Or who belittles in any fashion the gifts you labor so to bring into the world."[23] How I wish I had heard those words early in life, when I persisted in befriending people who diminished my person and my gifts by ignoring or belittling them! I was of course replicating several uncaring relationships I had grown accustomed to in childhood, and now that I have learned to love God's incarnation within my Self, I wonder how I ever put up with such diminishment. Being lesbian in a fundamentalist context of course exacerbated any tendency to accept unsupportive treatment. So I can certainly resonate with Wilchins's words about transsexuals: "Wanting desperately to be accepted, and unable to take on the

---

22. *Different for Girls*, a 1996 BBC romantic comedy available from Fox Lorber Home Videos, makes clear both the dangers and the joys of a male-to-female transitioning. Actor Steven Mackintosh does a sensitive, convincing performance as Kim, a heterosexual post-operative transsexual who had endured persecution as Karl but who faced down all opposition to secure for herself a fulfilled and happy life.

23. From Alice Walker, *In Search of Our Mother's Gardens: Womanist Prose* (San Diego: Harcourt Brace Jovanovich, Harvest/HBJ Books, 1983), 36, as quoted by Wilchins, *Read My Lips*, 47.

whole world alone, we have too often listened to those voices that were not our own." Wilchins also describes the journey of another male-to-female transsexual whose growth toward self-acceptance led through developing a sense of community, as mine also did: "She learned that although she might hate herself, she could not hate the fifty or one hundred other transsexuals she met, whose stories she heard, whose tears of frustration and rage she saw, whose everyday, one-day-at-a-time courage to survive she saw. And she understood, at last, the redemptive power of community" (48).

What sorts of injustices do transsexuals face? They may encounter severe judgment and abandonment by their families when their gender discomfort becomes evident. They often experience great loneliness and isolation because there are so few places where transsexuals can get together to share anecdotes and process information. Like other transpeople, transsexuals are sometimes assumed to be suffering from personality disorders, psychosis, or mental illness. Studies of transsexuals have been unreliable, lacking scientifically controlled comparisons with transsexuals who need no mental health care, and lacking a proper appreciation of the impact of transgenderphobic discrimination.[24] Susan Stryker, a well-known trans-theorist whose book *Changing Sex* is soon to be published by Oxford University Press, explains that during the Cold War era, candidates for sex reassignment surgery were required to spend months or even years proving to academically sanctioned "experts" that they could live in their "gender role of choice" once they were permitted access to hormones and surgery. "The obvious if unstated goal of these programmes was to produce transsexual men and women who conformed to heteronormative gender conventions, including the visual appearance of a conventional female or male morphology."[25]

When the time approaches to prepare for gender reassignment surgery by first living for a full year in the genetically-other sex role (usually required before such surgery can take place), many trans-

---

24. Israel and Tarver, *Transgender Care*, 26.
25. Susan Stryker, "Portrait of a Transfag Drag Hag as a Young Man," *Reclaiming Genders*, 69.

sexuals find it necessary to change jobs to ease the transition. Insensitive coworkers can make life unbearable for a transsexual. For that reason, some large companies now offer sensitivity training in which the transsexual worker, coworkers, and management can meet in a safe and structured environment to ask questions and receive clarification.

Like other transpeople, transsexuals face victimization by hostile strangers: murder, the possibility of arrest, the loss of their children after divorce, and loss of employment and housing. When arrested, transsexual women are often put into men's holding cells, where they are repeatedly raped.

Transsexuals are often presumed to be homosexual, but only about half of male-to-females end up as lesbians. Among females-to-males, an increasing number identify as bisexual or gay. But people cannot be sure where their change of gender may lead them because sexuality can be very fluid during the transitional time.[26]

Frequently, although times are better than those described by Stryker, transsexuals still must work hard to convince psychotherapeutic professionals that they really do need access to surgical and hormonal gender reassignment techniques. Once they have achieved access, they undergo tremendously expensive and complex procedures, most of them not covered by health insurance because the surgeries are considered elective—even if the individual is close to suicide without them. Many transsexuals work two minimum-wage jobs and engage in sex-work in order to pay for their surgeries. And God help them should they get involved in an accident! Emergency health technicians often refuse to help critically injured pre-operative transsexuals once they discover the "wrong genitals." Some transsexuals have even been left to die of their injuries.

---

26. David Harrison, "The Transsexual Mythtique," *Out in All Directions: The Almanac of Gay and Lesbian America*, ed. Lynn Witt, Sherry Thomas, and Eric Marcus (New York: Warner Books, 1995), 409. Just how fluid sexuality and gender identity may *continue* to be for many people is made clear by Bornstein in *My Gender Workbook*. Although I love Bornstein's playfulness and compassionate spirit, I do not think she has done justice to *long-term in-depth* relationships, in which gender freshness and freedom are explored within one relationship rather than in a series of sexual encounters.

When a transsexual and two of his friends were murdered in 1996, a comedian on the *Saturday Night Live* television program made fun of the murders. Yet when President Clinton signed the Hate Crimes Statistics Act in July 1996, hate crimes based on gender were still excluded.[27]

Even within the Queer[28] community, transsexuals have faced discrimination. In 1991, the National Lesbian Conference in Atlanta banned "nongenetic women" because the group had embraced the theories of Mary Daly and Janice Raymond[29] that transsexual women are surgically altered men created by patriarchal doctors in order to invade women's space.[30] I certainly agree with Raymond and Daly that patriarchal society has generated rigid sex roles, and I hope that if and when gender pluralism becomes a fact, fewer people will feel the need to seek gender reassignment surgery, although some will and should have the right to do so. But I oppose "women-born-women only" statements that have sometimes appeared in flyers for lesbian events because such statements discriminate against male-to-female transsexuals. In 1994 at the Gay Games in New York City, a transsexual woman was told she would probably have to compete as a man. It was only after much protest by the Transsexual Menace, Transgender Rights, and other organizations that the policy was overturned.[31] As a lesbian, I grieve that the lesbian community has involved itself in prejudice against transsexuals.

At the same time, I appreciate Kate Bornstein's distinction between *exclusion* and *oppression*.[32] The organizers of the Michigan Women's Music Festival were not oppressing transsexuals when they excluded them—they were seeking safe space for women in a culture that oppresses both women and transsexuals. Kate, herself a

27. Wilchins, *Read My Lips*, 208, 210.

28. See note 1 concerning the term *Queer*.

29. Raymond's book is *The Transsexual Empire: The Making of the She-Male* (Boston: Beacon Press, 1979).

30. Wilchins, *Read My Lips*, 110, 231.

31. Ibid., 74.

32. At a discussion of "Transgender Politics," sponsored by the Center for Lesbian and Gay Studies, New York City, Sept. 11, 1999.

transsexual, questioned why anyone would want to force entry into an event where they were not welcome—but I wondered what people are to do if they are not really welcome anywhere.

According to Martine Rothblatt, "The leading explanation of transsexuality is that a person's chromosomes triggered levels of testosterone and estrogen that resulted in the genitals of one sex and the thought patterns of the other sex."[33] Similarly, Susan Menking, M.D., says that "the basis for transsexual feelings is . . . most likely the result of some as yet unidentified prenatal hormonal influences on the developing brain."[34] For this reason, more than a thousand people every year undergo sex-change surgery, and many others stop short of surgery but use hormones to change their facial hair, voices, and physiques.[35]

Suzanne Kessler and Wendy McKenna claimed in 1978 that if society relaxed its basic rules about gender and learned to tolerate ambiguity, "there would be no transsexuals. There would be men with vaginas and women with penises or perhaps different signs of gender. Similarly, if men could wear dresses there would be no transvestism."[36] But their claims do not give adequate weight to the sense of incongruity between identity and body that is reported by many transsexuals. For instance, one female-to-male transsexual says he would still want surgery and hormones even if society were totally tolerant because he was uncomfortable having a vagina and breasts when he was so different socially and psychologically from others who had vaginas and breasts.[37]

Although most people are more aware of male-to-female transsexuals like Christine Jorgenson, Renee Richards, and Jan Morris,

---

33. Martine Aliana Rothblatt, *The Apartheid of Sex: A Manifesto on the Freedom of Gender* (New York: Crown, 1995), 7.

34. Susan Menking, "The Biology of Homosexuality and Transgendered," unpublished text available from the author by request at: MSmenking@aol.com.

35. Rothblatt, *The Apartheid of Sex*, 17.

36. Suzanne Kessler and Wendy McKenna, *Gender: An Ethnomethodological Approach* (New York: John Wiley & Sons, 1978), 181.

37. Henry S. Rubin, "Trans Studies: Between a Metaphysics of Presence and Absence," *Reclaiming Genders*, 181.

actual current statistics indicate an approximately equal number of females-to-males.[38] The latter are less noticed because they are more deeply closeted, because professional and transpeople's consumer resources have focused on the males-to-females, and also because females-to-males are more successful at "passing."[39]

In *Gender Outlaw*, Kate Bornstein points out that our culture tends to assume maleness unless there are at least four unambiguous female clues to outweigh the presence of one male clue (26). Furthermore, Bornstein feels that female-to-male transsexuals are more dangerous to the binary gender system than their male-to-female counterparts (245). They become part of the new, egalitarian, sensitive, caring kind of manliness currently being birthed in our culture. But "the group who still grunt and scratch" (Bornstein's words) use their power to silence and erase those presences who threaten their supremacy. Nevertheless, in *My Gender Workbook*, Bornstein insists that "Compassion is the foundation of a transgender politic, beginning with compassion for ourselves and extending outward to compassion toward other outlaws, friends, allies, families, and ultimately compassion even for those who recoil from us in horror" (262). Sounds like another Jewish person named Jesus of Nazareth!

Cross-Dressers (Transvestites)

Transvestites (who prefer the term *cross-dresser* because it sounds less clinical) dress in the clothing of the "other" gender for emotional satisfaction, for erotic pleasure, or for both. On the deepest level, cross-dressing is an attempt to live the full truth of one's nature in which the cross-dresser feels profoundly identified both with her/his own and with the "other" gender (i.e., the trans-dresser is bi-gendered to one degree or another). The cross-dresser has no desire to change biological sex characteristics but simply wants to explore the feelings and behaviors of the "opposite" gender. (I place "other" and "opposite" in quotation marks because I do not believe

---

38. Harrison, "The Transsexual Mythtique," 409.

39. Israel and Tarver, *Transgender Care*, 7; Kate Bornstein, *Gender Outlaw* (New York: Vintage Books, 1994), 244.

in a stark male/female opposition, but the limitations of language force the use of imprecise terminology at this transitional time.) Sometimes, but not always, the cross-dressing involves a sexual fetish. Sometimes the individual chooses to cross-dress completely for a certain period of time and quietly passes as the "other" gender.

However, certain women have cross-dressed all their adult lives in order to meet their inner needs and at the same time achieve the opportunities and freedoms of maleness. Billy Tipton, for instance, was a married jazz musician whose femaleness was discovered only after "his" death in 1989.[40] Murray Hall was a twice-married New York City politician. Lucy Ann Lobdell left her husband to become the Reverend Joseph Lobdell, cohabiting with Maria Perry.[41] These cross-dressers often convinced their partners that they had suffered severe abdominal injuries that made coitus impossible, thus protecting their secret.

Intermittent cross-dressers are usually heterosexual, although some few may be bisexual, gay, or lesbian. Many are heterosexually married. Over the years, I have seen numerous Ann Landers columns like the one that appeared on May 2, 1999, headlined "Cross-dresser leaves an anguished widow." It featured a letter from "Devastated in Texas" who discovered after his death that her "devoted loving" husband had had a secret habit of wearing women's clothes. As always, Landers counseled acceptance of cross-dressing husbands as the wisest and kindest course of action, since the cross-dressing is about the internal needs of these men and in no way compromises their loving responsibility toward their wives and families.

---

40. See Diane Wood Middlebrook, *Suits Me: The Double Life of Billy Tipton* (New York: Houghton Mifflin, 1998). Jason Cromwell objects to calling Billy Tipton a lesbian or someone who cross-dressed simply for socioeconomic advantage: "Does his life as a man have no meaning?" See Cromwell, "Passing Women and Female-Bodied Men: (Re)claiming FTM History," *Reclaiming Genders*, 34–61.

41. For more on these and many other cross-dressers, see Marjorie Garber, *Vested Interests: Cross Dressing and Cultural Anxiety* (New York: Routledge, 1992). Vern L. Bullough and Bonnie Bullough provide a six-page annotated bibliography in their *Cross-Dressing, Sex, and Gender* (Philadelphia: University of Pennsylvania Press, 1993).

Lord Robert Baden-Powell, founder of the Boy Scout movement, was well-known for his "skirt-dancing" and female impersonations both during his school years and during his long career in the British Army. Although he shared a residence for many years with Kenneth McLaren, Baden-Powell finally married at age 55, choosing a woman who preferred to wear a Boy Scouts' uniform rather than the uniform of the Girl Guides.[42] Yet this cross-dresser was a staunch upholder of binary gender and Victorian ideals of masculinity. In 1922 he wrote, "We badly need some training for our lads if we are to keep up manliness in our race instead of lapsing into a nation of soft, sloppy, cigarette suckers."[43]

Vanessa S., a heterosexually married Christian cross-dressing male, has a wife who is so accepting that she suggested the name "Vanessa" for her husband's feminine aspect and insisted that he cross-dress in a dignified and woman-respecting way. He has written about it in his book *Cross Purposes: On Being a Christian and Crossgendered* (Decatur, Ga.: American Educational Gender Information Service, 1996), where he testifies: "As my public exposure to femininity continued to increase, so did my sense of self-esteem. It's a wonderful thing to begin liking and accepting yourself for the person you are instead of trying to live up to someone else's idea of who and what you ought to be" (85-86).

Louise Kaplan, a psychoanalyst, sees cross-dressing as a perversion and defines transvestites as heterosexual males who are in dread of their female longings. Proud of his masculine identity, the transvestite gratifies his desire to be dependent, vulnerable, and submissive while still reassuring himself that he is a powerful and dominant male. He does this by dressing up as a "Phallic Woman."[44] But I am uncomfortable with Kaplan's definition because of its clinical and

---

42. Garber, *Vested Interests*, 170–71, 184.

43. As quoted by Sean Gill, "Christian Manliness Unmanned: Some Problems and Challenges in the Study of Masculinity and Religion in Nineteenth- and Twentieth-Century Western Society," *Is There a Future for Feminist Theology?*, ed. Deborah F. Sawyer and Diane M. Collier (Sheffield, England: Sheffield Academic Press, 1999), 160.

44. Louise Kaplan, *Female Perversions* (New York: Anchor Books, 1991), 242.

distancing tone. I prefer Leslie Feinberg's warmer, more empathetic definition that the cross-dresser expresses both "masculine" and "feminine" aspects: "We cross-dressers don't have to explain *why* we are the way we are. We have to explain *who* we are. How we see ourselves."[45]

Many cross-dressers feel bad about their cross-dressing; consequently, the International Foundation for Gender Education (IFGE) urges them to join one of the support groups available all over the United States. According to the IFGE, the urge to cross-dress "may be hard-wired into the brain. It will not go away. Unless you face your feelings, denial will cause frustration, anger, and depression."[46]

Because it is a felony to check the "M" box on identification papers if you were born female (or vice versa), when people are cross-dressed they are in the same danger that transsexuals and intersexuals face. Imagine being pulled over for driving too fast and having to hand the police officer a license that identifies you as the gender "opposite" to your hairstyle and the clothes you are wearing! Just as the Civil Rights and Black Liberation movements forced authorities to remove the boxes for identifying a person's race, cross-dressers of any gender or sexual orientation would be much safer if the M or F boxes were removed from documents such as driver's licenses and passports. A photograph should be sufficient for identification purposes, and a several-gendered person could be issued identification with several photographs to reflect all aspects of who they are. Of course, there might be great nervousness about criminal misuse of cross-dressed photographs; but photographs often do not resemble their subjects very perfectly, and there is no reason why several photographs would be more misleading than one—especially if accompanied by a disclosure letter.

Since cross-dressing is something done either occasionally or constantly across the whole spectrum of transgender identity, its

---

45. Feinberg, *Trans Liberation*, 29.

46. *About Cross-Dressers and Cross-Dressing*, brochure available from the International Foundation for Gender Education, P.O. Box 229, Waltham MA 02454-0229; phone 617-894-8340. Includes a bibliography and referral information.

meaning is complex and many-splendored. Marjorie Garber, who could never be accused of oversimplifying, puts it this way:

> [C]ultural observers have tried to make [cross-dressing] mean something, anything, other than itself. . . . Cross-dressing is about gender-confusion. Cross-dressing is about the phallus as constitutively veiled. Cross-dressing is about the power of women. Cross-dressing is about the emergence of gay identity. Cross-dressing is about the anxiety of economic or cultural dislocation, the anticipation or recognition of "otherness" as loss. All true, all partial truths, all powerful metaphors. But the compelling force of transvestism in literature and culture comes not, or not only, from these effects, but also from its instatement of metaphor itself, not as that for which literal meaning must be found, but precisely as that without which there would be no such thing as meaning in the first place.[47]

Garber has noticed that cross-dressing has been consistently avoided as a theoretical "third term" and made to disappear by seeing it merely as male or female manqué. But on the contrary, cross-dressing challenges "notions of binarity, putting into question the categories of 'female' and 'male,' whether they are considered essential or constructed, biological or cultural." Cross-dressing is currently as popular as it is in both art and criticism because we are coming to the realization that comfortable binary thinking is being destabilized—not just male and female, but also black and white, yes and no, Republican and Democrat, self and other, and so forth.[48] In other words, borderlines are becoming permeable.

Drag Queens and Drag Kings

Permeable, but not obliterated. Many heterosexual cross-dressers resent being confused with drag queens, regarding them as "nothing but gay men who dress in women's clothes." It is unfortunate to find homophobia among transpeople, but prejudice comes naturally

---

47. Garber, *Vested Interests*, 389–90.
48. Ibid., 11.

to any human being who has forgotten that all of us are manifestations of One Great Spirit and therefore that an attack on others is an attack on ourselves. Prejudice is no more ugly, and no prettier either, when expressed by transpeople than by anybody else.

Drag queens are males (usually gay) who impersonate females and enjoy displaying themselves as depictions of femininity. They are often as glamorously feminine as the most feminine women. There is usually a strong element of fun and elaborate pretense in the drag queen's performance, announced by names like "Divine," "Lady Bunny," "Miss Kitty," "Aurora Borealis," "Philthee Ritz," or "Tess Tosterone." As Henry S. Rubin points out, "Gay drag culture operates on a tension between appearance and reality where performers reveal they are parodying the real. If the 1991 film *Paris Is Burning* were released today, it would be more appropriate to call it a transgender film than a gay drag film, because the male to female people in *Paris* aspired to attain realness, whereas gay drag aspires to parody."[49] Gay drag enjoys great popularity: Every Labor Day thousands of participants and spectators flock to Manhattan's East Village for the annual drag celebration, "Wigstock."

Drag kings are females (usually lesbian) who cross-dress for entertainment purposes or perhaps permanently. Like their drag-queen brothers, they may at the same time consciously intend to challenge sexual stereotypes or to achieve personal satisfaction. But drag as entertainment is so far a predominantly male-to-female art form. If lesbians sponsor strip shows or erotic performances, it is difficult to code them as queer, lesbian, and deconstructive; therefore, drag kings frequently can wind up looking simply male and rather ordinary. I remember watching a TV performance in which lesbian singer k.d. lang dazzled an audience by swift changes of gender achieved through body language, facial expression, and clothing. But I later saw another k.d. lang performance in which she had cross-dressed in a tuxedo. She sang ballads in what seemed to me a disappointingly ordinary way. Judith Halberstam quite plausibly explains that

---

49. Henry S. Rubin, "Trans Studies: Between a Metaphysics of Presence and Absence," *Reclaiming Genders*, 173.

because mainstream definitions assume that male masculinity is nonperformative while "femininity reeks of the artificial," male impersonation did not achieve currency with the lesbian bar culture until very recently.[50] Certainly, wit of some sort is necessary to encode male impersonation as queer and/or destabilizing of binary gender. Deidre Sinott demonstrates the requisite wit by choosing for her drag name the words "Al Dente."[51] So do the women who perform as "Elvis Herselvis," "Justin Case," "Lizarace," or "Mo.B. Dick."

Performance artists differ from transvestites in their freedom to choose whether or not to cross-dress on any given occasion. Many male transvestites are serious and secretive about their preoccupation with women's clothing and cross-dress out of compulsion.[52] By contrast, drag queens are usually as open and flamboyant as possible.

Leslie Feinberg widens the definition of drag, describing it as a lifestyle or constant performance:

> The gay and lesbian drag communities . . . have always been 'out.' We are hounded virtually everywhere we go in public because of our gender expression. . . . The gay bars I first discovered in the 1960s in Buffalo, Niagara Falls, and southern Ontario are also transgender bars. They were filled with masculine females, feminine males, and our partners—who had their own highly stylized gender expression. A masculine female was referred to as "butch"; a feminine male as a "queen." If we cross-dressed, we were referred to as "drag." Drag queens and drag kings are gay and lesbian cross-dressers.[53]

Feinberg objects to the widespread notion that drag queens and kings over-exaggerate femininity and masculinity to the point of caricature. She insists that "each person's expression of their gender

---

50. Judith Halberstam, *Female Masculinity* (Durham: Duke University Press, 1998). Halberstam provides an in-depth discussion of Drag Kings in her chapter "Masculinity and Performance," 231–66.

51. See her essay, "My Goal Is to Change Society," *Trans Liberation*, 145–46.

52. Kaplan, *Female Perversions*, 242.

53. Feinberg, *Trans Liberation*, 23.

or genders is their own and equally beautiful. To refer to anyone's gender expression as exaggerated is insulting and restricts gender freedom."[54]

Plenty to think about there! And before I leave this topic, I must bear witness to the beneficial effects of a really first-rate drag show. When men of all shapes and sizes perform in drag with compassion, humor, and good will, the effect is to make everyone in the theater feel better about herself or himself. I remember a show in Portland, Oregon, that was not only sexy and funny but also teasing, tender, and remarkably wholesome—the absolute antithesis of the cold emptiness of the one and only pornographic show I ever attended. So far as I am concerned, drag is (or can be) a most liberating experience.

Transgenderists

This chapter has been devoted to the definition and discussion of the inequities suffered by transpeople, all of whom can be and currently are referred to as transgender people (or transgenderists). Inasmuch as there is a core group entitled to the original meaning of the term, it would be the people who live in role part-time or full-time as members of the "opposite" gender. Sometimes transgenderists utilize hormone or cosmetic surgery or even castration, but they do not seek gender reassignment surgery. Occasionally they self-identify as bi-gender.[55]

One of the most cogent descriptions of having a transgender core identity occurs in Leslie Feinberg's novel, *Stone Butch Blues*.[56] In that novel, Jess Goldberg, a working-class "butch," is beaten up and raped so often (usually by police), and lives so much in threat of yet more violence, that she takes male hormones in order to achieve the safety of "passing." And that ploy works fairly well,

---

54. Ibid., 24.

55. Israel and Tarver, *Transgender Care*, 15.

56. I am grateful to Paisley Currah of Brooklyn College, whose discussion of the novel as "a transgender narrative" (New York City, 9 October 1999) caused me to reread it and include it here.

except that Jess is forced to drive without a license and cannot leave the United States because "his" body and "her" birth certificate do not match. Jess also loses status in the lesbian community and loses "his" relationship with Theresa, who cannot stomach living with a "man" and being perceived as a heterosexual (i.e., losing her lesbian identity).

But the most serious problem Jess faces while passing as a man is the loss of "his" sense of "himself" as an authentic "he/she," what today we would call a transgenderist. "I didn't feel like a woman or a man, and I liked how I was different," Jess says about one of "her" dreams (143). "I don't feel like a man trapped in a woman's body," Jess explains, "I just feel trapped" (159).

When a young woman is attracted to "him," Jess ponders the fact that "Acceptance of me as a he felt like an ongoing indictment of me as a he-she" (178). When "he" meets an old friend who asks what "passing" is like, Jess responds, "Some of it is fun. I was tied up so tight all the time as a he-she. It feels good to do little things, like go to a public bathroom in peace or to be touched by a barber." But then he explains his sadness: "I feel like a ghost, Edna. Like I've been buried alive. As far as the world's concerned, I was born the day I began to pass. I have no past, no loved ones, no memories, no me. No one really sees me or touches me" (243).

A few minutes later, when Jess says that "he" doesn't like being neither male nor female, Edna expresses what may well be the essence of transgender politics: "There's other ways to be than either-or. It's not so simple. Otherwise there wouldn't be so many people who don't fit. You're beautiful, Jess, but I don't have words to help people see that" (218).

Looking into a mirror, Jess feels trapped behind "his" hormone-induced beard: "What I saw reflected in the mirror was not a man, but I couldn't recognize the he-she. My face no longer revealed the contrasts of my gender. I could see my passing self, but even I could no longer see the more complicated me beneath my surface" (222).

When Jess stops taking the hormones, "her" body begins to blend back toward a more mixed-gender appearance, and people notice. Some refer to "her" as *it*. Jess realizes, "The only recognition I can find in their eyes is that I am 'other.' I am different. I will always be different. I will never be able to nestle my skin against the comfort of sameness" (224).

When Jess makes friends with a transgenderist named Ruth, the two of them are afraid to go out in public together because of the trouble they might cause in people who are frightened of ambiguity. Jess sighs that she had wanted to do something really important in her life instead of fighting over which bathroom she could use, but Ruth reminds her, "I've seen people risk their lives for the right to sit at a lunch counter. If you and I aren't going to fight for the right to live, then the kids coming up will have to do it" (256). Ruth's words could well be taken as the manifesto for an omnigender revolution.

Discussing whether or not they could become lovers of one another, Ruth and Jess admit that even they are afraid to relate to each other's ambiguities and complexities. They are "neither night nor day" (270). And even in her difference, Jess admits that she "always wanted all of us who were different to be the same" (271). In other words, even people with a transgender core identity have been socialized to prefer binaries and to fear difference—so they must combat not only society's violent repudiation of themselves, but their own terror of one another.

At the end of *Stone Butch Blues*, Jess has a dream in which she feels proud to be sitting in a round hut with people like herself: "It was hard to say who was a woman, who was a man. Their faces radiated a different kind of beauty than I'd grown up seeing celebrated on television or in magazines. It's a beauty one isn't born with, but must fight to construct at great sacrifice" (300). In the light of that dream, Jess feels her whole life coming full circle: "*Growing up so different, coming out as a butch, passing as a man, and then back to the same question that had shaped my life: woman or man?*" And she decides, "I'm sorry that it's had to be this hard. But if I hadn't walked this path, who would I be?" (301) Her hopes soar as she remembers the challenge given to her by Duffy, a labor union organizer: "*Imagine a world worth living in, a world worth fighting for.*" Clearly, a world worth fighting for would be one in which people were appreciated in all their complexities instead of being rejected and attacked for not sorting out neatly into one of two possible genders.

Can we learn to live with gender ambiguity? It won't be easy, as I learned to my amusement recently. A transgender young person I know had told me that she'd recently done a drag performance at a gathering of CLOUT (Christian Lesbians Out Together). I assumed that the drag she referred to was masculine. But no: She wrote back to tell me, "When I wear a jacket and tie to church, I don't consider it drag. What I did at CLOUT was put on a Trans Elmo's wig, a pink taffeta semiformal and heels, and strut to Boy George's 'I'll Tumble for You.'"

She explained to me that her drag name, Christina Sabrina, refers to a drag queen, not a drag king: "Someone once told me I was an FTM (Female to Male) transsexual crossdresser, but I think the categories just get ridiculous after a while. . . . I'm with Kate [Bornstein] in terms of thinking gender is fluid, dynamic, and ever so complex."[57] But she admitted that as a Christian, she felt somewhat disoriented at a gender workshop for "secular queer folks."

Her feelings highlight the fact that Christians (and religious people generally) offer almost no safe faith-oriented space anywhere for transgender, gay, lesbian, or bisexual youth to sort themselves out. Kirkridge Retreat Center in Bangor, Pennsylvania; the Universal Fellowship of Metropolitan Community Churches; gay synagogues; and the denominational gay-friendly caucuses such as Dignity, Integrity, and the Welcoming Congregations in various denominations are the blessed exceptions.

Transgenderists frequently have trouble obtaining recognition, services, or validation from health-care providers, who may treat them as if they were transsexual and try to steer them toward gender reassignment surgery. What they need from professionals is what all transpeople need: to be listened to, to be assisted in defining their place within the gender spectrum (without nailing it down), and to be connected with others like themselves and with options that correlate with their unique needs.

---

57. Personal letter to the author, 7 October 1999.

Crimes against transgenderists are characterized by overkill and by underreporting. Brandon Teena, a Nebraska female-to-male transgender teenager, was gang-raped and beaten before being killed for having dared to usurp male privilege.[58] National media implied that Brandon deserved the attack; but more typically, there is little if any press coverage when a transgender person is victimized or killed. Very few people ever heard of the transgender San Francisco woman who was followed home, assaulted sexually, beaten to death, and left partially naked in a back alley. Most such cases go unnoticed, because law enforcement officers are hostile to transgenderists and sometimes the chief perpetrators of the abuse.[59] In the ten months between August of 1998 and June of 1999, there have been ten known murders in the United States of people perceived to be transgender; but only now is the media starting to pay attention.[60]

Apart from the physical violence, transgenderists face frequent humiliations that also can be difficult to bear. One male-to-female transgenderist (that is, a male who wear's women's clothes and hairdo to his/her work at the *New York Times*) told a 1999 transgender discussion group that at least once a month, gangs of young men follow him/her for blocks, yelling obscenities like "chicks with dicks!"

In a culture organized around binary gender, therefore, it is truly terrifying to be a transgender youth. Most such young people do all they can to remain invisible. Like most adolescents, they want to seem indistinguishable from their peers. But the overwhelming message they receive from their families, adult society, and their peers is that "gender nonconformity is a sick, mentally unstable condition to be feared, hated and ridiculed."[61]

In approximately one out of every 1,000 young people, transgender feelings reach a peak during the junior high and high school years. Parents who cannot accept the varieties of human experience attempt to control deviant behavior by punishment or

---

58. The 1999 film *Boys Don't Cry* is based on Brandon Teena's story.

59. Israel and Tarver, *Transgender Care*, 37–38.

60. *The Advocate* (22 June 1999), 6.

61. Israel and Tarver, *Transgender Care*, 132.

to cure it through mental health treatments. Some transgender youth are sent off to boarding schools, behavioral camps, or institutions where social conformity is rigidly enforced. But the fact remains that all children need to be accepted for who they are, not for what others think they ought to be. In particular, transgender youth need their family and friends to protect them from medical and governmental intervention. In her book *Gender Shock*, Phyllis Burke points out that the government has spent more than a million and a half dollars experimenting on children who do not fit the binary gender norm.[62]

According to the Larkin Street Youth Center, which serves homeless young people in San Francisco, more than seventeen percent of them test HIV positive, and most of them are gender and/or sexual minorities.[63] They were either thrown out of their homes or else ran away to escape abuse there. Without education, funds, employment, or much maturity, these youngsters are ripe for victimization, exposure to disease, and manipulation by sexually predatory adults.

Like every young person I know of, transgender youth need above all to be accepted. They also should be taught how to communicate effectively and how to counteract abuse from people who cannot or will not accept gender diversity.

Androgynes

Unlike transgenderists who may move from one gender to another on a full- or part-time basis, androgynes *simultaneously* adopt the characteristics of both males and females or else attempt to wear gender-neutral clothing in order to be identifiable as neither male nor female. Some young adults adopt androgyny for a while before moving toward a more clearly articulated gender orientation; and indeed, suggesting androgyny as a temporary option for transgender youth might be a helpful strategy.

---

62. Phyllis Burke, *Gender Shock* (New York: Anchor Books, 1996), as quoted by Bornstein, *My Gender Workbook*, 145.

63. Israel and Tarver, *Transgender Care*, 139.

Some people adopt androgyny to fulfill their own gender identity needs; others may want to challenge gender stereotypes.
Androgynes should not be expected to conform to transvestite or
transsexual models and should not be urged to seek gender reassignment surgery.[64]

In a work situation where an employee is about to make the transition from one gender to another, however, an androgynous gender presentation is sometimes wise. Presenting himself or herself as
both male and female (or neither male nor female) may be a way of
easing the shock to fellow employees. It also will buy time for elec-
trolysis, for the hormones to begin their work, and for the transperson
to learn the disclosure and communication skills that are vital to
success in "trans-ing" gender.

Like other transpeople, androgynes reject the pink-or-blue, either-or gender dichotomies of our culture. They are "shape-shifters"
who identify as either/or or neither/nor or perhaps as members of an
elusive Third Sex. They believe that expecting a human being to
embody only one of two possible genders truncates human gender
expression in ways we cannot even imagine.[65]

Homosexuals and Bisexuals

Strictly speaking, *sexual orientation* is one thing, *gender identity* is
another, and *gender expression* is still another. Although most sex
researchers focus on and recognize only three sexual orientations,
according to people's stories there would appear to be at least seven
(with many others if we were to include various fetishes): heterosexual, homosexual, bisexual, autoerotic, asexual, pansexual, and
pedophiliac. Pedophilia is radically unlike the others, because it
cannot achieve adult consent, being a proclivity toward sexual con-
tact with children. At least in our culture, pedophilia absolutely
cannot be expressed relationally, since everyone younger than the

---

64. Ibid., 15–16, 136.
65. Carol Queen and Lawrence Schimel, *PoMoSexuals: Challenging Assumptions
about Gender and Sexuality* (San Francisco: Cleis Press, 1997), 128.

age of consent deserves the right to develop without being tampered with.[66]

There are also eighteen basic preferences for sexual behaviors, each of which may be expressed actively or passively. It is unnecessary to list them all, but they include strong preference for such behaviors as oral or anal or group sex or sadomasochism.[67] Some people consider their preferences to be aspects of their sexual orientation and gender identity, which is the reason I mention them here.

Gender identity refers to a person's "core" *feeling* of maleness, femaleness, or otherwise. The term is often used concerning transgenderists as opposed to intermittent cross-dressers or people who "do drag."

Gender expression refers to the way people *present* themselves as masculine, feminine, androgynous, or however. Many people assume that sexual orientation is subsumed into gender expression, so that (for instance) sleeping with men is considered an expression of femininity no matter which gender does it (and vice versa). But the fact is that most lesbians, gay males, and bisexuals feel comfortable *identifying* with their birth-gender, although there will be many degrees of "masculinity" and "femininity" in their gender *expression*. Some people with transsexual conditions are able to satisfy themselves with same-sex relationships rather than undergoing the more drastic solution of gender reassignment surgery; but after such surgery, some turn out to

---

66. Having said that, I must also report Dr. Ralph Blair's statement that unless parents or other adults overemphasize incidents of childhood sexual experiences, even with adults, such incidents are not likely to have tragic repercussions. "[In their 1937 article in *The American Journal of Orthopsychiatry*] Bender and Blau concluded that the only guilt feelings which the boys in their study displayed were instigated by anxious adults who disapproved of the sexual contacts" (Ralph Blair, *Etiological and Treatment Literature on Homosexuality* [New York: Homosexual Community Counseling Center, 1972], 24). It is also important to mention that "pedophiliac abuse of both female and male children is committed 96 percent and 80 percent of the time, respectively, by heterosexual males" (Menking, "The Biology of Homosexuality and Transgendered"). Also relevant is the fact that the American Psychiatric Association classifies pedophilia as sexual behavior which is obsessive and compulsive (i.e. paraphilic).

67. Bornstein, *Gender Outlaw*, 37.

be heterosexual, some bisexual, some homosexual. Some intersexual children grow up to be homosexual or bisexual, some are asexual, and some are heterosexual. Nevertheless, the common perception tends to conflate lesbians, gays, and bisexuals with transpeople.

There are good reasons for that common perception. In the first place, since binary gender insists that "real men" desire only women and "real women" desire only men, homosexuals and bisexuals really *do* "trans" or cross over the gender boundary by loving people of their own gender. And among lesbians, butch-femme relationships often do *not* replicate patriarchal gender roles, but transform them into something more egalitarian.[68] In the second place, the heterosexuality of "real men" and "real women" is so bolstered by homophobia that society actually does define gender by sexual orientation. ("Masculinity" depends on *male dominant* heterosexuality, "femininity" on *female submissive* heterosexuality. And homophobia affirms male identity by rejecting whatever seems unmanly and affirms female identity by rejecting whatever seems not sufficiently deferential to males.) It is the fear of being considered homosexual that maintains rigid gender roles. It forces insecure men to pursue women incessantly and to dress sloppily. It forces insecure women to keep on wearing painful shoes and to manifest technical incompetence, especially in the presence of men. The profound connection between gender and sexual orientation is the reason why "femme" males and "butch" females are the most common targets of antigay hate crimes.[69]

And there are thousands of such crimes, most of them unreported. Nearly half of all gay men and lesbian women have been threatened with violence; thirty-three percent have been chased or followed; twenty-seven percent have had objects thrown at them; nine percent have been assaulted with a weapon; eighty percent have been verbally harassed.[70] I am one of the thirteen percent who have

---

68. See Lee Chiaramonte, "A Harrisonian Ontology of the Stone Butch as Process Relational *Imago Dei*," *Theology and Sexuality* 11, 75–90.

69. Richard Goldstein, "The Hate that Makes Men Straight," *Village Voice* (22 December 1998), 64, 67, 70.

70. Ibid., 64.

been spat upon. In New York City one day, I was walking arm in arm with my partner when a man spat directly into my face. I cannot begin to convey the feeling of contamination as we shakily sought a public rest room and washed my face again and again.

During 1998, antigay attacks increased dramatically—and no wonder: Hatred of gay males and lesbians (and bisexuals during their same-sex periods) is still an acceptable form of bigotry. It is a form of bigotry that is still validated by sermons, senate speeches, anti-sodomy statutes, prohibitions against gay soldiering and marrying and parenting, and local resolutions that make it legal to fire or evict homosexuals. Consequently, gay bashers commit their crimes with a feeling of righteousness so tremendous that they utilize overkill. Matthew Shepard, a gay student at the University of Wyoming, was brutally pistol-whipped, tied to a fence, and left to die in near freezing temperatures; his groin was black and blue from repeated kicking. And Allen Schindler (the gay sailor murdered by his shipmates) had had his penis severely lacerated.[71] When the predominantly gay Metropolitan Community Church in New Orleans was torched in 1973 in such a way that everyone inside was incinerated, police officers and newspapers joked about the "fruitflies" who had been cooked. It was 25 years later before the city officials apologized for the cruel callousness of New Orleans toward some of its own citizens.[72]

Berkeley psychoanalyst Nancy Chodorow describes the source of the hatred of homosexuals, a hatred that afflicts men far more than women:

> To the extent that a man's heterosexuality is defensive and threatened, he's more likely to be homophobic. To the extent that his heterosexuality feels more secure, he can contain and live with his homoerotic desires. And if you want to talk about hate, then it's

---

71. Ibid., 67.

72. I checked these facts with my friend the Reverend Elder Nancy Wilson, pastor of the mother church of the Universal Fellowship of Metropolitan Community Churches (West Hollywood, California).

what happens when you are confronted with contradictions in yourself that you can't tolerate. You project the bad out, and then you
want to destroy it.[73]

What I'm driving at is that binary gender assumptions, rules, and
roles are devastating to "masculine" men and "feminine" women
and to transpeople of every description, including homosexuals and
bisexuals. The only way to rid ourselves of homophobia would be to
espouse a more fluid sexuality, so that gender would no longer be an
issue. Eve Sedgwick's term for this state is *allosexuality*, "an arrange-
ment of many erotic patterns in no particular hierarchy."[74] My term
for it is *sexual and gender fluidity* operating under an *omnigender paradigm*. This does not mean that I would approve of all the erotic
patterns that are in use. Nor does it mean that churches and synagogues would have to approve equally of all erotic patterns. But it
does mean that we would have to accept reality and begin our theology and ethics with people *as they are* rather than *as we imagine
they ought to be*.

Frankly, I suspect that the acceptance of gender fluidity and pluralism will be as difficult for many homosexuals and bisexuals as for
many heterosexuals. Unfortunately, les-bi-gay people can sometimes
be as rigid and labeling as anybody else, defining our sexualities
through binaries like active and passive, top and bottom, butch and
femme. Sometimes stereotypes of "masculinity" and "femininity"
control gay lives almost as much as heterosexual lives. Colin Kreitzer,
a friend I met years ago at Kirkridge's annual Gay, Lesbian, and
Christian event, described for me his experience of having a friend
play back for him a tape of their conversation. Horrified that he
sounded "like a woman," at twenty-six years of age Colin retrained
his speech pattern and voice to be deeply "masculine." In his late
teens he had "embraced his maleness" by learning to be a jock, even
though during boyhood he had wanted to be a girl so that he wouldn't
be "threatened and pushed into sports." Having successfully matched

---

73. As quoted by Goldstein, "The Hate that Makes Men Straight," 70.
74. Ibid., 70.

himself to society's concept of "masculinity," except for his gayness, Colin is not amused by drag queens and is "uncomfortable with members of either sex who display overt characteristics of the 'opposite' sex." His personal taste runs to "masculine men and feminine women"; transpeople are "upsetting" to him.

Another gay friend, James Akers, was able to fit more easily into the binary gender construct, never in his life cross-dressing or wanting to be a girl. However, he expressed a fairly typical attitude when he told me, "I cringe when I learn of instances [of transgenderism which] the popular media or religious right are likely to sensationalize." In fact, many lesbians, gays, and bisexuals look on transpeople as "oddities who are a potential embarrassment to the push for mainstream acceptance."[75]

The chair of the Log-Cabin [Gay] Republicans claims that one-third of self-identified gays supported GOP candidates in 1994 and 1998 Congressional elections.[76] And like many heterosexual males, gay men are increasingly using steroids in pursuit of the perfect body—and harming their health in the long run in order to fit the "masculine ideal."[77] So some people in the gay community are more conservative and more eager to conform than most "straight" people might imagine.

Even a rigid dichotomy of homosexual versus heterosexual conforms to the binary model that is everywhere in our society. Bisexuals can be of assistance here by bridging the imagined chasm between homo- and hetero-sexualities; from at least one perspective, it's a sad limitation to be able to love only one gender—especially when we consider all the factors that nuance our perception of gender: not only external genitalia, hormones, chromosomes, and reproductive organs, but also family, community, the culture at large, age, race, the economy, beauty or lack of it, and the politics of choice.[78] Perhaps church people should be investigating the origins and problems of exclusive heterosexuality as well as exclusive homosexual-

---

75. Mubarah Dahir, "Whose Movement Is It?" *The Advocate* (25 May 1999), 50.

76. Robert Stears, letter to *The Advocate* (22 June 1999), 8.

77. Christian Walker, "Foul Shot," *The Advocate* (25 May 25 1999), 71.

78. See Bornstein, *My Gender Workbook*, 119.

ity, trying to explain the limitation of being able to desire only the "opposite" sex or only the same sex. As for lesbians and gay men, perhaps transpeople can assist us by reminding us that a respectable goal for people of faith would be freedom "from the boundaries created by expectations, roles, and fears."[79]

If gender is as fluid as the facts of intersexuality, transsexuality, and human experience would seem to indicate, then sexual orientation may not be as rigidly fixed as some of us used to believe. D. Travers Scott questions, "How can you be rigidly 'oriented' toward something that is amorphous, shifting, fluid, tricky, elusive?" And he warns, "Basing your identity on sexuality is like building a house on a foundation of pudding. . . . Fixed, strictly policed identities are a right-wing project."[80] For lesbian women and gay men, the greatest challenge of gender pluralism might be to accept the idea that, as Travers Scott dramatizes it, "Homosexuality's over," that "Queers are not a distinct minority group neatly parallel to ethnic, religious, or biologically based groups," and that the issue "isn't identity, it's ideology. It's about freedom, responsibility, and values."[81]

As hard as I have worked for more than two decades for gay, lesbian, and bisexual liberation, I identify with this statement by Riki Anne Wilchins: "I have no interest in being part of a . . . movement whose sole purpose is to belly up to the Big Table and help ourselves to another serving of Identity Pie, leaving in our wake some other, more marginalized group to carry on its own struggle alone."[82] I don't think that Wilchins's statement means we must or should abandon the struggle for les-bi-gay civil rights. It means that we must make common cause with transpeople against gender inequities and ultimately make common cause with all oppressed people everywhere, no matter *what* the cause of their oppression.

For those who may feel that solidarity with other oppressed people will dilute and delay our cause, we might remind ourselves that the

79. Michael Thomas Ford, "A Real Girl," *PoMoSexuals*, 159.
80. D. Travers Scott, "LeFreak, C'est Chic! LeFag, Quelle Drag!" *PoMoSexuals*, 66–67.
81. Ibid., 68.
82. Wilchins, *Read My Lips*, 97.

hetero/homosexual binary dates only from the end of the 19th century, when both terms were invented by the medical establishment. Prior to that dichotomizing act, sexuality was regarded as a vast smorgasbord of appetites and attitudes.[83] Not that there were no degrees of approval or disapproval of certain sexual behaviors; but the creation of the hetero/homosexual binary made it easier to glorify the one, repudiate the other, and oversimplify both. We can safely yield up our own dualisms in order to achieve sexual and gender justice.

On the one hand, homosexuality looks pretty "normal" when set in the context of all the varieties of intersexuality, transsexuality, and transgenderism. But on the other hand, accepting sexuality and gender identity and presentation as continua along which people may find what is comfortable for themselves (including the possibility of multiple identities, or shifts during various stages of life) would grant freedom to everyone by dispelling the whole concept of "binary normalcy." Those who want structure, order, and continuity in their gender lives (as I do) would be free to pursue that. Those who prefer to be able to express romantically with only one gender (as I do) would be free to do that. But those who feel and act otherwise would be free of the judgment and danger that currently dogs their lives as differently gendered beings. *Abnormality* would be defined as lack of caring, as callous irresponsibility, as inability to connect, rather than by object-choice, physical appearance, or legal certificate.

Dr. Anne Fausto-Sterling warns homosexuals not to place too much stock in research such as Simon LeVay's that finds evidence for an anatomical difference in the brains of homosexual men: "The full force of history tells us that if doctors and the courts think they understand the biochemistry of homosexuality they will compel people to undergo treatments to 'cure' it." She reminds us that "Fear of homosexuality helps to enforce heterosexual gender roles. Thus the political struggle about gay civil rights and gay acceptance inevitably becomes part of a power struggle about gender." And she

83. Goldstein, "The Hate that Makes Men Straight," 67.

offers some important advice: "Only by leaving behind fixed, linear models of the brain and behavior and progressing to complex, plastic, networked approaches will we get somewhere," because "the social acceptance of sexual difference is ground to be gained through the body politic, not the body biological."[84]

Transgender Politics

Although in this chapter I have been emphasizing the cruel injustices inflicted upon intersexuals, transsexuals, cross-dressers, drag queens and kings, transgenderists, androgynes, bisexuals, and homosexuals, I want to emphasize that the people I've met across the whole transgender spectrum are anything but pathetic. They are remarkably strong, resourceful, bright, resilient, and often good-humored. They have valuable gifts to offer society, and for that reason society should be willing to allow each person to reach his and/or her fullest potential.

Roz Kaveny, who writes for several British publications including *The Times Literary Supplement*, has formulated six axioms for a "workable transgender and transsexual politics." She finds them nonnegotiable, and so do I. The axioms are that everyone involved in transgender activism must

1. Display solidarity with *all* our transgender (including transsexual) brothers and sisters.
2. Build alliances by getting involved *as ourselves* in other areas of politics.
3. Don't let journalistic and intellectual attacks on our community go unanswered; we can have and keep the moral high ground.
4. Be creative, be smart, be ourselves, and don't let anybody tell us who we are and what we do.
5. Refuse the pathological medical model—we are not sick, just different.

---

84. Anne Fausto-Sterling, *The Myths of Gender*, rev. ed. (New York: Basic Books, 1992), 255–56.

6. Refuse those politics—heterosexism, body fascism—that work against all of the above, but most especially against no. 1.[85]

Although Kaveny speaks as a transperson to transpeople, her axioms would be useful for anybody of any gender or sexual orientation who would like to move society toward attitudes and policies favoring liberty and justice for all.

I particularly appreciate Kaveny's opposition to "body fascism," by which she means "the looksist agenda" that privileges the thin and/or beautiful over the fat and/or homely. Such "looksism" has emerged among many male-to-female transsexuals, where those who were small and slender before transitioning find it easier to be admired once they have become women. As Kaveny comments, "Human rights do not depend on . . . perfect teeth, hair and nails, or good dress sense, or on a thin waist or a bushy beard."[86] I trust Kaveny would agree with me that human rights don't depend on race, nationality, ethnicity, age, class, physical ability, mental ability, or religion, either.

Because Kaveny's conclusion makes me want to stand up and cheer, I will quote it at length, yearning for the day when Kaveny's "we" will include people of every sexual orientation, every religion and no religion, and every gender, including perhaps some that haven't even been tried yet: "We need to participate in the struggle for comprehensive across-the-board anti-discrimination measures and ensure that any such laws specifically include us; we need to join in the struggle for the option of all long-term partnerships to be recognized; we need to join the struggle for an ethic of fair and decent treatment for all in a just society. Why cry for the moon when we can have the stars?" And part of her postscript: "We need to move away from models of the transgendered condition that pathologize it towards ones that express it as part of the standard

---

85. Roz Kaveny, "Talking Transgender Politics," *Reclaiming Genders*, 146–47. Emphasis mine. Used by permission.

86. Ibid., 155.

range of human variation . . . part of the rich harvest of the evolution of the human brain."[87]

When all the variations of human gender and sexuality become acceptable, provided they do not harm oneself or others, then everyone will be "normal" and "normalcy" will lose its coercive power.

Are we ready to grant ourselves that kind of freedom? Only by granting it to others can we bring it home to ourselves.

---

87. Ibid., 157–58.

CHAPTER FOUR

≋ Judaism and Christianity on Creation, Cross-Dressing, and Sexuality

I N *My Gender Workbook*, transsexual Kate Bornstein describes how s/he sought spiritual guidance from her rabbi at the time she was beginning the transition from male to female: "He quoted me the Old Testament saw that 'A woman shall not put on the garments of a man, nor shall a man put on the garments of a woman.' I explained to him that I wasn't a man. He said, 'In the eyes of the Lord, you are and always will be'" (113). No empathy, no entering into the lifelong pain of a boy who had always known he was a girl, just legalistic pontificating. Similarly, Leslie Feinberg was unable to finish her religious education because of her insistence on cross-dressing when s/he was a girl.[1]

But Bornstein and Feinberg, as they fully recognize, wouldn't have fared any better with most Christian priests or pastors. Typical is the response of both the Vatican and the Protestant press to the Platform for Action drafted by the United Nations Conference on Women in 1995. An article in the *Baptist Press*, for example, said that the document "fails to describe gender as male and female, though the word [gender] appears more than 200 times. Some critics have charged [that] the drafters want to include homosexuals, bisexuals, and transsexuals under the definition of gender. . . ."[2] Similar concerns were expressed by a Catholic group, which sponsored a newspaper advertisement to express their dismay. They characterized the document's questioning of an exclusively male-female

---

1. Feinberg, *Transgender Warriors: Making History from Joan of Arc to RuPaul* (Boston: Beacon Press, 1996), 49.

2. Tim Strode, *Baptist Press*, as quoted in Bornstein, *My Gender Workbook*, 113.

dichotomy as "maddening," because "every sane person knows there are but two sexes, both of which are rooted in nature."[3]

In other words, the attitude of many religious leaders has been that gender is fully and adequately defined by the male-female binary. Anyone who does not fit that binary doesn't even exist in any reality worthy of religious recognition: Hence, there is no need for pastoral concern, listening, or support. But far from being "rooted in nature," the binary gender system is not only unjust to "normal" males and females (chapter 2), it doesn't fit the basic facts of biology, let alone psychology (chapter 3). The common understanding of gender is woefully inadequate.

I wish I could believe that as soon as religious people learn in detail the plight of intersexuals, transsexuals, and other transgender people, they will repent of their oppressive attitudes and open their hearts to a transformation. That's really all this book is asking for— a collective change of attitude that would lift from millions of shoulders burdens too heavy for human beings to bear. I have no question where Jesus would stand on this issue, for he told the disciples that "the religious scholars and the Pharisees have succeeded Moses as teachers; therefore perform every observance they tell you to. But don't follow their example: even they don't do what they say. They tie up heavy loads and lay them on others' shoulders, while they themselves will not lift a finger to help alleviate the burden"(Matt. 23:1–4, *The Inclusive New Testament*).

However, I sense that the gender mountain will be very difficult to move, especially in religious circles. In all probability, official church policies will be the rear guard on gender, being dragged toward gender justice kicking and screaming when the secular society will no longer tolerate anything else. History has repeated itself, alas, concerning the church and racial issues, women, sexual orientation, peace, capital punishment, and corporal punishment. Why should gender be any different?

---

3. An advertisement in the *New York Times* (3 September 1995), paid for by the Catholic League for Civil and Religious Rights.

Still, hope does spring eternal in my heart, and I must invest my pen as well as my money and my prayers toward moving the gender mountain. I see four major reasons why the religious community will be the hardest to convince regarding an omnigender paradigm: First, there really is a lack of awareness regarding gender oppression, and education is the only cure for that. This book is my attempt to assist the educational process.

Second, religious people are as involved in the culture as anybody else, and there is a huge commercial investment in the binary gender construct. Women and men as sexual objects for one another are used to sell almost everything, and material success is often conflated with divine approval and blessing. It is also very easy to turn a blind eye to one's own special privileges by calling them God's will, so that others are "defined out" and seem by definition to deserve their less privileged fate. Thus, if gender really does mean only "masculine" male versus "feminine" female, each attracted only to the other, billions of people are automatically "defined out" of any gender protection and deprived of various civil and human rights—unless they are willing to shrink or stretch themselves to fit. The religious community can easily assume that to require other people's conformity is to support God's creative order. Therefore, people can feel positively righteous about applying pressure to conform.

Third, we human beings really do tend to create God in our own image. If we are judgmental and vindictive, we assume that God is an angry, judgmental, punishing God. Never mind that Jesus was called "the express image of God's person" (Heb. 1:3) and was not at all judgmental except when it came to the cruel use of power over other people (as shown in the Matthew 23 passage). It is well known that racism stems from projecting onto races other than one's own the traits one fears and despises in oneself—and then hating the other races for having those traits. The same process plays itself out with gender: men projecting onto women those traits they fear and despise within themselves; heterosexuals projecting onto homosexuals and bisexuals; and "normal" people projecting onto intersexuals, transsexuals, and transgenderists.

The projection of our disowned traits is performed in the hope of making ourselves feel better about ourselves. But ironically, the projection only makes us feel worse because as we condemn others, we ourselves feel condemned. On a largely unconscious level, we assume God feels about us the way we feel about others, and the downward spiral continues—self-condemning feelings, projection, judgment of the other, feeling judged ourselves (self-condemning feelings), projection again, and on and on and on. Therefore Jesus said we should not judge, so we would not *be* judged (Matt. 7:1; Luke 6:37). The church will never be able to experience a full out-pouring of God's grace until it stops rejecting aspects of itself by judging certain categories of people as unacceptable. But that day seems far removed, and gender seems to be even less negotiable than other humanly constructed boundaries.

Fourth, there are certain interpretations of scripture that may block otherwise loving people from acting as loving as they might like to act. Granted, with the human ego being as chameleonic as it is, some people who are opposed to omnigender for one or more of the other reasons just cited may use scripture to rationalize attitudes they already hold for those very unscriptural reasons. But in order to avoid the trap of judging and feeling judged, I am going to engage the scriptural reasoning as if it were sincerely held by people who are psychologically and spiritually whole.

The "Great Theological-Ethical Divide" among Christians

Charles Colson, who maintains a Web site called *Breakpoint* that purports to give "A Christian Perspective on the News and Trends," is horrified at the "bizarre fantasy" that there might ever be restrooms labeled *intersexual* alongside those labeled *men* and *women*. He is aware that some babies are born "afflicted with a deformity" (hermaphroditism) but sees no alternative for them except to undergo plastic surgery and hormone therapy, which would enable them to function as either male or female. Why does Colson dictate that intersexuals must go through the anguish of multiple operations and therapies? Because Congress has passed the Defense of Marriage Act (DOMA) that limits marriage to unions between one man and one woman. But if those who study sexuality are correct, Colson recognizes, there would no longer be opposite sexes but rather a vast continuum from male to female, and everything in between. And in that case, DOMA could not be sustained.[4]

If this sounds like rejection of scientific evidence in order to deny to others the privileges he values for himself, Colson is quick to explain his reasoning: Christians cannot permit biology to dictate behavior because the Bible teaches that the Fall into sin affected biology. Nature itself is now distorted from God's original perfect plan. This belief gives Christians a basis for fighting evil, including the alleviation of disease—and helping those unfortunate children who are born with unusual genitals.

Colson denies that the binary division of the sexes is a social construct, calling it a divine creation. Therefore, he concludes that all we'll ever need is two kinds of rest rooms, one for men and one for women. Presumably, those who are neither male nor female, or both, are to stay out of public places—or at least out of public rest rooms. Ironically, that would include all those who are "in Christ," where according to Galatians 3:28, "there is no longer male and female."

Colson's argument sets in stark relief perhaps the most basic theological rift within contemporary Christianity—the disagreement between those who believe that creation remains good because God's sovereign and loving will cannot ultimately be controverted by human agency, and those who believe that in the Fall, human sinfulness succeeded in creating a real separation between creation and Creator. (This separation can be overcome only through individual repentance and faith in the saving work of Jesus' death on the cross, which is interpreted as paying the penalty for human sinfulness.)

Every Christian denomination contains people on either side of this great theological divide. However, in many people, disposition or temperament affects behavior more fully than do doctrinal beliefs, and for that reason Christian behavior patterns appear more

---

4. Charles Colson, "Blurred Biology: How Many Sexes Are There?" <www.breakpoint.org/scripts/61016.htm>. Accessed 9 August 1999.

like a continuum than two sides of a huge chasm. Some people's innate kindliness casts a gentle light that enables them to accept diversity regardless of their theology. But for other temperaments, a theology of separation from God exacerbates judgmentalism. So the difference runs deep.

Those who subscribe to "creation spirituality," as I do, hold that God's connection to the creation is just as unalterable as a mother's relationship to her child—mother and/or child could deny their connection all they liked, but the fact of their relationship would remain. If Ephesians 4:6 is correct that the eternal God is "above all, and through all, and in you all," then there is no *eternal* or *real* separation between Creator and creation. Indeed, if the traditional Christian teaching of God's omnipresence is true, then surely an intersexual or transgender sexuality is as sacred as anyone else's sexuality, because God's presence inhabits every entity.

How then to account for all the terrible events that occur in the world? They stem from the human ego which has imagined itself separate from its source, imagined itself to be its own creator, and which then fears retaliation from the God whose authority it thinks it has succeeded in usurping. There is no end to the human cruelty that can occur once people have projected their undesired traits onto others and then have sought to eradicate those traits by oppressing those who "represent" them. As for natural disasters such as earthquakes, destructive storms, avalanches, and so on, the sheer *intensity* of them may originate in a similar problem: a cavalier use of natural resources, including nuclear testing and accidents, or carelessness about carbon emissions, with little concern for the outcome to others and to the environment as a whole.

Christians who believe the Fall brought about an utter separation from our Source feel that the gulf can be crossed only through faith in the redeeming death and resurrection of Jesus. Salvation is something God provides from the outside; it is external to any human effort other than acceptance. Although St. Paul testifies that there is nothing that can ever separate us from the love of the Christ (the Anointed One), Christians who emphasize the Fall as an objectively real sundering would say that Romans 8:38–39 applies only to Christians who interpret scripture as they do. However, there is something so cosmically inclusive about Romans 8:38–39 that such an interpretation seems much too narrow: "I'm certain that neither death nor life, neither angels nor demons, neither the present nor the future, neither heights nor depths—nor anything else in all creation—will be able to separate us from the love of God that comes to us in Jesus Christ, our Savior" (*The Inclusive New Testament*).

What then is the salvation that is embodied in our Savior Jesus Christ? For those who believe in Original Blessing, it is that we and our divine Source are and always have been one, that the imagined separation never occurred, that God's sovereign will could not be overturned, and that God's love for us is endless, irrevocable, and unconditional. From a religious perspective, Jesus was crucified because he insisted that he and his divine Source were one, which sounded like blasphemy to the religious leaders of his place and time. And he prayed that his followers would know that they too are one with God (John 17), an affirmation that still sounds too blasphemous to be taken seriously by a good many Christians.

Not surprisingly, those who are convinced of the truth of God's absolute omnipotence and omnipresence find it easier to accept all aspects of creation, including people who are markedly different from themselves. But those who regard the Fall as ultimately real have to struggle with the feeling that God is angry about being displaced and must be placated. Trying to cope with fear and guilt causes a tendency to project outward the traits we fear and loathe within ourselves. Bruce Bawer has described this process as "stealing Jesus" and thus creating a church of law in place of a church of love. His book *Stealing Jesus: How Fundamentalism Betrays Christianity* (New York: Crown Publishers, 1997) is well worth reading. As a person who spent the first thirty-some years of life in fundamentalism, I can testify that Bawer's grasp of details is accurate.

But what amazes me is that despite widespread belief in sin's power to separate us from God, there are still so many kind and compassionate Christians, eager to share the blessings of life with those less fortunate than themselves. It is when theological belief in separation combines with guilt-ridden judgmentalism that cruelty results—such as picketing the funerals of murdered gay men with signs proclaiming that "God hates fags."

So, then, there is a great theological divide within Christendom. The doctrine of Original Sin interprets Genesis 3 as describing the real, objective perversion of God's original plan by human disobedience and sinfulness. Salvation then comes from a Jesus who is uniquely divine among human beings and who must be invited to enter the human heart; and millions of beautiful lives have been lived within that belief system. By contrast, Christians who believe that the goodness of God's creation could not be subverted see Genesis 3 as describing a body-identified *imagined* separation from God. It is the terrifying sense of separation that sets every body against every other body and pits humankind against the natural environment as well. Salvation comes from recognizing the Sacred Presence within the human core of ourselves and all other creatures and learning to abandon the ego in favor of communion with that Presence.

Faced by two mutually exclusive interpretive communities, one might be tempted to simply walk away. It seems impossible to reconcile those who emphasize law (with salvation through Christ's satisfaction of law's demands) and those who emphasize love (with salvation as the acceptance of a familial divine-human relationship that no angel or demon could ever destroy). Again (fortunately), human kindliness, good humor, and compassion can often bridge the gap. But for those who care about theological matters, the "great divide" can cause great puzzlement. Does one simply join the interpretive community that best satisfies one's personal preferences and agendas? Is there no way to establish one interpretation of scripture as more authoritative than another?

The Genesis Creation Accounts

While it is impossible to convince anyone of an authoritative reading of a text if their questions, concerns, and assumptions are drastically different from our own, it *is* possible to ask of readers that they interpret any given passage consistently with the interpretive structures they themselves have set up. I propose to do that with the Genesis creation accounts as they impact gender issues. By doing this, I will be covering somewhat similar ground as that already covered by Letha Dawson Scanzoni and me in the 1994 expansion of our book *Is the Homosexual My Neighbor?*[5] But my focus will differ in order to address broader gender issues as opposed to the focus on sexual orientation in the earlier discussion.

This revisiting of Genesis 1 and 2 is necessary because, as we have seen, the Religious Right is using the same "order of creation versus the fallen world" arguments to oppose omnigender as it has used to oppose the granting of full human and civil rights to people who are lesbian, gay, or bisexual.

One non-controversial rule of hermeneutics is that a reader must pay attention to the genre or literary type of whatever is being interpreted. A historical treatise should not be read as if it were a lyric poem, a novel, a letter, or a doctrinal treatise. By this standard, chapters 1 and 2 of Genesis belong to the genre of creation accounts, stories intended to describe origins and reassure people who are feeling threatened in an endangered world. Genesis 1:1—2:4 is an elegant poem or hymn of creation; Genesis 2:5–24 is an older account, an earthy folktale of creation emphasizing the interests of a peasant society.[6] Neither account is a scientific treatise. Both are religious statements intended to glorify God and to suggest God's involvement with humankind.

The efforts of "creationists" to exclude the teaching of evolution from public schools (citing Genesis 1 and 2) are violations of the rule that, like any other piece of literature, biblical passages must be read in accordance with their own genre. To teach Genesis 1—2 during science classes is therefore a violation of scriptural intent revealed through the author's choice of literary genre. Poems and folktales of creation must not be treated as if they were scientific textbooks. As a matter of fact, in Genesis 1:11–13, the description of the creation of plants and animals according to species ("of every kind") would seem to leave some room for evolutionary theory. But the question of God's precise methodology is simply not addressed. Genesis 1—2 affirms *that* God created without stating *how* God created.

---

5. See especially pages 81–83 and 149–52. I would urge any reader concerned specifically with homosexuality to read this book; there is no way I could recapitulate all its insights here.

6. J. R. Porter, "Creation," *The Oxford Companion to the Bible*, ed. Bruce M. Metzger and Michael D. Coogan (New York: Oxford University Press, 1993), 140–41.

Similarly, Genesis 1 and 2 do not address the astonishing biodiversity of human gender and sexuality. All we are told is that "God created humankind in [God's] image . . . male and female [God] created them" (Gen. 1:26). And we are given the details of the deep sleep during which Adam, the creature of earth, was divided into the human male and female (Genesis 2:18–22).

Upon this slender evidence, Kate Bornstein's rabbi based his assertion that "in the eyes of the Lord" s/he is and always will be a man. Upon this slender evidence, the Vatican and the Protestant Right base their horror that homosexuals, bisexuals, transsexuals (and transgenderists) might ever be included in the definition of the word *gender* and thus win human and civil rights protections. On this slender evidence, Charles Colson bases his confident assertion that intersexual babies are not part of God's created order but are a result of the Fall, so that they must submit to surgical correction in order to function as either male or female, no matter whether the surgery robs them of erotic sensation forevermore.

Other Understandings of Genesis 1—2

Ironically, there is a traditional method of reading Genesis 1—2 that provides a stronger sanction for omnigender than for the binary gender construct. According to W. Gunther Plaut's commentary on Genesis, the teaching of Jewish midrashim is that "Men and women were originally undivided, i.e. Adam was at first created bisexual, a hermaphrodite." Plaut explains that an English equivalent for the Hebrew of Genesis 2:7 would be "God fashioned an earthling from the earth."[7] When this hermaphroditic earthling is

---

7. W. Gunther Plaut, *The Torah: Genesis—A Modern Commentary* (New York: Union of American Hebrew Congregations, 1974), 24, 19. See also John Elwolde, "Human and Divine Sexuality: The *Zohar* on Genesis 5:2," *Religion and Sexuality*, ed. Michael A. Hayes, Wendy Porter, and David Townes (Sheffield, England: Sheffield Academic Press, 1998), 64–84. Elwolde quotes the *Zohar* 34b.30–33 to the effect that "the name Adam" comprehended "male and female. The female was fastened to his side, and God cast the male into a deep slumber, and he lay on the site of the Temple. God then cut the female from him and decked her as a bride and led her to him" (83).

later placed under a deep sleep, he/she is divided into the human male and female. From this perspective, intersexuals are not only part of God's original plan, they are *primarily* so!

Scholarly Christian interpretation takes a slightly different approach. Arguing in *God and the Rhetoric of Sexuality* (Philadelphia: Fortress Press, 1978) that proper analysis of form yields proper articulation of meaning (8), Hebrew professor Phyllis Trible explains that the earth creature formed by God in Genesis 2:7–8 is "not the male," and not "the first man," but rather "precisely and only the human being, so far sexually undifferentiated" (80). It is only after God performs radical surgery during the earth creature's "deep sleep" that the human male and female emerge simultaneously: "two creatures where before there was only one."

In an earlier article, Trible had seen the earth creature as androgynous until the differentiation of male and female in Genesis 2:21–24.[8] But in *God and the Rhetoric of Sexuality* she renounces that view because "the word *androgyny* assumes sexuality, whereas the earth creature is sexually undifferentiated" (141). She insists that the original earth creature is "one creature who was . . . neither male or female nor a combination of both" (98).

For our purposes here, the important point is that both Jewish and Christian scholarship has recognized that the original created being is either hermaphroditic or sexually undifferentiated, a "gender outlaw" by modern terms, closer to a transgender identity than to half of a binary gender construct. According to this very ancient interpretation, binary gender would be a later development, not the first intention of the Creator but provided subsequently for the sake of human companionship. From this angle, hermaphrodites or intersexuals could be viewed as reminders of Original Perfection.

Also ironically, religious conservatives seek to deny human companionship to transpeople on the basis of the very chapters that describe the Creator's awareness that "it is not good for ha-'adam

---

8. Phyllis Trible, "Depatriarchalizing in Biblical Interpretation," *Journal of the American Academy of Religion* 41 (1973): 35, 37–38.

[the earth creature] to be alone/ I will make for it a companion corresponding to it" (Genesis 2:18).[9]

Charles Colson is typical of the Religious Right in his claim that the male-female gender binary is grounded in the image of God. He says that scripture tells us exactly how God created us before the Fall and "how He intended us to live: as males and females reflecting His own image" (see note 4). This reference to Genesis 1:26–27 is ironic on the face of it, since naming God's image as both male and female actually depicts God as either androgynous or hermaproditic—far more supportive of transgender identity than of the "opposite sex" theory.

Trible warns, however, that "the metaphorical language of Genesis 1:27 preserves with exceeding care the otherness of God. . . . God is neither male nor female, nor a combination of the two. And yet, detecting divine transcendence in human reality requires human clues. Unique among them, according to our poem, is sexuality. God creates, in the image of God, male and female" (21).

Thus the text shows that male metaphors for God, such as father, king, or warrior, are only *partial*, as are female metaphors for God, such as the mother (Isa. 66:13), the pregnant woman (Ps. 22:9), or the mistress (Ps. 123:2). The image of God male-and-female presents an equality that has been dreadfully lacking in the actual workings of our society's gender system—to the detriment of everyone, as we have seen in chapter two.

If Trible is correct (and I think she is), we cannot argue for omnigender on the basis that God is literally androgynous or intersexual, any more than we can depict God as literally male or literally female. But neither can anyone legitimately claim, as Colson and others do, that our current male-female polarization is based on

---

9. Trible, in *God and the Rhetoric of Sexuality*, emphasizes that although "the English word *helper* suggests an assistant, a subordinate, indeed . . . an inferior . . . the Hebrew word . . . carries no such connotation. . . . In our story the accompanying phrase, 'corresponding to it' . . . tempers this connotation of superiority to specify identity, mutuality, and equality" (90). Thus the value judgment involved in binary gender (male superior to female) is not supported by the Hebrew of Genesis 1 and 2.

the image of God. It isn't. God is not literally male and female and neither is the human race. People's experience, biology, and psychology have alerted us to the facts of human gender diversity, and the creation accounts of Genesis 1 and 2 do nothing to undercut or refute those facts.

Additional Implications of Genesis 1 and 2

If religious people choose to reject the claims of transpeople to full human and civil rights, they cannot rationally claim the Genesis text as their authority. In addition to the textual details we have already examined, the following facts must be considered.

First, the Genesis narratives in no way indicate that the sexual relationship and parenthood of Adam and Eve are to be considered normative for all sexual experience forever and ever. (Are all childless heterosexual marriages sinful? sick? I don't think so, especially on an already overpopulated planet.)

Second, Genesis 2:24 implies matrilocal marriage when it says, "a man leaves his father and mother and clings to his wife"—that is, it echoes "the custom of having the man become part of his wife's family and household."[10] (Are those who see Adam and Eve's relationship as sex-and-gender normative willing to return to matrilocal customs, as consistency would require of them? After all, if Adam and Eve's special circumstances are normative for everyone everywhere, matrilocal marriage would be an important part of those circumstances.)

Third, there is no wedding ceremony recorded in Genesis 1 and 2. Adam and Eve simply recognize one another and come together sexually without benefit of clergy. Of course, they had God as clergyperson; but so by their own testimony do many lesbian, gay, and other transgender partners.

Fourth, if the relationship of Adam and Eve really does signify that genital relating may properly take place only within heterosexual marriage, as many national church bodies currently insist,

---

10. Plaut, *The Torah*, 22, n24; cf. 309, n43.

then there is no sex ethic for single people other than celibacy. But in fact many thousands of unmarried heterosexuals are cohabiting while clergy pretend not to notice (or, in some cases, do the same themselves). Adrian Thatcher has brought together some facts that ought to help church leaders develop a more realistic attitude. For instance, the Roman Catholic Church did not require wedding ceremonies until 1563, and weddings were not a legal requirement in England and Wales until 1754. Until the late 18th century, engaged lovers often cohabited before their wedding day, and fully half of the 18th century brides in Britain and North America were pregnant when they walked the aisle.[11] Wouldn't it be more honest all around to develop an ethic that teaches singles, heterosexual or otherwise, to honor and be tender with one another's vulnerability?

Fifth, Genesis 1 and 2 have been used to teach a *complementarity* of male and female, as if neither could be a whole person without the other. But the text says no such thing. On the contrary, the Hebrew makes clear that Adam and Eve are powers equal to one another, "fitting helpers" for one another, equally placed in charge of the remainder of creation (Gen. 1:28–31). Both owe their lives solely to God, but each looks to the other for companionship and assistance in caring for the ecosystem in which they live. The point is not complementarity, but *cohumanity*—a cohumanity, I am convinced, in which every person of every gender is meant to partake.

Sixth, and finally for now, it is important to honor the Jewish understanding of Genesis because the text is part of the *Hebrew* Scriptures. Reform Rabbi Robert Saks acknowledges that for Orthodox and Conservative Jews, as for right-wing Christians, the Genesis creation accounts are by far the strongest argument in favor of compulsory heterosexuality within a binary gender system. (The story of Sodom is not relevant to sexual ethics for Jews, because all branches of Judaism interpret the sin of Sodom as a lack of hospitality. And the word *abomination* applied in Leviticus to same-sex intercourse seems to Jews to mean something no stronger than

---

11. Adrian Thatcher, *Marriage after Modernity: Christian Marriage in Postmodern Times* (Sheffield, England: Sheffield Academic Press, 1999), 108–14. See also the Sex and Gender issue of *The Witness* (April 2000).

degrading.) By contrast, to Reform or Reconstructionist Jews, the Genesis emphasis on the pairing of male and female (including Gen. 5:1–2) reflects a cultural understanding which has subsequently been modified by human experience and research. To these Jews, the symbolic meaning of the creation of Adam and Eve is primarily two-fold: that it is important to behave in line with our natures, and that life is intended to be pleasurable.[12]

Such interpretations offer considerable support to those gay and lesbian people to whom engaging in heterosexual intercourse seems unnatural (out of line with our own nature), to those bisexuals and transgenderists who cannot fit neatly into the male-female binary, and to all who seek pleasurable companionship in ways other than heterosexual marriage. Had Kate Bornstein's rabbi subscribed to the Reform and Reconstructionist Jewish consensus described by Rabbi Saks, Kate would have found some human kindness toward her transitioning. Had Leslie Feinberg's rabbi been more open to that consensus, her/his religious education would not have been cut short because of cross-dressing.

The Biblical Prohibition against Cross-Dressing

Religious leaders often condemn transvestites under the rubric of Deuteronomy 22:5: "A woman shall not wear a man's apparel, nor shall a man put on a woman's garment; for whoever does such things is abhorrent to the Lord your God" (NRSV). Or they might refer to David's curse upon the house of Joab, wishing that Joab's family might always contain someone with gonorrhea, someone leprous, someone violent, someone hungry, and someone who holds a spindle

---

12. Speaking as a panelist on the topic, "The Bible and Homosexuality," at the Fourth Sharing Our Rainbow of Light Conference, Foundry United Methodist Church, Washington, D.C., 11 November 1999. See also the outstanding essay by a Brown University professor of Judaic studies, Saul M. Olyan, "And with a Male You Shall Not Lie the Lying Down of a Woman: On the Meaning and Significance of Leviticus 18:22 and 20:13," *Que(e)rying Religion: A Critical Anthology*, ed. Gary David Comstock and Susan E. Henking (New York: Continuum, 1997), 398–414. And cf. Elwolde, "Human and Divine Sexuality," 64–84.

[that is, a man who enacts female behaviors, a transgender person]" (2 Sam. 3:29). They might also refer to Paul's comments about hair length, which seem to be based on anxiety about gender boundaries: "Does not nature itself teach you that if a man wears long hair, it is degrading to him? But if a woman has long hair, it is her glory?" (1 Cor. 11:14–15). It would appear that in ancient Judaism and in the early Christian church, there were people whom we today would call transgender. And apparently they were surrounded by social disapproval. But does that mean that all these centuries later, and in entirely different cultures, God is dead-set against people who cross-dress or enact gender roles that do not match their bodies of birth?

In his book on sex ethics in the New Testament and their contemporary implications, L. William Countryman provides an extended discussion of Israel's Holiness Code as it is reflected in Deuteronomy 22:5. He explains that cross-dressing was prohibited because it was felt that pollution occurred whenever two things were mixed that did not belong together. It was "confusion" (not "perversion," despite the NRSV) if human beings had sexual intercourse with animals, or if different species of domestic animals were mated, or if a field was used for several different kinds of seed, or a fabric were woven from several different kinds of fibers, or if a male acted like a woman by having sex with another man (Lev. 18:22, 20:13), or if people cross-dressed. Thus, as Countryman emphasizes, the male who fulfills the "female" or receptive role in same-sex intercourse is "a combination of kinds and therefore unclean, like a cloth composed of both linen and wool," and precisely the same reasoning applies in the prohibition against cross-dressing.[13] In a culture like ours, which seems to prefer mixed fibers for "permanent press"

---

13. L. William Countryman, *Dirt, Greed, and Sex: Sexual Ethics in the New Testament and Their Implications for Today* (Philadelphia: Fortress Press, 1988), 26–27. Countryman points out that according to Jude 6–7, the sin of Sodom was that of males wanting to have sex with angels, which would transgress a purity code analogous to that which prohibits bestiality. There must be no such mixing of kinds (134).

clothing, it is ludicrously selective to invoke Deuteronomy 22:5 against cross-dressers.

Countryman also points out that "anxiety over the polluting potential of women may well have contributed to the rejection of cross-dressing . . . and homosexual acts among men . . . both of which seemed to confuse the purer male with the 'dirtier' female."[14] In right-wing Protestantism, there are churches that still do not allow women to be ministers; in Eastern Orthodoxy, girl babies still cannot be brought to the altar for blessing as boy babies can; and the Vatican remains opposed to female priesthood or even to a married clergy. But few of our contemporaries would admit that these prohibitions stem from a belief in female *impurity*. (In politics, there are references to premenstrual syndrome as skewing female judgment, despite the fact that properly conducted double-blind experiments fail to show cyclical mood alterations.[15] Those references are the modern equivalent to codes of female impurity.)

On a personal level, few males would speak openly about having an aversion to females because females are desecrating; but some women have internalized a sense of their own impurity. I have never forgotten a letter I received from a woman who had read my book *The Divine Feminine*. She wrote, "How *dare* you speak of God as female? Don't you know that God is *holy?*" I wrote in return: "My dear sister, please consider what you are implying about yourself, and me, and all the women and girls you know."

Any sincerely religious person who believes that women and men are equally created in God's image should think twice before invoking biblical prohibitions against cross-dressing and same-sex love. Because these prohibitions are associated with the attitude that femaleness is a pollutant, they have no place within a democratic and fair-minded society, let alone in a contemporary church, synagogue, or mosque.

---

14. Ibid., 30.

15. Anne Fausto-Sterling, *The Myths of Gender* (New York: Basic Books, 1992), 105.

Connections with Polytheism

In the *New Revised Standard Version* of the Bible (1989), Deuteronomy 23:17 is translated, "None of the daughters of Israel shall be a temple prostitute; none of the sons of Israel shall be a temple prostitute." This translation contradicts the findings of recent biblical scholarship that the *qadesh* was a male Canaanite priest, not a prostitute, and that the female *qedeshah* was in all probability also a priest, not a prostitute.[16] Nevertheless, the vehemence of Deuteronomy 23:17 illustrates the fact that for about three centuries, the monarchs of Israel and Judah conducted campaigns to eradicate the religions of Canaan, especially deploring the gender-variant priests and priestesses of the god Baal and his consort Asherah. It took a great deal of vigilance and persecution to root out of Israel all allegiance to the Canaanite religion, and that vigilance explains the absolute tone of prohibitions against "temple prostitutes" (priests), homosexual activity, and cross-dressing, all of which were associated with Canaanite worship.

Despite the fact that the love between David and Jonathan, and Ruth's devotion to Naomi, were celebrated in the Hebrew Scriptures, by the late second century the *Mishnah* (the first text of rabbinical Judaism) said that sexual intercourse between men was punishable by stoning; and in the late twelfth century, Moses Maimonides wrote that "Women are forbidden to engage in lesbian practices with one another, these being the doing of the land of Egypt."[17] So Hebrew repudiation of homosexuality, cross-dressing, and transgenderism is

---

16. Tikva Frymer-Kensky, "Deuteronomy," *Women's Bible Commentary*, ed. Carol A. Newsom and Sharon H. Ringe (Louisville: Westminster John Knox Press, 1998), 64–65. In her excellent book, *In the Wake of the Goddesses: Women, Culture, and the Biblical Transformation of Pagan Myth* (New York: Free Press, 1992), Frymer-Kensky clarifies that "The religion of Israel's contemporaries did not offer a choice between monotheism and the goddesses, but rather between monotheism and a male-dominated polytheism" (5–6). Monotheism was a great improvement over that kind of paganism.

17. "Judaism," *Cassell's Encyclopedia of Queer Myth, Symbol, and Spirit*, ed. Randy P. Luncunas Conner, David Hatfield Sparks, and Mariya Sparks (New York: Cassell, 1998), 21.

linked to its attempt to distinguish monotheistic worship from the paganism of surrounding territories. And in contrast to the earlier goddess religions that regarded sex as sacred, "one of the characteristics of biblical [Old Testament] religion is the radical separation of the sexual from the sacred."[18] Tikva Frymer-Kensky, a prominent scholar of ancient Near Eastern religion, points out that "The monotheist God is not sexually a male. . . . God is asexual, or transsexual, or metasexual . . . but 'he' is never sexed. . . . Sexual activity brings people into a realm which is *unlike* God; conversely, in order to approach God one has to leave the sexual realm."[19] What a contrast to the goddess-worship of ancient Sumer, where "divine vaginas bring birth and renewal"![20]

So there is an ancient tradition behind the refusal of Kate Bornstein's rabbi to support in any way her transition from male to female and the refusal of Leslie Feinberg's synagogue school to tolerate her/his transgender clothing. What is surprising is that so many clergy at the opening of the third millennium of the Common Era do not find it necessary to seek out accurate information about the lives of the people to whom they attempt to minister. This culture is a far cry from that of the ancient Israelites trying to differentiate monotheistic worship from the polytheism of their neighbors and to that end drawing certain religio-social boundaries.

It is also a far cry from the culture in which Paul urged long hair for women and short hair for men (1 Cor. 11:14). At that time, Greek and Roman male deities who were transgender (Adonis, Apollo, Dionysus, and others) were portrayed with long flowing hair, and the male priests of the goddess Cybele were called the "long-haired ones." By contrast, goddesses and Amazons were typically portrayed with short hair cut in a traditionally masculine fashion or else with disheveled hair.[21] In his eagerness to differentiate Christianity from Greek and Roman paganism, Paul directed that

---

18. Frymer-Kensky, "Deuteronomy," 65.
19. Frymer-Kensky, *In the Wake of the Goddesses*, 188–89.
20. Ibid., 37.
21. "Hair," *Cassell's Encyclopedia*, 167–68.

Christian men wear their hair short and Christian women, long. He may also have sought differentiation from the young men of Judaism, for whom long hair was an admired characteristic, as witness Song of Solomon 5:11.[22]

It made sense for ancient Israel to draw boundaries between its own customs and beliefs and those of surrounding cultures. And it made sense for the apostle Paul to draw boundaries between a nascent struggling Christianity and the religions that surrounded it. But in our society, both Judaism and Christianity are so well established that they need no self-protective definition. And people who are truly full of faith in God have no need to fear people who differ from themselves. So it is time to let go of the tendency to condemn homosexuality, bisexuality, and transgenderism because of historic associations with polytheism.

Transgender within Judaism

To condemn human beings because their sexual or gender-orientation seems pagan, anti-Jewish, or anti-Christian is to forget the many profoundly Jewish and Christian people who have been transgendered. According to rabbinic commentary, not only was the original Adam hermaphroditic, but both Abraham and Sarah were intersexual. Isaiah 51:1–2 says that Israel owes its existence to God's intervention, because God hewed Israel out from a metaphorical rock (Abraham) and dug Israel out of a metaphorical quarry (Sarah). This is understood to mean that Abraham had no apparent genitals and Sarah had no womb, so that both of them were congenitally incapable of procreation. Although this reading may seem fanciful to modern readers, at the very least it shows that rabbis who cherished the Hebrew Scriptures did *not* view intersexual conditions as being condemned by those scriptures.[23] Otherwise they

---

22. William Smith, "Hair," *A Dictionary of the Bible* (New York: Pillar Books, 1976), 219.

23. Sally Gross, "Intersexuality and Scripture," *Theology and Sexuality* 11 (September 1999), 71–73.

would never have described their father Abraham and their mother Sarah as intersexuals who required a miracle to bring forth their beloved children, the Israelites.

The Hebrew hero Joseph (Gen. 30—50) is described in the biblical exegesis of the *Midrash* (5th century B.C.E. through the 2nd century C.E.) as a beautiful young man whom Potiphar purchased for the pharaoh of Egypt precisely because of his beauty. Potiphar is described in the *Midrash* as one of the eunuch priests of a pagan goddess; and we are told that both he and his wife desired Joseph. Although the *Midrash* denies that Joseph ever yielded, some scholars question that and instead assume that he and Potiphar enjoyed a transgender relationship. Furthermore, Joseph's famous coat may have been his mother Rachel's wedding dress, and several scholars claim that its possession links him to the transgender priests of Asherah.[24]

Then there is the famous relationship between David and Jonathan as recorded in 1 Samuel, chapter 20. Tom Horner provides an interesting discussion of Saul's jealous outburst because of his son Jonathan's love for David (1 Sam. 20:30–31), an outburst that clearly implied a homosexual bond[25] between these apparently bisexual men (both were married, David many times, and both had offspring). David's grief at Jonathan's death included the passionate statement of 2 Samuel 1:26:

> I am distressed for you, my brother Jonathan;
> greatly beloved were you to me;
> your love to me was wonderful,
> passing the love of women.

Years later, King David invited Jonathan's lame son Meribbaal (Mephibosheth) to eat at the royal table, "for Jonathan's sake" (2 Sam. 9:1–13).

---

24. "Joseph," *Cassell's Encyclopedia*, 193.

25. Tom Horner, *Jonathan Loved David: Homosexuality in Biblical Times* (Philadelphia: Westminster Press, 1978), 32.

Although many interpreters are at pains to explain away the passionate details of the David and Jonathan story, their love is in the tradition of great warrior-lovers such as Gilgamesh and Enkidu or Achilles and Patroclus. And their presence in the Bible renders untrue the often-repeated assertion that the Bible has nothing good to say about same-sex love.

So does the presence of Ruth and Naomi. Whether or not their love included a sexual dimension would be hard to say, because "female homosexuality, not once singled out for mention in the Old Testament, was not a subject of any concern."[26] We do know that they lived together for a brief time, that Ruth refused to part from her mother-in-law, that the two of them connived to get a second husband for Ruth and a home for them both, and that Ruth presented Naomi with the son she bore by Boaz. We know also that the women of Bethlehem said to Naomi, "Blessed be the Lord, who has not left you this day without next-of-kin . . . for your daughter-in-law *who loves you, who is more to you than seven sons*, has borne him" (Ruth 4:14–15, NRSV, emphasis mine). Their words constitute strong community recognition of the love between Ruth and Naomi. And we know that the commitment Ruth made to Naomi has been part of many thousands of wedding ceremonies:

> Do not press me to leave you
> or to turn back from following you!
> Where you go, I will go;
> Where you lodge, I will lodge;
> your people shall be my people,
> and your God my God.
> Where you die, I will die—
> there will I be buried. (Ruth 1:16–17)

As Horner comments, "There are . . . not sufficient grounds to say with certainty . . . that a homosexual relationship existed between Naomi and Ruth, but there are enough to point out that the

---

26. Ibid., 45.

possibility of such a relationship cannot be overlooked."[27] Again, their presence in Holy Scripture makes it inaccurate to claim that the Bible is totally negative toward same-sex love. Taken together, the presence of Abraham, Sarah, Joseph, David and Jonathan, and Ruth and Naomi constitute rather strong support for transgender and omnigender in the Hebrew Scriptures.

I am happy to be able to report that as I write, all branches of Judaism except the Orthodox are registering a growing acceptance and support of their transgender congregants. Reconstructionist, Reform, and Conservative rabbis have adopted resolutions supporting gay, lesbian, bisexual, and transgender rights; queer Jews have formed congregations in most metropolitan areas and have been welcomed in "straight" synagogues; and since the 1980s, the World Congress of Gay and Lesbian Jewish Organizations has served as a coordinating body.[28] And as of March 29, 2000, Reform Jewish leaders "overwhelmingly approved a resolution giving rabbis the option of presiding at gay commitment ceremonies." Reform Judaism has approved the ordination of gay and lesbian rabbis for a decade; Rabbi Eric Weiss voices the hope that the new decision will serve as "a call to all religious denominations to bring the same prophetic voice to lift our nation from the bonds of prejudice and to embrace all members of the American family."[29]

---

27. Ibid., 43.

28. Lewis John Eron, "Homosexuality and Judaism," *Homosexuality and World Religions*, ed. Arlene Swidler (Harrisburg: Trinity Press International, 1993), 124–25.

29. Estes Thompson, "Reform Jewish Group Backs Rites for Same-Sex Unions," *The Record* (30 March 2000), A-6.

CHAPTER FIVE

≋≋ *Omnigender Confronts Scripture and Church History*

I N ADDITION TO THE SCRIPTURE passages from the Hebrew Bible
discussed in the last chapter, there are many passages in the Christian scriptures that contain transgender images, and church history
is replete with transgender figures. In this chapter we will examine
some of the biblical passages, historical figures, and doctrines that
have implications for transgender theology.[1] As we explore these
sources, we will see the ways in which some Christians have denied
these realities and participated in doublespeak in order to defend
the binary gender construct.

As a beginning, I cannot resist mentioning the irony that, despite its conscious condemnation of transgender appearances and
behaviors—especially its burning of witches, who were thought to
have the power to change their sex—the church still dresses its
male priests in full-length gowns or frocks (and "defrocks" them if
they get too out-of-line) and still assigns to them the "feminine"
work of preparing and distributing communion and washing up the
"dishes" afterwards. If the medium is the message, what is the message here?

---

1. For a breezy, readable survey of biblical transgender people (especially lesbians and gays) from a Christian perspective, I recommend *Our Tribe: Queer
Folks, God, Jesus, and the Bible* by the Reverend Nancy L. Wilson (San Francisco: HarperSanFrancisco, 1995).

The Christian Doctrine of Jesus' Virgin Birth

One of the primary narratives in the Christian scriptures, the annunciation to the Virgin Mary and the subsequent birth of Jesus, introduces an intersexual theme into the heart of the Christian story. Let me explain.

In its September 1983 issue, the *Journal of the American Scientific Affiliation* published an article by Edward L. Kessel, emeritus professor of biology at the University of San Francisco, entitled "A Proposed Biological Interpretation of the Virgin Birth" (129–36). In that article, Kessel explained that if we believe scripture that Mary had never been with a man when she conceived Jesus, then "Jesus' conception, gestation, and birth were parthenogenetic." He cites the views of several research scientists who separately reached the conclusion that virgin birth is "probable among humans." He also explains that virgin-conceived offspring are always chromosomal females, and that "because human beings have the same X-Y kind of sex determination found in other mammals, with the female . . . possessing two X chromosomes, Jesus was conceived as a chromosomal female." And because "no animal can change the genotype that it receives at conception, Jesus remained female always in this chromosomal sense."

How then to account for Jesus' maleness according to the gospel witness? Kessel explains that Jesus underwent a sex reversal to the male phenotype, adding that "Biologists are generally agreed that sex reversal, like parthenogenesis, may sometimes occur in human beings as it does in lower animals." He describes several scenarios by which the sex reversal might have occurred, and several genetic scenarios concerning the probable genotypes of Mary and Jesus. But for our purposes, the important factor is Kessel's conclusion: "The female embryo Jesus of the Virgin Conception and Incarnation became the two-sexed infant of the Virgin Birth who was the androgynous Christ, bearing both the chromosomal identification of a woman and the phenotypic anatomy of a man."

Kessel goes on to champion female ordination on the basis of his findings: "No one can longer argue effectively against the ordination of women in the church on the grounds that Christ was a man. Christ was also a woman"—and to Kessel, that amounts to "a Perfect Human Being."[2]

No wonder Jesus of Nazareth has always been regarded by mystics as androgynous! And in the theology and liturgy of the Orthodox Christian Church, the wound in Christ's side is analogous to female genitals, so that Christ gives birth to "his" bride, the Church, through the wound in "his side, just as Eve was drawn from the side of Adam."[3] Talk about transgenderism!

While Kessel himself is careful to deny that Jesus was bisexual, hermaphroditic, or pseudohermaphroditic (all of which he considers pathological and/or defective), I cannot help making a connection to the Genesis depiction of a God who is imaged as both male and female and yet is literally neither the one nor the other. A chromosomally female, phenotypically male Jesus would come as close as a human body could come to a perfect image of such a God. And since I do not share Kessel's view that hermaphrodites or intersexual people are necessarily pathological or defective, it seems to me that from the perspective of his findings, intersexuals come closer than anybody to a physical resemblance to Jesus—unless perhaps we grant that honor to post-operative female-to-male transsexuals who remain chromosomally female after their transition to maleness.

Certainly the least that can be said about Kessel's work is that if he is correct, any church that worships in Christ's name should be

---

2. In 1988 Kessel incorporated and expanded his research into a book: Edward L. Kessel, *The Androgynous Christ*, privately printed and available only from the author (Apartment 337, Rose Villa, 3505 S.E. River Rd., Portland OR 97222).

3. "Jesus," *Cassell's Encyclopedia of Queer Myth, Symbol, and Spirit*, ed. Randy P. Luncunas Conner, David Hatfield Sparks, and Mariya Sparks (New York: Cassell, 1998, 190. See also Graham Ward, "The Gendered Body of the Jewish Jesus," *Religion and Sexuality*, ed. Michael A. Hayes, Wendy Porter, and David Townes (Sheffield, England: Sheffield Academic Press, 1998), 180 and 187; Luce Irigaray, *Speculum of the Other Woman* (New York: Cornell University Press, 1985), 199–200; and Caroline Walker Bynum, *Fragmentation and Redemption: Essays on Gender and the Human Body in Medieval Religion* (New York: Zone Books, 1992).

willing to let go of an inaccurate and unjust binary gender construct that does not allow room for a Christ Himself who is also Christ Herself!

Kessel's understanding of Jesus' birth as literally parthenogenetic accords well with a recent emphasis within the academic field of *thealogy* (discourse concerning the Goddess), an emerging field of study in England and elsewhere.[4] Thealogians understand the fabric of the cosmos to be "originally and fundamentally, metaphorically and actually, parthenogenetic—generating or reproducing without sexual union." Goddess-feminists understand sexuality to be "nonordinary," referring "above all to the quasi-parthenogenetic power of women to generate power and matter in and of themselves."[5]

Similarly, Kessel's description of Jesus as phenotypically male and chromosomally female accords well with contemporary transgender politics. Professor Gerard Loughlin of the University of Newcastle puts it this way: "It is only in the complex, fecund and fluid matrix of Christ-become-the-Church that Christian theology may refigure masculinity. . . . [S]ince the body of Christ is . . . both the crucified, risen, and ascended Lord, the mother who nurtures her children, and each and every one of them, it cannot be supposed that Christian masculinity is [exclusively any] one thing. . . . This understanding of how identities are destabilized in Christ also explains the appropriateness of thinking Christ hermaphroditic, and in certain strands of medieval monasticism and mysticism . . . Christ is at one and the same time male and female, masculine and feminine." Emphasizing that such an understanding of Jesus could bring about a "possible refiguring of our sexed identities," Professor Loughlin asks an important question: If "the male Christ is both feminine and masculine, can we any longer be certain as to what constitutes masculinity and femininity?"[6]

---

4. See Melissa Raphael, *Introducing Thealogy: Discourse on the Goddess* (Cleveland: The Pilgrim Press, 2000).

5. Raphael, "Thealogy and Parthenogenetic Reproduction," *Religion and Sexuality*, 214.

6. Gerard Loughlin, "Refiguring Masculinity in Christ," *Religion and Sexuality*, 410–11.

Eunuchs, Homosexual Love, and Same-Sex Couples

Although it has been claimed that Jesus never said a word about homosexuality, that is not strictly accurate if we understand the term *eunuch* not only in its literal but also in its symbolic meaning. Literally, the term *eunuch* refers to those who have been physically castrated; but the Bible also uses the term in its symbolic meaning of "all those who for various reasons do not marry and bear children."[7] According to John J. McNeill, Jesus' reference to those who have been eunuchs from birth (Matt. 19:12) is "the closest description we have in the Bible of what we understand as homosexual."[8] McNeill continues, "It should come as no surprise, then, that the first group of outcasts of Israel that the Holy Spirit includes within the new covenant community is symbolized by the Ethiopian eunuch (Acts 8:26–40)." Unfortunately, Christian churches have not continued to embody the kind of inclusion that was practiced by Jesus and the early church and celebrated by Paul in Galatians 3:28 ("There is no longer male and female").

Not only did Jesus pointedly praise all of those who for various reasons do not marry and bear children, not only was the baptism of one such person pointedly described in Acts 8:26–40, but Jesus performed a miracle on behalf of a Roman centurion who was distraught over the illness of a boy who may have been his lover (Matt. 8:5–13). Tom Horner points out that Matthew uses the Greek word *pais* to describe the centurion's servant. The word means *boy*, but it is "the same word that any older man in Greek culture would use to refer to a younger friend—or lover." Luke tells the same story in his Gospel (7:1–10), but being Greek and aware of how *pais* would be heard by his Hellenistic readers, Luke uses the word *doúlos* (slave) three times to identify the boy. Matthew, less aware of Hellenistic nuances, has probably used the nearest Greek equivalent of what the centurion actually said: my *pais*—my boy/my friend/my lover.

---

7. John J. McNeill, *The Church and the Homosexual*, 4th edition (Boston: Beacon Press, 1993), 64. See also the Rev. Nancy Wilson's discussion of eunuchs in *Our Tribe*, 120–31, 281–85.

8. McNeill, *The Church and the Homosexual*, 65.

Certainly the great concern of the centurion would seem unusual if the boy meant nothing more to him than an ordinary slave. And as Horner points out, "if the homosexual element were present, he [Jesus] was not disturbed by it. Instead, he was overwhelmed by the man's faith, which is clearly the paramount element in the story."[9]

Mary Rose D'Angelo adds yet another cautionary note for those who insist the Bible is uniformly negative about any committed love outside of heterosexual marriage. D'Angelo, who teaches theology at the University of Notre Dame, writes about "the early Christian practice of missionaries working in couples," some of whom were married but many of whom were same-sex couples. Describing a first-century sculpture of two women, Eleusis and Helena, clasping hands (a sculpture which was later recut to remove the women's veils and make them look like a male and female with a wedding ring), D'Angelo explains that "What [the] handclasp announces is a commitment between women: not necessarily a commitment that is exclusive or primarily erotic in character, but one that is major, that bears the weight that a family commitment would have borne."[10] In this context, D'Angelo discusses the partnerships of Tryphena and Tryphosa (Romans 16:12), Euodia and Syntyche (Philippians 4:2), and Martha and Mary (Luke 10:38–42; John 11:1—12:19).

D'Angelo comments that "the choice of women to work and live together rather than with a man emerges as a sexual as well as a social choice." And she quotes with approval Bernadette Brooten's speculation that in Romans 1:26–27, Paul's remarks about homoeroticism arose in part "from the need to defend the early Christian mission's practice of missionary couples, including his own practice and the women cited in Rom. 16:12 and Phil. 4:1–2."[11] D'Angelo adds, "Like female leadership in the early Christian mission, the practice [of female partnerships] raised the spectre of the unnatural woman who plays the role of a man."[12]

---

9. Horner, *Jonathan Loved David*, 122.

10. Mary Rose D'Angelo, "Women Partners in the New Testament," *Que(e)rying Religion: A Critical Anthology*, ed. Gary David Comstock and Susan E. Henking (New York: Continuum, 1997), 444.

11. Ibid., 453.

12. Ibid., 454.

While D'Angelo makes no claim that the partnerships were necessarily what we today would call lesbian, or that either or both of the women partners would today be described as transgender, she emphasizes that the commitments between these women were real and strong and only represent "the tip of a very deeply submerged iceberg."[13] Women's New Testament missionary partnerships form one more reason why it is perilous to claim that the Bible says nothing good about same-sex love and/or transgender roles.

Transgender Imagery in the New Testament

Years ago, long before I had any conscious interest in transgender issues, I noticed that the New Testament epistles addressed all members of various local congregations as members of God's family and therefore as brothers (as in, for instance, Rom. 14:10 or 1 Cor. 6:5–6). Clearly there were women in the congregation at Rome (16:3–15) and Corinth (1 Cor. 11:2–6) and elsewhere; so there were many "female brothers" in the early Christian community. At the same time, I noticed that the New Testament depicts all believers, viewed collectively, both as the bride of Christ (Eph. 5:25–27) and as members of Christ's body (Eph. 5:30). If the body of Christ is assumed to be a male body, then Christian women, by putting on Christ like a garment, are imaged as either androgynous he/shes or as transvestites.

And if Christ's body is assumed to be a male body (as the power structures of many churches would still seem to indicate), yet the church itself is assumed to be female (as the numbers in the pews would still seem to indicate), then the church itself is a he/she, a transgender entity. Furthermore, since the men in Ephesus were called Christ's bride—and by extension, all Christian men were called Christ's bride—then the New Testament has used imagery of a same-sex marriage in which a "male" Christ marries not only Christian women but millions of male brides. John Donne, the great seventeenth-century poet and Dean of St. Paul's Cathedral, fearlessly made use of this imagery when he asked God to use a batter-

---

13. Ibid., 454.

ing ram on his stubborn heart, indeed to "ravish" (rape) him, because his will was so conflicted that he could not easily yield to his Divine husband.[14]

Of course, I was aware that this imagery resulted more from subsuming women into male identity (immasculating women[15] or else depicting male souls as female) than of deliberate gender blending. And as a member of a Plymouth Brethren Assembly during my youth, I heard vastly more about everybody, including women, being "brethren" than I did about everybody, including men, being "Christ's bride." So one time when I was addressing a large conference of people from the Church of the Brethren, I quipped that we Christian women would be more willing to identify as "brothers" if more Christian men were willing to identify as "Christ's brides." Unfortunately, the women in that conference felt so oppressed by their supposed inclusion in the term *brethren* that after my speech a group of them literally backed me against a wall, tears in their eyes, entreating me never to say that again. And recognizing their pain and rage, I never did.

Now, however, that I am trying to open religious minds toward a more fluid concept of gender, I am returning to that transgender imagery for another look. Natalie Watson of the Cuddeson Theological College at Oxford, England, has commented that although "the disembodied androgyny that is created by identifying the essentially feminine church as the body of the male Christ appears absurd to a feminist understanding of embodied reality, it points to the significance of considering the relationship between ecclesiology and bodies, essentially between ecclesiology and women's bodies."[16] That's certainly true; but the transsexual imagery also asks us to consider the relationship between the church and gendered bodies of all sorts—male, female, and everybody in between.

---

14. John Donne, "Holy Sonnet 10, 'Batter my heart, three-personed God,'" *John Donne*, ed. John Cary (New York: Oxford University Press, 1990), 177–78.

15. Natalie Watson, "A Feminist Critical Reading of the Ecclesiology of 'Lumen Gentium,'" *Is There a Future for Feminist Theology?*, ed. Deborah F. Sawyer and Diane M. Collier (Sheffield, England: Sheffield Academic Press, 1999), 77.

16. Ibid., 80.

We have already seen that Jesus of Nazareth is not exclusively a male Savior after all, judging from his/her parthenogenetic birth. Now we see that Holy Scripture depicts Christian men as his/her brides and Christian women as his/her brothers. At the very least, such biblical gender blending ought to encourage those who take scripture seriously to become less rigid about gender identities, roles, and presentations.

Consider also Jesus' implication that his/her suffering on the cross was to initiate the labor pangs (travail) of bringing forth a New Humanity (John 16:21–22). Referring to the onset of a woman's painful contractions as the moment when "her hour is come," just minutes later Jesus announces that "the hour is come" (John 17:1) and goes forth to face his trial and crucifixion.[17] Similarly, Paul writes of himself as a mother in labor suffering the pangs of giving birth (Gal. 4:19).

Consider too that the early church understood Jesus to be the human embodiment of Sophia, the Wisdom of God, always depicted as female in the Hebrew Scriptures. Apparently Jesus understood himself that way also, responding to his critics with words that identified him with Sophia herself: "Wisdom is vindicated by her deeds" (Matt. 11:19, NRSV).

And consider the fact that Jesus is called the "son of *man*" because of his *mother*, not because of Joseph.[18]

For that matter, would the frequent biblical imagery of God as female have been included in the canon of Scripture if all the people made in His/Her image were required to be exclusively one or the other? This is not the place to repeat all that I wrote in my 1983 book *The Divine Feminine*. It is easily available, as is a vast amount of other feminist scholarship about the nature of God Herself, who is also God Himself and God Itself.[19]

---

17. Virginia Mollenkott, *The Divine Feminine: The Biblical Imagery of God as Female* (New York: Crossroad, 1983), 16–17.

18. This was first pointed out in 1622 by Marie de Jars de Gournay in "Egalité des hommes et des femmes"; see Elizabeth Gossman, "The Image of God and the Human Being in Women's Counter-Tradition," *Is There a Future for Feminist Theology?*, 40.

19. See especially Elizabeth A. Johnson, *She Who Is* (New York: Crossroad, 1993).

Brigitte Kahl's essay, "Gender Trouble in Galatia? Paul and the Rethinking of Difference" in *Is There a Future for Feminist Theology?* is a fascinating description of the way Paul in Galatians "consciously or subconsciously constructs gender and other identities by confusing them," blurring boundaries in a way that "implies a tremendously transforming potential, which mostly has been kept under cover throughout the centuries of Christian Pauline interpretation" (73). She argues that Galatians 3:28, "Paul's most fundamental statement on border-transgressing unity of race, nation, class and sex, is not just to be considered as a lighthearted aside but as an integral part of the Pauline text—even if Paul quoted it from somewhere else" (59).

Stating that "the oneness of Jew and Greek, slave and free, and male and female proclaimed in Galatians 3:28 seems to produce something like a masquerade of identities" (61), Kahl cites many illustrations: Paul's becoming a mother (Gal. 4:13), slaves becoming free with a freedom defined as enslavement to one another (Gal. 5:13), non-Jews transmuting into Jews (Gal. 3:7, 29; and 4:31), Jews presented with an Arab grandmother, Hagar (Gal. 4:21–31), "difference that is not opposed to sameness/identity but to non-difference, implying pluriformity and oneness-in-difference" (65), and non-Jewish men who become Jews but remain uncircumcised, "a description previously reserved for Jewish women" (72).

It is certainly true, as Kahl charges, that "By 'clothing' Paul with a Christian identity in the later sense, and after driving the circumcised out of the church, we have silenced and buried this highly challenging discourse on identity and difference, which today could be one of the most precious contributions of Paul to the dialogue of religions and cultures, especially to the Jewish-Muslim-Christian encounter" (71).

But for my purposes in this book, it is Kahl's emphasis on the pluriformity and the depolarizing effect of Galatians that is helpful: "The symbolic superiority of male over and against female, which is marked by circumcision, loses theological foundation and dignity" (71). Kahl muses that non-circumcised Jewish men "must have been perceived as 'different,' irregular, even abnormal . . . not real Jews and not real men. . . . Maybe a 'third sex' in between?" (72). Maybe as irregular as intersexuals? Transsexuals? Transgenderists? In Christ, no male and female: It is time for Christianity to regain Paul's vision.

Transgender in Church History

Turning to the history of Christianity, we discover that the Irish Catholic abbot Saint Abban (5th century c.e.) performed a miraculous transsexualizing of a girl into a boy on behalf of an older couple who were desperate for a male heir. This transsexual miracle proved no bar to canonization, for Saint Abban's feast day is celebrated on March 16, although some sources say October 26.[20] We may also be surprised to find that the church has canonized many female-to-male saints—women who cross-dressed, lived, studied, and worshiped as men throughout adulthood or for significant lengths of time. Leslie Feinberg claims to have uncovered more than twenty such transgender saints.[21]

Among them was Saint Pelagia, who had been a courtesan in Antioch before she converted to Christianity and began to identify as Pelagius. When the "wise brother Pelagius," monk and eunuch, was discovered after "her" death to have female anatomy, the mourners chanted, "Glory be to thee, Lord Jesus, for thou hast many hidden treasures on earth, female as well as male." "Her" transgender identity did not prevent canonization, and Pelagius/Pelagia's feast day is October 8.[22]

There is also Saint Marina, who assumed the name Marius in order to become a monk. Evicted from the monastery when a woman accused "him" of fathering her child, Marius brought up the child without disclosing "his" gender of birth. Despite the discovery of "his" femaleness after death, Marina was canonized some time later— not as St. Marius, but as St. Marina.

---

20. "Abban, Saint," *Cassell's Encyclopedia*, 39.

21. Leslie Feinberg, *Transgender Warriors: Making History from Joan of Arc to RuPaul* (Boston: Beacon Press, 1996), 71.

22. "Pelagia, and Saint Pelagia," *Cassell's Encyclopedia*, 264. Unless otherwise indicated, information about other Christian transgenderists is drawn from this fascinating volume.

Saint Eugenia of Alexandria was a noblewoman who adopted Christianity, took a male identity, and entered an abbey. When another woman tried to seduce Eugenia, and failing that accused "him" of making sexual advances toward her, the abbot revealed "his" femaleness. After dying a martyr's death, Eugenia was canonized despite full awareness of his/her transgenderism.

Saint Anastasia was a sixth-century Byzantine noblewoman to whom the Emperor Justinian was attracted. To escape his attentions, Anastasia withdrew into a convent; but when Justinian began to search for her after his wife's death, Anastasia took a male identity and became a hermit monk. Her feast day is March 10.

Saint Galla was a Roman noblewoman who became a hermit monk on Vatican Hill after her husband's death. To do that she, of course, had to assume a male identity, and legend has it that no sooner had she done so than she began to grow a beard. She is fêted on October 3 or 5.

Similarly, St. Paula of Avila was miraculously granted a beard and possibly a complete sex change when she asked Christ to shield her from a man who was pursuing her sexually. Known as St. Paula the Bearded, she is fêted on February 3.

Saint Wilgefortis, whose name means "strong virgin," was also granted a long beard when she asked Jesus to save her from the marriage her father had arranged. Determined to marry her off anyway, her father forced her to come heavily veiled to the wedding ceremony. But when the veil was lifted, her suitor was horrified by the beard and refused to go through with the wedding. Her father had her crucified, no doubt for her "unnaturalness." Her feast day is July 20.

And let us not forget St. Joan of Arc (1412–1431), who was told in a vision that she was to relinquish female attire and behavior in order to assume a transgender, Amazon-like identity as a warrior for France. When she was on trial at Rouen and sufficient evidence could not be found to condemn her as a witch, it was her insistence that her cross-dressing and soldiering were divinely inspired that subsequentally sent her to the flames. Executed on May 30, 1431, she was found innocent of heresy in 1456 and canonized in 1920. Ironically, her feast day is May 30, the same day the canonizing church had permitted her enemies to burn her to death.

Except for St. Joan of Arc, the many female-to-male transgenderists who were canonized as saints lived during the Middle
Ages; yet throughout that period the church continued to invoke
Old Testament laws against same-sex love *and cross-dressing*. How
could that be? Was it Janus-faced deception, as in the case of the
many powerful bishops, archbishops, and even popes who pretended
celibacy but carried on active sex lives? I don't think so. For one
thing, Christian women were often told on the basis of Matthew
22:30 that if they embraced celibacy on earth, their reward would
be to become males in heaven. (The unmarried male clerics apparently reasoned that if there is no marriage in heaven, that must mean
that everyone there is free from the temptations of lustful female
sexuality.) Even during this life, "by renouncing the body and sexuality and following ascetic ideals, women in effect transcended their
femaleness" and "became, so to speak, 'honorary males.'"[23] Therefore, although to my knowledge the church never canonized a male
to female transgenderist, sometimes the hierarchy was willing to assume that certain Christian celibate women had made the transformation to maleness early, so to speak, before reaching heaven. From
another perspective, ascetic transvestite women were viewed as having obeyed injunctions like that of Romans 13:14: "*Put on* the Lord
Jesus Christ, and make no provision for the flesh to gratify its
desires"(NRSV, emphasis mine). Hence, their transgenderism was
no bar to canonization.

Even churchly language in praise of women was sometimes what
we would call transgender. For instance, Bishop John Chrysostom
heaped praise on his patron, the wealthy ascetic Olympia, by ex-
claiming about her, "Don't say 'woman' but 'what a man!' Because
this is a man, despite her physical appearance."[24] This discounting
of *women's* spirituality by co-opting it for maleness is yet another
result of patriarchal gender dualism: If maleness and masculinity are

---

23. Karen Jo Torjesen, *When Women Were Priests: Women's Leadership in the
Early Church and the Scandal of Their Subordination in the Rise of Christianity* (San
Francisco: HarperSanFrancisco, 1993), 210.

24. Ibid., 211.

construed as superior, rational, and noble, what is left for female-ness except to be inferior, irrational, and degraded?

Add to all this the closely guarded secret that throughout church history, there have always been a large percentage of gay, bisexual, lesbian, or transgender pastors, nuns, and priests. Some of the gay priests have even risen to the pinnacle of the hierarchy: For instance, Pope Paul II (1417–1471), who was known for his effeminate behavior, vanity, beauty, and extravagant clothing, is said to have died of a heart attack during homosexual intercourse. His successor, Pope Sextus IV (1414–1481), whose good works included founding the Sistine Chapel, granting asylum to Spanish Jews, and establishing the first hospital for orphans, appointed his nephew and beloved, Raphael Riaro, to the offices of Papal Chamberlain and Bishop of Ostia.[25] Furthermore, according to many scholars, a cross-dressing heterosexual woman was elected Pope during the mid-ninth century: Pope Joan, her papal name being Pope John VIII, Angelicus. S/he died in childbirth or shortly thereafter.[26] And the church's insistence that s/he never existed is symbolic of the religious erasure of transgender experience.

As for nuns, the case of Sister Benedetta Carlini (1590–1661) has been well documented by Judith C. Brown in *Immodest Acts: The Life of a Lesbian Nun in Renaissance Italy* (New York: Oxford University Press, 1986).[27] More general coverage is offered by Rosemary Curt and Nancy Monahan in *Lesbian Nuns: Breaking Silence* (Tallahassee, Fla.: Naiad Press, 1985).

Concerning gay or lesbian Protestant pastors, a readable and compelling survey is provided by Dann Hazel in *Witness: Gay and Lesbian Clergy Report from the Front* (Louisville: Westminster John Knox Press, 2000).

My point here is simply that it makes no sense for contemporary Christians or Jews to recoil from an omnigender construct because

---

25. See "Paul II, Pope" and "Sixtus IV, Pope," *Cassell's Encyclopedia*, 263, 306–07.

26. "Joan, Pope," *Cassell's Encyclopedia*, 191–92.

27. Since Benedetta was said to take on the appearance either of Jesus or a beautiful adolescent male, along with a deepened voice, when she made love to Sister Bartholomea, s/he was transgendered as well as lesbian.

they associate a rigidly binary gender system with orthodox beliefs and practices and associate transgenderism (including homosexuality) with "pagan unbelief." Although guilt by association may seem a useful tactic, there have been so many honored and honorable transgenderists (including homosexuals) during the course of Jewish and Christian history that the guilt-by-association argument will no longer work.

Prohibition of Genital Surgery

Deuteronomy 23:1 reads, "No one whose testicles are crushed or whose penis is cut off shall be admitted to the assembly of the Lord" (NRSV). Does this mean that even men injured in an accident through no fault of their own were prohibited from entering the temple? Apparently, yes. But it must be noted that the great Hebrew prophet Isaiah advocated restoring congregational membership to such men:

> . . . do not let the eunuch say,
> "I am just a dry tree."
> For thus says the Lord:
> to the eunuchs who keep my sabbaths,
>   who choose the things that please me
>   and who hold fast my covenant,
> I will give, in my house and within my walls
> a monument and a name
> better than sons and daughters;
> I will give them an everlasting name
> that shall not be cut off. (Isa. 56:3b–5)

Isaiah's words have given comfort to many thousands of people who for many reasons cannot or do not marry and have children—intersexuals, transsexuals, lesbian women, and gay men among them.

For our purposes at this time, the Big Question is whether Deuteronomy forbids genital reassignment surgery and, if so, whether that law should be applied to contemporary transsexuals. Leslie Feinberg, who calls him/herself a "Jewish, transgender, working-class revolutionary" and who has undergone both female-to-male surgery and its reversal, assumes that Deuteronomy 23:1 does indeed prohibit sex-change surgery. But he/she considers such laws "trans-phobic" and "gender-phobic," written sometime between the eleventh and seventh centuries B.C.E., and no longer applicable. She asserts that the very presence of such laws does, however, indicate that self-castration and sex-change were widespread enough at that time to be a religious issue.

Feinberg argues that like the prohibition against cross-dressing, the one against genital surgery stemmed from repudiation of cross-gendering among priests of the various goddesses. The prohibitions were also part of a worldwide consolidation of patriarchal rule that required making class distinctions between women and men and eliminating any blurring or bridging of those categories. In order to accomplish that patriarchal consolidation, the communalism of goddess-worshiping societies had to be overthrown in favor of the private ownership of property and the accumulation of wealth.[28] This is *not* to say that the Jews invented patriarchy. They were not the first society to organize into class hierarchies—and the patriarchal system that manifested itself in Hebrew culture was at the same time manifesting itself all over the world.

Nevertheless, the Hebrew Scriptures do reflect the rise of a patriarchal ruling class, and they do imply that rules against genital surgery were related to the self-mutilations practiced by some of the priests in Canaanite religion (for instance, Deuteronomy 14:1 [NRSV] says, "You are the children of the Lord your God. You must not lacerate yourselves").

---

28. Feinberg, *Transgender Warriors*, 50–51. I do not agree with those who *dismiss* Feinberg as Marxist because of her insistence on the redistribution of wealth. Although she may in fact identify as Marxist, a concern about economic justice is far larger than any one thinker such as Marx; and the collapse of Communism in the Soviet Union does not excuse us from seeking to solve the horrors of hunger and poverty. In my opinion, she is like a Hebrew prophet (see Isa. 58, for example). If Feinberg is exclusively Marxist, then so is Shakespeare (see *King Lear* III. iv. 33–41; IV. i. 60–73; etc.); so was Jesus (Luke 6:24, etc.); and so am I.

So if Feinberg's assumption is correct that Deuteronomy 23:1 is indeed a trans-phobic law prohibiting sex-change surgery no matter how it is achieved or how desperately it may be needed, there is no longer any need to apply it that way. Judaism is no longer in a survival mode, it is clearly differentiated from other religions, and patriarchal power and capitalistic economies have triumphed to a fault.

As for Christians, the conservative *Wycliffe Bible Commentary*, edited by Charles F. Pfeiffer and Everett F. Harrison (Chicago: Moody Press, 1962) makes clear that no ruling against sex-reassignment surgery should apply within the Christian community: "In New Testament times such disabilities [i.e., being a eunuch, having endured accidental or deliberate castration] no longer enter into consideration even in the external administration of the church (cf. Isaiah 56:4–5 and Acts 8:27–38)" (186).

Jesus' words about eunuchs in Matthew 19:12 reveal an accepting, respectful attitude that ought to be the norm for the modern church: "For there are eunuchs who have been so from birth" includes at the very least all intersexual people; "and there are eunuchs who have been made eunuchs by others" includes post-operative transsexuals; "and there are eunuchs who have made themselves eunuchs for the sake of the kingdom of heaven" includes not only pre-operative and non-operative transsexuals but all other transgenderists, celibates, and homosexuals who do not engage in reproductive sex. The kingdom of heaven is located within us (Luke 17:21); so perhaps what Jesus means by being eunuchs "for the sake of the kingdom of heaven" is the Jewish counsel of being true to one's deepest nature. As Jesus went on to say, "Let anyone accept this who can."

But Sally Gross, an intersexual scholar, offers a startlingly different perspective on the meaning of Deuteronomy 23:1—namely, that it explicitly forbids the removal of gonads and the reshaping of a "too large" clitoris and other such surgeries that are routinely performed on intersexual babies and children. Writes Gross, "[B]iblical literalists should be persuaded by the letter of Scripture to be very suspicious indeed of genital surgery imposed upon intersexed infants when no intrinsic risk to life and physical health demands it."[29] Rather than arguing that intersexuals are required by scripture to seek surgery that will fit them acceptably into society's binary gender system, Christians like Charles Colson should show their respect for an explicit scriptural prohibition against genital surgery of a cosmetic nature. And they should show their respect for the Creator's biodiversity by welcoming "the notion of a spectrum which includes people who are intersexed."[30]

I heartily agree with Gross's conclusion: "Biblical literalists are indeed arguably bound by Scripture to respect the sense of many people who are intersexed that violence was done to them by the imposition of what was in effect cosmetic surgery, and to accept that it is right and proper that those who are born intersexed are enabled to remain physically as they are and to identify as intersexed [if they so desire]."[31]

And obviously, if proper attention to scriptural injunctions requires movement toward omnigender acceptance by all who take the Bible seriously, then human compassion and empathy require such movement by everyone else as well. Indeed, the movement is already underway not only in Judaism, as we saw earlier, but also in Catholic and Protestant branches of Christianity. In Catholicism, the Vatican continues to tighten the reins, describing the homosexual orientation as an "objective disorder" and characterizing all extramarital sexual activity as aberrant; but American Catholics increasingly depart from the Vatican perspective, with forty-five percent currently believing that "homosexuals can be good Catholics," according to recent Gallup research.[32] In Protestantism, church debates over the meaning and place of sexuality have become so intense that according to the World Council of Churches, "appar-

---

29. Sally Gross, "Intersexuality and Scripture," *Theology and Sexuality* 11 (September 1999), 74.

30. Ibid., 71–74.

31. Ibid., 74.

32. Charles Austin, "Christians Grappling with Sin's Shifting Face," *The Record* (8 March 2000), A-1 and A-14; Denise and John Carmody, "Homosexuality and Roman Catholicism," *Homosexuality and World Religions*, ed. Arlene Swidler (Harrisburg: Trinity Press International, 1993), 144.

ently God is calling us to rethink it." Presbyterian ethicist Marvin Ellison comments that, in all probability, "the great divide is not denominational but rather theological-ethical in character,"[33] a phenomenon I have explained in the previous chapter.

Avoiding Christian Doublespeak

I predict that despite the mounting evidence presented in this book and elsewhere, some Christian leaders will oppose omnigender with the same doublespeak that has characterized the narrower discussion of homosexuality and the church. Other religions will no doubt replicate Christian problems in their own ways, but I want to limit myself to the controversy I know best.

Gerard Loughlin's critique of gender and ethics in the influential theology of Karl Barth provides an excellent example of Barth's Christian doublespeak.[34] Loughlin makes clear that binary gender is a non-negotiable aspect of Barth's theology: "Each of us is either male *or* female, while at the same time being oriented to the sex we are not."[35] Barth writes, "in obedience to God, man will be male or female" because God created "an inward, essential and lasting order of being as He and She, valid for all time and also for eternity."[36] Yet Barth, writing in the late 1940s and early '50s, also insists that women must not define themselves in terms of "traditional preconceptions" or the "uncalled for illusions of man." Like every man, every woman must construct her own identity—but in doing so, she must "always and in all circumstances be woman . . . she must feel and conduct herself as such and not as man . . . is the command of the Lord, which for all eternity directs both man and woman to their own sacred place and forbids all attempts to violate this order."[37]

---

33. Marvin Ellison, "Homosexuality and Protestantism," *Homosexuality and World Religions*, 171.

34. Loughlin, "Sex Slaves: Rethinking 'Complementarity' After I Corinthians 7:3–4," *Is There a Future for Feminist Theology?*, 173–92.

35. Ibid., 182.

36. As quoted by Loughlin from Karl Barth's *Church Dogmatics* III/4, ibid., 183–84.

37. Ibid., 183.

Which is it, I want to ask Karl Barth: Are women and men free to feel their authentic feelings and to become fully realized selves, the selves we most deeply recognize ourselves to be? Or must we hew to our society's male-female polarities, imagining them to be God's will "for all time and also for eternity"? Barth tries to have it both ways; but in practice, that is impossible for millions of people. Barth's doublespeak reminds me of men who coached girls' sports teams in the mid-twentieth century, insisting that the girls must play to win but also insisting that they must always behave like ladies, preferably never even perspiring.

A further illustration of what I mean by Christian doublespeak comes from a well respected mainline Protestant book by Richard B. Hayes, *The Moral Vision of the New Testament: A Contemporary Introduction to New Testament Ethics* (San Francisco: Harper-SanFrancisco, 1996). Touted as showing "how the New Testament provides moral guidance on the most troubling ethical issues of our time," Hayes's book uses as test cases the issues of violence in defense of justice, divorce and remarriage, homosexuality, anti-Judaism and ethnic conflict, and abortion. His treatment of homosexuality shows little or no awareness of the transgender movement, but it is enough to clarify what his position on omnigender would no doubt be.

I chose Hayes's book because there is so much good about it that the doublespeak is all the more painful. Here's an instance of the positive aspects of this work: Hayes admits that homosexual behavior is a minor concern in the Bible—"perhaps half a dozen brief references in all of scripture"—and then makes this excellent statement:

> What the Bible does say should be heeded carefully, but any ethic that intends to be biblical will seek to get the accents in the right place, not overemphasizing peripheral issues. (Would that the passion presently being expended in the church over the question of homosexuality were devoted to urging the wealthy to share with the poor! Some of the most urgent champions of biblical morality on sexual matters become strangely equivocal when the discussion turns to the New Testament's teachings about possessions.) (381)

To which I say a heartfelt *Amen.*

But when it comes to actual exegesis of biblical references to homosexual acts, Hayes refuses to wrestle with the scholarly evidence that disagrees with his gay-negative interpretations. Instead he sweeps aside all such evidence by calling it "wishful"—not in his own voice, either, but in the voice of a non-self-accepting gay Christian named Gary, spoken when Gary was dying of AIDS. The few times Hayes refers to the work of "gay apologists," his dealings are sketchy, non-contextual, and sometimes appallingly inaccurate. Perhaps the most astonishing example is his statement about John Boswell's award-winning *Christianity, Social Tolerance, and Homosexuality* (Chicago: University of Chicago Press, 1980). Hayes claims that "As Boswell's study amply documents, the mainstream of Christian ethical teaching has been relentlessly hostile to homosexual practice" (397). My friend and colleague John Boswell has long since gone to his reward, but he would have been most surprised to learn that *that* was the point of his book!

That Hayes would oppose an omnigender paradigm is evident from his assertion that Genesis 1 and 2 "describes man and woman as created for one another" and that "Thus the complementarity of male and female is given a theological grounding in God's creative activity" (386). Ignoring the verifiable fact that thousands of gay, lesbian, bisexual, and transgender Christians live beautifully ethical and faith-filled lives, Hayes makes an ugly claim on the basis of his interpretation of Romans 1: "When human beings engage in homosexual activity, they enact an outward and visible sign of an inward and spiritual reality: the rejection of the Creator's design" (386). Are intersexual newborns also a "sacrament of antireligion" because they too reject the Creator's design?

And this brings us to the topic of doublespeak. Hayes admits that "self-righteous judgment of homosexuality is just as sinful as the homosexual behavior itself" and that "no one has a secure platform to stand upon in order to pronounce condemnation on others" (309). Those seem to me amazing admissions from an author who has just defined my highest and holiest expressions of love to be sacraments of antireligion! When I was thirteen, I attempted suicide because of judgments like that. I marvel that people like Hayes seem unconcerned about the thousands of suicides and murders that are prompted by their rhetoric.

Elsewhere, in his discussion of abortion, Hayes argues that "As God's creatures, we are stewards who bear life in trust. To terminate a pregnancy is not only to commit an act of violence but also to assume responsibility for destroying a work of God 'from whom are all things and for whom we exist'(1 Cor. 8:6)" (450). Leaving aside Hayes's non-contextual condemnation of that which under certain circumstances might be more loving than giving birth, I wonder whether Hayes views intersexual, homosexual, and transsexual fetuses as the work of God which ought not to be destroyed? If they (we) exist "from God" and "for God," how dare anyone consign them (us) to lives without loving companionship, consigning them (us) to nothing warmer than "disciplined abstinence" (403)?

Hayes says that "Even if it could be shown that same-sex preference is somehow genetically programmed, that would not necessarily make homosexual behavior morally appropriate" (398). So, according to Hayes, even if the Creator has genetically programmed His/ Her creations to love people of their own gender, for them to obey the Creator's program would be morally reprehensible! See what I mean by doublespeak?

Furthermore, Hayes must surely be aware that some Christians have proudly announced that if a "gay gene" is ever isolated and can be determined *in utero*, they will seek to abort such fetuses. Whether or not he intended to do so, Hayes's remark about genetic mis-programming lends moral support to such attitudes, contradicting his own stance regarding abortion and the use of violence to support a "just cause." Doublespeak again!

Ultimately, I wish Hayes were able to stay consistent with his own best insights. In the context of racial and ethnic differences, for instance, Hayes asks,

> how is it possible for the community of Christ's people to participate in animosity toward "outsiders"? If God is the Creator of the whole world who will ultimately redeem the whole creation—if the death of Christ was the means whereby "God was pleased to reconcile to himself all things, whether on earth or in heaven, by making

peace though the blood of his cross" (Col. 1:20)—then how can the church that is called to bear God's message of reconciliation to an unredeemed world (2 Cor. 5:17–20) scorn or reject people of any race or tongue, whether they are Christian or not? (441)

Indeed!

And, I would add, how can the church that is called to bear God's message of reconciliation scorn or reject people of any sexual orientation or gender identity? I believe that moving toward an omnigender construct is a work of reconciliation and making peace.

CHAPTER SIX

≋ *Precedents for Increased Gender Fluidity*

ALTHOUGH IT MIGHT BE A little much to say that any recent culture has embraced transgender people as within the "standard range of human variation," there are and have been many cultures that are more gender-flexible and inclusive than our own. In some cultures, transgenderism is recognized simply as a personal attribute. In others, it is considered a by-product of religious ecstasy. And in still others, it is acceptable as a response to particular economic circumstances, such as the case of a family with only one child, a daughter, who is needed to care for cattle and must be granted male status in order to do so.[1] In this chapter, I hope to describe ways in which binary gender has been disregarded in various cultures while bringing about none of the dreadful results certain people seem to fear, including the demise of heterosexual families and the gradual extinction of the human race.[2]

Obviously, this book would not be the place for an exhaustive description of all such cultures, even if I had the knowledge and expertise to provide it. I will simply try to introduce enough evidence to show that gender fluidity has been practiced for centuries and has not had disastrous effects on the societies in which it has occurred.

1. Roz Kaveny, "Talking Transgender Politics," *Reclaiming Genders: Transsexual Grammars at the* Fin de Siècle, ed. Kate More and Stephen Whittle (New York: Cassell, 1999), 157.

2. My profound thanks to Dr. Janet Pollak, Professor of Anthropology at William Paterson University, for reading and making helpful suggestions concerning this chapter.

If we may take seriously John Milton's depictions of angelic relationships in *Paradise Lost*, the "heavenly culture" is characterized by utter gender fluidity. In Book One of this profoundly theological epic, the narrative voice explains that angels are sometimes male, sometimes female, sometimes both:

> For spirits when they please
> Can either sex assume, or both; so soft
> And uncompounded is their essence pure,
> Not tied or manacled with joint or limb,
> Nor founded on the brittle strength of bones,
> Like cumbrous flesh; but in what shape they choose
> Dilated or condensed, bright or obscure,
> Can execute their airy purposes,
> And works of love or enmity fulfil.
> (I.423–431)[3]

In other words, Milton's angels are shape-shifters with instantaneous transsexual and hermaphroditic capacities. Furthermore, they use these capacities to make love with one another and are able to achieve a more total embrace than any human coupling can because angelic lovers never meet with bodily obstructions of "membrane, joint, or limb" (VIII. 620–29).[4]

Milton did not envision a static heaven in which the greatest activity is either eating or singing in the heavenly choir. He envisioned an erotic and active heaven of "blessed dances" and "rapturous . . . joyous revels" and "immortal nuptials" enacted again and again.[5] Presumably, since Milton believed in correspondences between things heavenly and earthly ("as above, so below"), redeemed human beings might also "either sex assume, or both" and might

---

3. John Milton, *Paradise Lost*, I. 423–431, *The Oxford Authors: John Milton*, ed. Stephen Orgel and Jonathan Goldberg (New York: Oxford University Press, 1990), 366.

4. Milton, *Paradise Lost*, VIII. 620–629, *Oxford Authors*, 522.

5. Milton, "Damon's Epitaph," *Oxford Authors*, 161.

make love in any of those genders, although *instantaneous* shape-shifting would not be possible until the assumption of resurrection bodies.

Where did Milton get such gender-fluid concepts? No writer on angels prior to Milton had ever asserted that they make love with one another,[6] let alone that they could do so as either male or female or both simultaneously. Bearing in mind that Milton said *Paradise Lost* was dictated to him during his sleep by the special inspiration of a heavenly muse (IX. 20–24),[7] and that he awarded final authority to the Bible in any conflict between the classics and the scriptures,[8] we may assume that Milton had noticed and adopted the gender-fluid New Testament imagery described earlier in this book.

As Elizabeth Stuart said in her inaugural lecture as a professor of Christian theology, "Two millennia before the invention of queer theory early Christian theologians played around with concepts of gender in order to subvert them. In Ephesians 5, to give but one example . . . the male Christ is said to have a female body—the Church. . . . Again and again in early Christian writings gender is played out and broken open in order to reveal the nature of the redeemed, ecclesial person."[9] Christ, the "husband" or "male," is the head or source of the "wife," the "female" body, which in turn is instructed to grow up into the "male" head (Eph. 4:15). As members of the church, Christian men are Christ's "bride" as much as women are and Christian women, like men, are embodiments of the "male" Christ and therefore Christian "brothers." Steeped in such imagery, Milton interpreted Jesus' remark about no heavenly marrying or giving in marriage (Matt. 22:29-30) to mean *not* that

---

6. "Angels," *A Milton Encyclopedia*, ed. William B. Hunter Jr. (Lewisburg: Bucknell University Press, 1978), I. 49b.

7. Milton, *Paradise Lost*, IX. 20–24, *Oxford Authors*, 524. Milton's muse was feminine, a "celestial patroness," who brings the words of the poem "nightly to my ear" (IX. 47): an image of a male poet's being impregnated by a female muse.

8. Milton, "Of Education," *Oxford Authors*, 232.

9. Stuart's lecture, delivered at King Alfred's College, Winchester, on 14 October 1998, was published as "Sexuality: The View from the Font (the Body and the Ecclesial Self)," *Theology and Sexuality* 11, 9–20.

there would be no sex in heaven, but rather that sex in resurrection bodies would have none of the binary possessiveness and constriction of marriage in a fallen world. Instead, as Jesus put it, resurrection bodies would be "as the angels in heaven"—a vision of astonishing freedom.

Ancient Religions

Similarly, the erotic was regarded as a holy and life-sustaining power in early Mesopotamia (c. 2500–1500 B.C.E.). There was a relaxed attitude toward sex and gender that seems almost unthinkable to contemporary American minds. Julia M. Asher-Greve presents evidence of a multiple gender system in which castrates and people without sexual organs were assigned specific social tasks; "gender taxonomy tolerated ambiguity beyond the 'normative' masculine-feminine"; and "body and mind were a inseparable unity, denoted by the same Sumerian word."[10] For many centuries, the sacred marriage between the goddess Inanna and her consort Dumuzi was central to the religion of Sumer, while in Babylon and Israel the couple was known as Ishtar and Tammuz. In one wedding narrative, Inanna focuses admiringly on her own genitals, calling upon her female attendants to praise them musically so that everyone might be able to join in the singing. Soon, we are told,

> The young lady was praising her parts
> and the elegist was weaving it into a song,
> Inanna was praising them,
> had her parts extolled in song.
>
> "My crescent-shaped 'Barge of Heaven,'
> So well belayed,
> full of loveliness, like the new moon,
> my untilled plot,

---

10. Julia M. Asher-Greve, "Feminist Research and Ancient Mesopotamia: Problems and Prospects," *A Feminist Companion to Reading the Bible*, ed. Athalaya Brenna and Carole Fontaine (Sheffield, England: Sheffield Academic Press, 1997), 234.

left so fallow in the desert,
my duck field so studded with ducks,
my hillock land, so well watered,
my parts, piled up with levels,
well watered."[11]

In her commentary on this hymn, Starhawk points out that not only does Inanna find herself beautiful in her own eyes and eager for sex with her male consort, but she invites other women to sing praises to her sexual parts, and in doing so they demonstrate intimate knowledge of them. Hence, Starhawk comments, "Inanna represents the woman who is neither heterosexual nor lesbian but simply sexual—and proud of it."[12]

Furthermore, Inanna lives what is essentially the free life of a young man and is called "hero" and "manly." The Sumerian scholar Tikva Frymer-Kensky says that "Inanna transcends gender polarities and is said to turn men into women and women into men. . . . [A]t her festivals, men dress as women and women as men, and cultic dancers wear outfits that are men's clothes on the right and women's on the left."[13] As the patron of sexuality—brides, prostitutes, eunuchs, and homosexuals alike—Inanna would make a good patron for the contemporary transgender movement. In fact, at a recent California State University conference on transgenderism,

---

11. Thorkild Jacobsen, *The Treasures of Darkness: A History of Mesopotamian Religion* (New Haven: Yale University Press, 1976), as quoted by Starhawk, *Truth or Dare: Encounters with Power, Authority, and Mystery* (San Francisco: Harper & Row, 1987), 43. See also Tikva Frymer-Kensky's descriptions of the sacred marriage: *In the Wake of the Goddesses: Women, Culture, and the Biblical Transformation of Pagan Myth* (New York: Free Press, 1992), 45–69. Jeremiah 49:19 refers to Inanna/Ishtar/Astart as "the queen of heaven"; her consort Dumuzi is referred to as Tammuz in Ezekiel 8:14; but in Syria his name would be Adonis.

12. Starhawk, *Truth or Dare*, 44.

13. Frymer-Kensky, *In the Wake of the Goddesses*, 29.

Dr. William Dragoin distributed a tracing of a cave painting over 15,000 years old that depicted a transgendered priest/ess.[14]

None of this about Inanna will come as a surprise to those who are familiar with the scholarship concerning the many centuries when the supreme deity was adored in female form. Archeologist Marija Gimbutas, Merlin Stone, Riane Eisler, and others have traced Goddess reverence as far back as the Paleolithic era through evidence including multitudes of female figurines and cave paintings. Some incised drawings in the Addaura Cave near Palermo appear to honor the Bird Goddess, a transgender manifestation of the divine that is also depicted in hosts of figurines with the torso of a bird, female human breasts, and a neck that is human, male, and phallic.[15]

Furthermore, many of the priests and priestesses who dedicated their lives to various goddesses were gender-variant, either homosexual or otherwise transgendered. For instance, within the spiritual household and center of learning led by Sappho at Lesbos (approximately 620 B.C.E.) lesbian priests served the goddess Aphrodite, who is sometimes depicted as hermaphroditic, with both female breasts and an erect phallus.[16] And the transgender *Qedeshim* who served Asherah, the primary goddess of the Canaanites, also served her consort Baal, who was depicted as a golden calf and who loved both women and men.[17]

---

14. Dallas Denny, "Transgender: Some Historical, Cross-cultural, and Contemporary Models and Methods of Coping and Treatment," *Gender Blending*, ed. Bonnie Bullough, Vern Bullough, and James Elias (Amherst, N.Y.: Prometheus Books, 1997), 35.

15. "Addaura," *Cassell's Encyclopedia of Queer Myth, Symbol and Spirit*, ed. Randy P. Luncunas Conner, David Hatfield Sparks, and Mariya Sparks (New York: Cassell, 1998), 42. See Marija Gimbutas, *The Goddesses and Gods of Old Europe, 6500–3500 B.C.: Myths and Cult Images* (Berkeley: University of California Press, 1982), and the astringently skeptical description of "The Rise and Fall of Women's Power" by Cynthia Eller in *Living in the Lap of the Goddess: The Feminist Spirituality Movement in America* (New York: Crossroad, 1993), 150–84.

16. "Thiasos," 322, "Goddess Reverence," 17–18, and "Aphrodite," 64, *Cassell's Encyclopedia*.

17. "Atherat," 75, "Qadesh," 274, and "Baal," 80, *Cassell's Encyclopedia*. It took 300 years of active campaigning for Israel's leadership to banish the *quedeshim* and goddess-reverence from Israel.

The Phrygean and Greco-Roman goddess Cybele was served by *galli*, male priests who were eunuchs and transvestites. Ironically, the highest-ranking galli wore miters—ribboned turbans or tiaras associated with effeminacy—the irony being, of course, that Western Christianity still uses the term *miter* for a bishop's liturgical cap. When the galli were being initiated they were referred to as "those who are being born again"—another irony, considering the frequent use of that term by the Evangelical Right. Once initiated, the galli were called sometimes "half men," sometimes "not men." But they were never called women, despite their feminine attire, their earrings, their castrati voices, and their tendency to lisp.[18]

Both Axel Persson and William Tyrell point out that like the galli, the Amazons were consecrated to Cybele, as were other lesbian women.[19] Archaeological evidence may eventually prove that the legendary Amazons were not as fictional as many scholars have thought: Graves of priestesses in Sarmatian cemeteries (in the Russian steppes) have been found to include their armor and weapons, marked, quite uniquely, with even more ancient symbols of Indic myths, indicating "the far greater antiquity of their warring faith." Jessica Salmonson therefore concludes that "there is good reason to suppose that their cult did actually exist."[20]

In stark contrast to monotheistic patriarchal religions, women, transgender people, and same-sex oriented people were welcome to serve as spiritual functionaries not only for Inanna/Ishtar, Aphrodite, Asherah, and Cybele, but also for Artemis/Diana, the Phoenician goddess Astarte, the Scythian goddess Artimpasa, the Teutonic deities Freyja and Freyr, and many others. Mesopotamians

---

18. "Gallos," *Cassell's Encyclopedia*, 146–153.

19. See Axel W. Persson's *The Religion of Greece in Prehistoric Times* (Berkeley: University of California Press, 1942); and William Blake Tyrell, *Amazons: A Study in Athenian Mythology* (Baltimore: Johns Hopkins Press, 1984).

20. Jessica Amanda Salmonson, *The Encyclopedia of Amazons: Women Warriors from Antiquity to the Modern Era* (New York: Paragon House, 1991), 10. See also Guiniviere Curfman, "Funerary Practices of the Sauro-Sarmatians of Pokrova [Russia]," *Real Amazons NetZine* (summer 1999) <http://www.fc.net/~arachne/>. Despite the jazzy title, Curfman is doing serious research as a student of archaeology.

considered transgenderism and homosexuality to be essential characteristics bestowed by a god or goddess; and they were not alone
in that belief.[21]

None of this gender fluidity appears to have damaged heterosexual relating, human reproduction, or the human tendency to bond
within families. Quite the contrary: Frymer-Kensky comments that
in the cultic "confusion of genders" and "hymnic acknowledgment
of it" that surrounded Inanna/Ishtar, the ultimate effect was "not
only to transcend gender, but also to protect it. As in all rituals and
occasions of rebellion, the societally approved, scheduled, and regulated breaking of a norm actually serves to reinforce it."[22] While
contemporary transgender people have no desire to reinforce the
binary gender construct and would not appreciate being socially
scheduled or regulated, nevertheless, the benign results of ancient
gender fluidity should prove reassuring to those who, for whatever
reason, fear it would cause disaster.

Africa and the Diaspora

As I write, newspapers are full of reports that AIDS is spreading
with desperate rapidity in Africa and among African Americans in
the United States (among Hispanics also, but that is a different
topic about which I have little information). Various concerned
clergy in African American denominational churches are admitting that a large aspect of this problem has been the silence surrounding sex outside of marriage (whether heterosexual, bisexual,
or homosexual), combined with the notion that gender-variant behavior, especially homosexuality, was unknown in Africa until it
was introduced by white colonialists. Womanist scholar Renita
Weems comments that to say the vast majority of the black community is homophobic may be an oversimplification, but it is also
an understatement.[23] And womanist theologian Delores S. Will-

---

21. "Ancient Near Eastern and Western Antiquity," *Cassell's Encyclopedia*, 5–7.

22. Frymer-Kensky, *In the Wake of the Goddesses*, 29.

23. Renita Weems, "Just Friends," *Que(e)rying Religion: A Critical Anthology*, ed.
Gary David Comstock and Susan E. Henking (New York: Continuum, 1997), 351.

iams names two of the "daily sins" of black denominational churches as "encouraging homophobia" and "responding to the AIDS crisis with denial."[24] Because precious lives could have been saved if AIDS had been met with swift acknowledgment and education, it is tragic that the gender fluidity of African culture has been either forgotten or else deliberately obscured by Afrocentric leaders.[25] Had people known the honorable role of homosexuals and transgenderists in African religion and culture, perhaps they would not have felt ashamed to acknowledge the homosexuals and transgenderists in their midst or to acknowledge the human tendencies toward extramarital sexuality in general.

Leslie Feinberg mentions that "African spiritual beliefs in intersexual deities and sex/gender transformation among their followers have been documented among the Akan, Ambo-Kwanyama, Bono, Chokwe, Dohameans (of Benin), Dagon, Bambara, Etik, Handa, Humbe, Hunde, Ibo, Jukan, Kimbundu, Knoso, Kunama, Lamba, Lango, Luba, Lulua, Muso, Nuba, Ovimbundu, Rundi, Shona-Karonga, Venda, Vili-Kongo, and Yoruba." And s/he adds that "transgender in religious ceremony is still reported in the twentieth century in West Africa. And cross-dressing is a feature of modern Brazilian and Haitian ceremonies derived from West African religions."[26]

Renowned social anthropologist Edward E. Evans-Pritchard, who studied the Azande people of today's southwestern Sudan and northern Zaire, points out that intergenerational homoeroticism was prac-

---

24. Delores S. Williams, *Sisters in the Wilderness: The Challenge of Womanist God Talk* (Maryknoll, N.Y.: Orbis, 1993), 208.

25. For a powerful indictment of black heterosexism by an African American professor of pastoral theology at Seabury-Western Seminary, see Horace Griffin, "Their Own Received Them Not: African American Lesbians and Gays in Black Churches," *Theology and Sexuality* (March 2000): 88–100.

26. Leslie Feinberg, *Transgender Warriors: Making History from Joan of Arc to RuPaul* (Boston: Beacon Press, 1996), 44. Feinberg's sources include Randy P. Conner, *Blossom of Bone: Reclaiming the Connections between Homoeroticism and the Sacred* (San Francisco: HarperCollins, 1993); and Joseph Campbell, *The Way of the Animal Powers* (San Francisco: Harper & Row, 1983).

ticed among them "from remote antiquity" until the early twentieth century. A male warrior married a boy-wife until the boy was old enough to become a warrior himself and take his own boy-wife. Commanders were permitted several boy-wives if they so desired. Evans-Pritchard explains that these practices were indigenous, not the result of any foreign influences.[27] He also found that the wives of Azande nobility often established deep and long-lasting relationships with other women in their husbands' court, although they kept the sexual element hidden from their husbands' awareness.[28]

Anthropologist S. F. Nadel points out that among the Nuba tribes of the Nilotic Sudan, transgender homosexuality is common enough to be referred to by a variety of terms. Among the Nuba, Nadel says, "homosexuals . . . wear women's clothing, do women's work, and adopt women's ways." Among the Korongo and Mesakin, transgendered "wives" and "husbands" live together and "keep a common household."[29]

Sociologist David F. Greenberg describes the *mugawe* among the Kenyan Meru people as a powerful religious leader who is "a complement to . . . male political leaders, and consequently must exemplify feminine qualities." The mugawe, who wears women's clothing and hairstyles, is "often homosexual and is sometimes married to a man." Greenberg comments also that "religious transgenderal homosexuality is reported for a number of tribes across Africa."[30]

---

27. Edward E. Evans-Pritchard, *The Azande: History and Political Institution* (Oxford: Oxford University Press, 1971), 183, 199–200.

28. Evans-Pritchard, "Sexual Inversion Among the Azande," *American Anthropologist*, no. 72 (December 1970): 1428–34, as cited by Robert M. Baum, "Homosexuality and the Traditional Religions of the Americas and Africa," *Homosexuality and World Religions*, ed. Arlene Swidler (Harrisburg: Trinity Press International, 1993), 25.

29. S. F. Nadel, *The Nuba: An Anthropological Study of the Hill Tribes in Kordofan* (London: Oxford University Press, 1947), as cited in *Cassell's Encyclopedia*, 1; cf. Baum, "Homosexuality and the Traditional Religions of the Americas and Africa," 29.

30. David F. Greenberg, *The Construction of Homosexuality* (Chicago: University of Chicago Press, 1988), 60.

Among the four Bantu-speaking societies, transgenderism is closely associated with religious authority, prophet-status, and spiritual healing. He-Shes or men-women are perceived to be especially powerful because they combine masculine and feminine powers just like the original creative deity. In Zambia, among the Ila, the *mwaami* or prophet can be a man or a woman or a man-woman, in which case he wears women's clothes and sleeps among (but not with) the women.[31]

The Yoruba religion, which is rooted in Nigeria, has been practiced for centuries and may be associated with the ancient religions of Egypt and Phoenicia. It was brought to the New World along with the twelve million Africans of the slave trade. Known as *Santeria* in the United States, and as *Candomblé* in Brazil, it was influential upon and influenced by *Vodou* (often spelled *voodoo* by those who conflate it with witchcraft). The Yoruba religion in the Americas has made room for bisexual, homosexual, and transgendered practitioners. Babaluayé is the Yaruba-diasporic *orisha* or deity who rules life-threatening illnesses, including HIV/AIDS. He is often identified with the Catholic Saints Lazarus and Sebastian and therefore is especially venerated by people with AIDS and those who love them.[32]

In New York City during the period 1920–1935, African Americans developed a homosexual and transgender subculture that played an important role in the Harlem Renaissance. Their presence was recognized in the Blues. Bessie Smith sang about two things she didn't understand, "a mannish-acting woman and a lisping, swishing, womanish-acting man." The lyrics of "Sissy Man Blues," usually sung by males, pleaded, "If you can't bring me a woman, bring me a sissy man," implying (correctly) that although cross-gender behavior was cause for amusement, homosexuals were accepted as a

---

31. Baum, "Homosexuality and the Traditional Religions of the Americas and Africa," 29. Baum provides many other specifics about gender fluidity in African and American traditional religions in this essay in *Homosexuality and World Religions*, 1–46.

32. "Babaluayé," 80, and "Africa and African-Diaspora," 2–3, *Cassell's Encyclopedia*.

natural fact of life. Many of the writers, intellectuals, performers, and artists of the Harlem Renaissance were "homosexual, bisexual, or otherwise sexually unorthodox."[33] It is painful to think about how many lives might have been spared if the African American community had known and remembered these facts, honored the contributions of their own transgendered, lesbian, gay, and bisexual people, and confronted AIDS decisively. The price of early silence is now being paid chiefly by black women and children who have been infected through either drugs or heterosexual intercourse.

T. Dunbar Moodie, Vivienne Ndatshe, and British Sibuyi have written about the fact that during the 1930s–1950s in the gold mining compounds of South Africa, homosexual relationships were familiar to miners, company officials, and missionaries. In these "mine marriages," a man chose a younger man to live with him and be his "boy" or "wife," not only as a bed partner but also as a provider of domestic services in exchange for "substantial remuneration." An entire set of rules governed the "mine marriages," rules that were enforced by black mine authorities. In more recent years, however, there has been a decline in homosexuality among miners, partly because country wives have moved to town to be with their husbands, and partly because same-sex congress has been pathologized as a personality disorder.[34]

Stephen O. Murray and Will Roscoe have recently edited a volume of seventeen essays by various scholars that "unequivocally refute claims that African societies lacked homosexual patterns and had no words for those who desire their own sex." These essays report or review the evidence of same-sex patterns in some fifty African societies, in every region of the continent, among women as well as men, and find "substantial evidence that same-sex patterns were 'traditional' and 'indigenous.'" Murray and Roscoe conclude

33. Eric Garber, "A Spectacle in Color: The Lesbian and Gay Subculture of Jazz Age Harlem," *Hidden from History: Reclaiming the Gay and Lesbian Past*, ed. Martin B. Duberman et al. (New York: New American Library, 1989), 318–31.

34. T. Dunbar Moodie, Vivienne Ndatshe, and British Sibuyi, "Migrancy and Male Sexuality on the South African Gold Mines," *Hidden from History*, 411–25.

that the future for African homosexualities is one of "greater visibility, greater dialogue—and greater risks."[35]

Granted the vast evidence of homosexuality and other transgenderism in African indigenous society and the Americas as well, I became curious to see what Martin Bernal might have said about the topic in his monumental study *Black Athena: The Afroasiatic Roots of Classical Civilization* (New Brunswick, N.J.: Rutgers University Press, 1987). Bernal, who teaches government studies at Cornell University, won a 1990 American Book Award for Volume I, in which he argued that although classical civilization has deep roots in the East in general, and Egypt in particular, since the eighteenth century these Afroasiatic influences have been ignored, denied, or suppressed, chiefly because of racism. The term *transgender* was not well known in 1987, so I was not surprised to find no such reference in the index, nor was I surprised by the absence of *hermaphrodite*, *transvestism*, or *transsexuality*. But there were only two references to homosexuality, and they state that Egypt was "intolerant of homosexuality" (71), whereas ancient Greece appreciated homosexuality, and modern Hellenism still contains a "major homosexual strand" which is associated with the writings of John Winckelmann, himself a homosexual (213).

Since the classical Greek construction of sex was not about intimacy but about a superior free male expressing his power over women, boys, slaves, or foreigners,[36] it bears absolutely no resemblance to homosexual love as it is now understood. But my concern here is that Martin Bernal has given the impression that homosexuality, and presumably other gender variance, is indigenous to Greece, whereas the black influence via Egypt was totally intolerant and therefore virtually free of such gender fluidity.

Lena Troy offers a much more nuanced picture of gender in ancient Egypt, where in one creation paradigm the mother indepen-

---

35. Stephen O. Murray and Will Roscoe, *Boy-Wives and Female Husbands: Studies of African Homosexualities* (New York: St. Martin's Press, 1998), 266, 278.

36. David Halperin, "Sex before Sexuality: Pederasty, Politics, and Power in Classical Athens," *Hidden from History*, 37–59.

dently gives birth, while in the other paradigm "the father is equipped with a feminine element that enables him to reproduce himself."[37] And Winnie Brant has shown that Akhenaten, husband of Queen Nefertiti and monotheist worshipper of Aten, was either a transvestite woman masquerading as a male, or a transgendered male, transfigured by Aten. Indeed, if Moses was Egyptian, then Hebraic monotheism "may have been derived from the Aten religion, founded by a transgendered king."[38] Furthermore, Jessica Salmonson writes about Hatshepsut (d. 1479? B.C.E.), a great female transgender pharaoh who fought at the head of her troops, laid claim to full masculine power and prerogative, and was worshiped for eight centuries after his/her death.[39] And in the early first century B.C.E., Egyptian marriage contracts often forbade husbands from keeping either concubines or boy-lovers, something that must have been happening for the prohibitions to have been deemed necessary.[40] David F. Greenberg supplies several other examples of hermaphroditic deities and homosexual kings of Egypt, explaining that the critical category was not sexual orientation but gender: to penetrate was to be male and honorable, to be penetrated was female and disgraceful.[41]

Despite such facts, when a popularly acclaimed scholarly book like Bernal's *Black Athena* offers erroneous impressions about Egyptian and African history, lack of awareness of transgender history among grassroots African Americans becomes understandable. Yet the deadly consequences for black lives calls for immediate change.

---

37. Lena Troy, "Engendering Creation in Ancient Egypt," *A Feminist Companion to Reading the Bible*, 267.

38. Winnie Brant, "The Gender Heresy of Akhenaten," *Gender Blending*, 62.

39. Salmonson, *The Encyclopedia of Amazons*, 112.

40. Roscoe, "Precursors of Islamic Male Homosexualities," *Islamic Homosexualities: Culture, History, and Literature*, ed. Stephen O. Murray and Will Roscoe (New York: New York University Press, 1997), 62.

41. Greenberg, *The Construction of Homosexuality*, 127–35. See also Terrina J. Deakin, "Evidence for Homosexuality in Ancient Egypt," *International Journal of Greek Love* I (1966): 31–38.

Buddhism

During a recent public conversation between the distinguished African American poet/novelist Alice Walker and the equally distinguished Tibetan Buddhist nun Pema Chödrön,[42] someone asked their opinion of the Dalai Lama's statement that homosexuality was a hindrance to the spiritual life. Chödrön laughed, called the statement "nonsense," and explained that the Dalai Lama had no knowledge of homosexuality and therefore no experience from which to speak. Walker, who identifies herself as "homosocial" and/or bisexual, expressed immediate agreement. Thus Chödrön and Walker would have no argument with gay poet John Giorno, who was profoundly influenced by the Dalai Lama and also by Dudjom Rinpoche. Asked how Buddhism had affected his sexuality, Giorno said, "making love is meditation. . . . It seems to me gayness is just two people who are Buddhas."[43]

Similarly, Robert Aitken, a renowned Zen Master, teaches that the "Buddha nature is neither homosexual nor heterosexual, 'it is both.'" Buddhists have therefore been active in the struggle against HIV/AIDS while at the same time teaching the Buddha's Second Noble Truth, that suffering stems from being unable or unwilling to accept life exactly as it presents itself. In other words, as lesbian Buddhist Jeanne Du Prau wrote after the untimely death of her lover, "I can say, no, this isn't what I wanted . . . or I can say, yes, I see. This is my life. It is being revealed to me, little by little. It could not be other than it is."[44]

These contemporary responses reflect the historic realities of Buddhism at its inception in the 6th and 5th centuries b.c.e. José I. Cabezón describes the Buddha's loving relationship with his disciple Ananda by quoting one of the *Jataka* tales of early Indian Buddhism: The two "always went about together . . . ruminating and

---

42. Available on audiotape cassette from Sounds True, P.O. Box 8010, Boulder CO 80306. Phone: 303-665-3151. Web site: <www.soundstrue.com>.

43. From an interview conducted by Winston Leyland for a gay newspaper in 1974, as cited in *Cassell's Encyclopedia*, 11.

44. "Buddhism," *Cassell's Encyclopedia*, 7–12.

cuddling together, very happy" and in another tale, refusing to marry so they could stay together.[45] But some later Buddhist scholars nevertheless contend that same-sex intimacy and transgenderism were condemned in Indian Buddhism.[46] Knowing how radically Christianity departed from the gender-inclusive "discipleship of equals" of Jesus of Nazareth, I have no trouble believing that Indian Buddhism also may have rapidly departed from the gender fluidity of its founder and his earliest disciples.

Among the *Bodhisattvas*—enlightened human beings who decline *nirvana* in order to help heal the planet and enlighten humankind— several are associated with transgender or homosexual experience. For instance, Avalokitishvara, a male, transforms into the female Kuan Yin when he is overwhelmed by compassion for children; but she soon changes back into her male form in order to defend his/her devotees.[47] Tara, the Star-Goddess and Bodhisattva revered in Hinduism and Tantra as well as Tibetan Buddhism, causes men who meditate upon her to undergo a transsexual process as she enters their bodies in a ray of light.[48] And in a 17th century drama reminiscent of the biblical Ruth and Naomi, two women (one single, one married) fall in love in a Buddhist convent and covenant with one another in front of the Buddha's image. Later, the single one becomes a second wife to the married woman's husband so that they may continue in their relationship.[49]

Two psychologists and an endocrinologist recently observed and wrote about the *acault* males in the country of Burma (now renamed Myanmar). In Burma, regarded as one of the most profoundly Buddhist of countries, the acault are well known for their cross-gender

---

45. José I. Cabezón, "Homosexuality and Buddhism," *Homosexuality and World Religions*, 89.

46. Ibid., 88–89.

47. Elémire Zola, *The Androgyne: Reconciliation of Male and Female* (New York: Crossroad, 1982), as cited in "Avalokitishvara," *Cassell's Encyclopedia*, 78.

48. "Tara," ibid., 317.

49. Lei Yu (1611–1680), in the drama *Lian Xiangban* (the meaning of that in English is "pitying the fragrant companion"), as described by Cabezón, "Homosexuality and Buddhism," 84.

behavior. It stems from the belief that they have been chosen by a female spirit named Manguedon, who interceded to bestow fortune on the Burmese through acault lives. They go through a marriage ceremony with Manguedon, after which they will never be like other men because they take on her characteristics. In the West, the acault might be considered male-to-female transsexuals, and/or transvestites, and/or homosexuals.

The Burmese, who are Theraveda Buddhists, believe that only a man can reach nirvana, and the acault are not considered men. But on the other hand, the acault are revered and given money and other gifts because their blessing brings good fortune. They do not have sex with one another but only with "real men," with whom they take a "passive" or "female" role. If they live with a man, the man is considered heterosexual; and the acault is usually responsible for taking care of "his/her husband," both sexually and financially. The only stigma for the "heterosexual" husband is that he is considered lazy for not working toward nirvana in this lifetime; and there is no stigma attached to the acault because s/he has been possessed by Manguedon. Interestingly, because their social constructs do not match Western ones, the Burmese people were adamant that there is absolutely no homosexuality in Burma.[50]

In north and central Thailand, Buddhist myths of origin refer to three basic sexes—male, female, and hermaphrodite (called *kathoey*, an independently existing third sex). Only in the twentieth century did kathoey come to mean a "deficient" male. Although kathoeys are effeminate and have sex only with men, they are not viewed as gay, but rather as a second kind of woman, or midway between a man and a woman.[51]

As for Buddhism in Japan, Father Francis Xavier was so outraged by the widespread homoeroticism among Buddhist monks that he called it the "Japanese vice." When he tried to preach the evils of sodomy on various occasions, he was either laughed at or expelled

---

50. Eli Coleman, Philip Colgan, and Louis Gorran, "Male Cross-Gender Behavior in Myanmar (Burma)," in *Que(e)rying Religion*, 287–93.
51. Nanda, *Neither Man Nor Woman*, 142.

from Buddhist monasteries or Japanese courts. Although some Japanese Buddhists might have agreed with Xavier's condemnation of homoeroticism, the fact remains that homosexuality was "a preferred form of expression among the Buddhist priesthood."[52]

Zen Buddhism, which developed in Japan during the ninth century, also permitted passionate friendships between priests and novices despite a thirteenth century attempt to eradicate that practice. The beauty of the novices was celebrated in Japanese Noh theater, and a body of homoerotic poetry emerged from Zen monasteries and colleges.[53]

All in all, while Buddhist attitudes toward gender fluidity have varied from culture to culture and from one historical epoch to another, the contemporary Buddhist is usually accepting of gender and sexual diversity. José Cabezón says that homosexuality is openly practiced in Western Buddhist communities and no North American Buddhist institution has ever impeded full participation of homosexuals by requiring abstinence.[54] That acceptance accords well with Buddhism's central teachings concerning compassion, transformation, individual responsibility, enlightenment, and empowerment.

Hinduism

Traditional Hinduism often refers to sexual ambiguity and alternative sexes, not just among human beings but also among deities. According to ancient Hindu teaching, there is a third sex subdivided into four categories: the "waterless" (male eunuch from birth); the "testicle voided" (castrated male); the hermaphrodite (intersexual); and the "not woman" (usually a woman who does not menstruate, a female eunuch or intersexual). To these people, Hindu

---

52. Noguchi Takenori and Paul Schalow in *The Kodansha Encyclopedia of Japan* (1983), as quoted in *Cassell's Encyclopedia*, 8.

53. Martin Colcutt, *Five Mountains: The Rinzai Zen Monastic Institution in Medieval Japan* (Cambridge: Harvard University Press, 1981), as cited in *Cassell's Encyclopedia*, 9.

54. Cabezón, "Homosexuality and Buddhism," 94.

society assigns the function of providing alternative sexual gratifications, some of them spelled out in the classical sex manual known as the *Kama Sutra*, compiled somewhere between the third and fifth centuries. Although homosexuality was condemned in certain law books, the *Kama Sutra* permitted "mouth congress" for eunuchs, and in reality homosexuals were tolerated within Hindu society. Vatsyayana, author of the *Kama Sutra*, answered critics of oral and anal sex by saying that in all things connected with love, people should act "according to what is agreeable to [their] nature and [themselves]."[55]

The *Hijras* of India perform an alternative gender role that attracts people the West would differentiate as eunuchs, homosexuals, transsexuals, hermaphrodites, and transvestites. Classified as neither men nor women, the hijras are castrated males who dress in female clothing, wear their hair long, and pluck out facial hair to make their skin as smooth as a woman's. They walk, sit, and stand like women, and within their communal households call one another "sister," "aunty," or "grandmother." In public accommodations, they request "ladies only" seating; some of them marry men and live with their husbands; but they are free to act in sexually suggestive ways that would be off-limits to the ordinary woman of India.

Although men become hijras because they are impotent, they are not fully hijras until they have had their genitals surgically removed. It is through this emasculation and the initiation/rebirthing that accompanies it that the hijras are sanctioned to play their ritual role as performers at marriages, male births, and temple festivals. The collections they receive in return for their blessing, dancing, drumming, singing, and comedy are a major means of support, along with sex-work, begging, and performing everyday jobs.

Hijras are sometimes feared, abused, ridiculed, or pitied; but they are not regarded as ordinary. They are special, sacred beings because of their castration/new birth and their dedication to the Indian Mother-goddess Parvati and their own special goddess,

---

55. Nanda, *Neither Man Nor Woman*, 21–22. The dating of the *Kama Sutra* is from Reay Tannahill, *Sex in History* (New Tork: Stein & Day, 1982), 200.

Bahuchara Mata. One of their major functions is to "call into question the basic social categories of gender on which Indian society is built. . . . While Western culture strenuously attempts to resolve contradictions and ambiguities by denial or segregation, Hinduism appears content to allow opposites to confront each other without resolution," perhaps in celebration of the concept that in a boundless universe, "any and all possibilities may be permitted without excluding one another."[56]

A professor of comparative religions has recently claimed that although classical Hinduism considered homosexuality only a matter of marginal disapproval, modern Hindus associate it with Euro-Westerners with whom some encounters have been unpleasant and less than peaceful. "Neo-Hinduism is now so hostile to [homosexuality]," he asserts, "that no community admits homosexual practices, though each accuses the others."[57]

But since there are about fifty thousand hijras living openly in India, perhaps the professor has overstated his case. He also seems unaware that between 1920 and 1950, Gandhi and Nehru did everything they could to eradicate from Hindu and Indian culture all positive references to transgenderism and same-sex desire. Gandhi even sent his devotees to 11th century Hindu temples to destroy carvings of same-sex coupling, in an attempt to convince people that any queerness in India was entirely the result of European or Western influence. (Tagore succeeded in halting that violence; hence, at a later date, Alain Danielou was able to take photographs of sculptures depicting same-sex eroticism and transgender themes.) Nehru's government was responsible for passing the first law in Indian history that made same-sex intimacy a criminal act.[58] Yet there is still plenty of demand for the sexual services of hijras.

---

56. Nanda, *Neither Man Nor Woman*, 23. Information about the hijras is drawn from Nanda's excellent book. See especially 1–54.

57. Arvind Sharma, "Homosexuality and Hinduism," *Homosexuality and World Religions*, 70.

58. "Hinduism," *Cassell's Encyclopedia*, 18.

Not even Gandhi and Nehru could erase from Hindu mythology such figures as Shiva, a deity who incorporates both male and female characteristics; or Vishnu, who transforms himself into a beautiful woman in order to reclaim the sacred nectar that demons have stolen; or Krishna, Vishnu's avatar (incarnation), who takes female form to destroy a demon. Hijras claim that when Krishna returned from female to male form, he told the other gods, "There will be more like me, neither man nor woman, and whatever words come from the mouths of these people, whether good [blessings] or bad [curses], will come true."[59]

Nor could Gandhi and Nehru totally erase memories of Arashanarishvara, "The Lord whose Half is Woman," the transgendered offspring of Shiva and Shakti. In artistic representations, Arashanarishvara's left or Shakti side is female, tan-skinned, dressed in red, and holding a lotus; the right or Shiva side is male, blue-skinned, and wearing a tiger pelt. Like the Chinese Tao, symbolized by the union of Yin and Yang, Arashanarishvara represents the totality or wholeness that lies beyond duality. He/she is associated with the *chakra* or sacred energy-center located in the throat, and also with homoeroticism. Danielou writes that "the hermaphrodite, the homosexual, and the transvestite have symbolic value and are considered privileged beings, images of the Arashanarishvara."[60]

It seems to me that Serena Nanda, who spent so much time in thorough and sensitive fieldwork among the hijras of India, deserves the last word about gender fluidity within Hinduism. She writes, "Whereas Westerners feel uncomfortable with the ambiguities and contradictions inherent in such in-between categories as tranvestism, homosexuality, hermaphroditism, and transgenderism, and make strenuous attempts to resolve them, Hinduism not only accommodates such ambiguities, but also views them as meaningful and even powerful."[61]

---

59. Nanda, *Neither Man Nor Woman*, 20–21.
60. As quoted in "Arashanarishvara," *Cassell's Encyclopedia*, 67.
61. Nanda, *Neither Man Nor Woman*, 20.

Islam

Several years ago, I was a panelist at the most conservative Episcopal seminary in the United States. Apparently I was the first openly lesbian (or transgender, gay, or bisexual) person to speak from that platform and was permitted to do so only because of a very special set of circumstances. One compassionate student sought me out beforehand, tears in her eyes, to tell me she hadn't been able to sleep for fear of what the faculty and students would "do" to me. For the most part, the panel was a civilized exchange, although after we had left, the chapel was exorcised to free it from our demonic influence. But during the question-and-comment period after the panel, a male student expressed his anger that a lesbian had been permitted to speak as if she were Christian instead of an unrepentant sinner. Explaining that he came from an Islamic homeland, he commented to the effect that whereas Christians in America do not know how to punish sinners, in Islam they *do* know what to do with sinners. The seminary audience burst into applause.

I sat there wondering whether those who were applauding knew that the student was referring to the summary executions recently carried out by the Iranian government against those accused of homosexuality.[62] It felt strange to be among people who would applaud the idea of killing me for being who I am and loving whom I love. And I find it ironic that any Muslim government can take such a stance, considering the extensive gender diversity within Islamic culture.

In his 1985 book *Sexuality in Islam*, Abdelwahat Bouhdiba makes clear that although a masculine-feminine heterosexual binary is

---

62. The oppression of homosexuals and transgendered people was increased exponentially after the rise of Islamic fundamentalism during the late 1970s. Khomeini's revolutionaries tortured and put to death hundreds and perhaps even thousands, many of whom were political opponents and not necessarily homosexual: see Khalid Duran, "Homosexuality and Islam," *Homosexuality and World Religions*, 194. Yet Khomeini's followers did not hesitate to use anal rape as a punishment. A group of them gang-raped a male Iranian student who dared to laugh during one of their demonstrations, just as men caught in harems were punished by anal rape: see Greenberg, *The Construction of Homosexuality*, 181.

understood to be "an absolutely universal divine wish," there is a great deal of deviation from that norm. He speaks, for instance, of the "highly frequented pleasure gardens where singers, dancers, gamblers . . . [and] homosexuals of both sexes taught the art of pleasure."[63] And in their book *Islamic Homosexualities*, Stephen O. Murray and Will Roscoe find "consistent patterns of Islamic homosexualities that can be traced over the course of centuries, from age-differentiated relations . . . to alternative gender statuses represented by the male *khanith* of Oman, the female *mustergil* of southern Iraq, and the sworn virgins of the Balkans."[64] David F. Greenberg summarizes the Islamic situation succinctly: "Despite Islamic opposition to homosexuality, it has been widely practiced and accepted. The current imposition of the death penalty in the Islamic Republic is a historical aberration."[65]

Everett K. Rowson points out that during Islam's first century, for a period of several generations, a group of male musicians called *mukhannathun* ("effeminates") held a social position of exceptional prestige and visibility. They were men who resembled or imitated women's body language and voices, and during the years of their highest prestige were depicted as sexually uninterested in either women or men. However, by the ninth and tenth centuries this perception had changed, and the "effeminates" were understood to be inclined toward homosexuality.

Rowson explains that in classical Islamic culture, "active" (penetrating) and "passive" (penetrated) homosexuals were regarded in two different ways, the active partner being subject to less disapproval than the passive one. So extensive was homosexual practice and anal intercourse that separate terms were used to describe passive partners who were paid, those who traded passivity for an opportunity at activity, and those who preferred the passive role. The mukhannathun were regarded as the latter.[66]

---

63. Abdelwahat Bouhdiba, *Sexuality in Islam*, trans. from the French by Alan Sheridan (London: Routledge & Kegan Paul, 1985), 7, 131.

64. Murray and Roscoe, *Islamic Homosexualities*, 5–6.

65. Greenberg, *The Construction of Homosexuality*, 189.

66. Everett K. Rowson, "The Effeminates of Early Medina," *Que(e)rying Religion*, 61–88.

In Islamic Oman (located on the Saudi Arabian Peninsula), the *xaniths* or *khanith* perform a function similar to that of the hijras of India, although the xaniths are not castrated. The term xanith means "impotent, effeminate, and soft,"[67] and xaniths are regarded as neither male nor female but as both. They worship in the mosque with men, support themselves by acting as male prostitutes, but are classified as women socially—except that they do not have to follow purdah. Xaniths are recognized as homosexual, but if they marry a woman and can display the bloody towel that proves they have deflowered her, they become men and no longer xaniths. Appearance-wise, the xanith is carefully intergendered, managing to look like a woman even though Omani law forbids him to wear female clothing.[68] So he constitutes a true third gender in Omani society.

According to Vern and Bonnie Bullough, the case of Oman is by no means unique in the Islamic world. Despite the fact that Muhammad said some things were appropriate only to men and others only to women, there is plenty of cross-dressing. A famous ninth-century commentator on the Koran spent an entire section describing men who wish to resemble women and women who wish to resemble men.[69] Some of the Muslim female impersonators dressed like dancing girls and performed at festivals in Upper Egypt during the nineteenth century.[70]

Aditionally, at least as late as the nineteenth century, boys in female garb were part of the harems kept by rich men of Afghanistan. Sir Richard Burton reported that these boys rode luxuriously in camel panniers and were called "traveling wives."[71]

Then of course there are the Muslim mystics known as Sufis, who accepted various forms of transgendered and homoerotic behavior. Abdelwahat Bouhdiba says that the Sufis were persecuted by reactionary Islamic authorities not only for homoeroticism but

---

67. Nanda, *Neither Man Nor Woman*, 130–31.

68. Bullough and Bullough, *Cross-Dressing, Sex, and Gender*, 12–13. See also Stephen O. Murray, "The Sohari Khanith," *Islamic Homosexualities*, 244–55.

69. Bullough and Bullough, *Cross-Dressing, Sex, and Gender*, 12.

70. Greenberg, *The Construction of Homosexuality*, 179.

71. Bullough and Bullough, *Cross-Dressing, Sex, and Gender*, 13.

especially because they looked on the beloved as a reflection of God.[72] That attitude is evident in the poems of Jalal al-Din Rumi (1207–1273), whose passionate and sacred love for another male, Shams al-Din Tabrizi, is enshrined in mystical poems of great beauty. Fortunately, these poems have recently been popularized in the United States through the dramatic, powerful English translations of Coleman Barks.[73] The Sufi dance ritual performed in a trance by dervishes (who are sometimes transvestite) had its origin in the whirling dance of lamentation and love performed by Rumi for forty days after Shams had been murdered by some of Rumi's followers, who were jealous of the intimacy.[74]

As for intersexuality within Islam, eunuchs were used for many centuries to guard the harems and perform many other services in royal and/or wealthy households. Eunuchs (castrati) were still in service during the first decades of the twentieth century. And about eight thousand eunuchs were imported *each year* into Arabia, Egypt, and Turkey during the late nineteenth century.[75]

In her well-researched book *Sex in History*, Reay Tannahill remarks that some sultans "made use of women concubines for dynastic reasons, while preferring boys when only pleasure had to be considered" (244). Certainly many Islamic gender arrangements leave nothing for Western women to desire. During the 1970s, I met a woman who taught in a British military school in an Islamic country and was at one point permitted to visit a harem. She found that the women were very open about their experience. They said they were always thrilled to be chosen for sex during the male's visits despite being unable to sit comfortably the next day because of the abrupt nature of the sex act, without foreplay or romantic dalli-

---

72. Bouhdiba, *Sexuality in Islam*, 20.

73. Coleman Barks, *The Essential Rumi* (San Francisco: HarperSanFrancisco, 1995).

74 "Rumi," *Cassell's Encyclopedia*, 287. See also Jim Wafer, "Vision and Passion: The Symbolism of Male Love in Islamic Mystical Literature," *Islamic Homosexualities*, 167–31.

75. Tannahill, *Sex in History*, 246–54. On eunuchs, see Roscoe, "Precursors of Islamic Male Homosexualities," 64–76.

ance. Although they knew that males reserved most of their affection for one another, nevertheless the women competed for male sexual attention. (If this is heterosexuality, make the most of it!) Tannahill claims that in the game of love and desire, the only serious rival a courtesan (not wife!) might encounter would be "the 18-year-old boy, whose attractions the Arabs felt as keenly as their predecessors the Persians and Greeks had done" (236).

In the Holy Koran, there are three mentions of *wildan* (or *ghilman*)—handsome young men who will serve as cupbearers to the souls of Muslim males after they have died and entered into Paradise. How can this be aligned with Article 123 of Iran's penal code, which requires the death penalty for same-sex activity? Even the anonymous authors of the article on "sodomy" in *The Encyclopedia of Islam* are forced to admit that the Koran seems ambiguous about the topic, condemning homoeroticism, yet promising to give faithful males some Ganymede-like menservants in Paradise.[76] Remembering that the Buddhist Burmese deny any homosexuality in their culture because of the way they construct or define the coupling of men with acault males, I suspect that similar redefining and restructuring goes on in the Muslim culture.

Shahid Dossani, a gay Muslim, points out that the Koran mentions homosexuality only five times. In one reference, the prophet Muhammad says, "If two men commit indecency, punish them both. If they repent and mend their ways, let them be. God is forgiving and merciful." The other four passages refer to the words of Lot to the men of Sodom: "You lust after men instead of women." (Unlike the Jews, including Jesus, who view Sodom's sin as lack of hospitality to strangers, Muslims are certain that Sodom's sin was homosexuality, and particularly anal intercourse.)

Dossani comments that the Koran contains much less intolerance than Muslims generally imagine, and that "the roots of gay

---

76. "Wildan," *Cassell's Encyclopedia*, 346. These beautiful serving boys were also called *al-fatà* or *houri* (the latter including girls as well as boy-servants; see Murray and Roscoe, conclusion, *Islamic Homosexualities*, 307). The Koran does not specify that these boys and girls offer *sexual* services, but later Muslim literature does: see Greenberg, *The Construction of Homosexuality*, 173.

intolerance [in Islam] seem to be more sociological and cultural than religious." Islam is intrinsically more evolutionary-minded than other religions, says Dossani, because it accepts that Judaism was right for its time and Christianity for its time, until Muhammad came along to teach the "best" way. Therefore Muslims should be able to recognize that evolution did not end with Muhammad's death in 632 C.E. Dossani's message to other gay, lesbian, bisexual, and transgender Muslims is this: "You have to look at Islam as a religion which is meant to help you evolve, not keep you in a mental straitjacket."[77]

Shamanism

Shamanism is narrowly defined as the spiritual practices of the traditional cultures of Siberia, but more broadly it is understood as a cross-cultural or multicultural spiritual path that emphasizes the interrelatedness of everything that lives, a reverence for nature, and the recognition of spiritual or divine entities who take an active interest in human life. Many shamanic traditions also honor transgenderism and same-sex eros as being just as natural and just as sacred as heterosexual eros and/or gender conventionality. The shaman is a spiritual facilitator who may trigger a trance-like state through chanting, drumming, ecstatic dancing, or mind-altering substances, and who, while in that trance, visits or communicates with the spirit world. He/she also functions as a healer and/or intercessor, a diviner, a magic-worker, a teacher of divine mysteries, and/or a guide of souls. Today's channelers—spiritual mediums who bring people messages from discarnate entities such as angels or master teachers—could also be regarded as shamans.[78]

Because shamanism has been practiced in so many cultures and centuries—since the Paleolithic Era, to be precise—the topic is immense. Here I can mention only a few facts relevant to gender fluidity. And I will make a very artificial distinction between Na-

---

77. Shahid Dossani, "Being Muslim and Gay," *Que(e)rying Religion*, 236–37.
78. "Shamanism," 27, "Channeling," 108–09, *Cassell's Encyclopedia*.

tive American shamanism and that of other cultures, mainly because the topic *is* so vast.

As I wrote earlier in this chapter, many of the priests who served the Great Mother or other goddesses were cross-dressers and/or transsexual males-to-females, often castrated, who possessed shamanic powers and prestige. Leslie Feinberg notes in this connection, "our earliest ancestors do not appear to have been biological determinists" because societies all over the world allowed for more than two sexes, and transgenderism, transsexuality, and intersexuality turn up everywhere in creation stories and oral histories.[79] Here I will mention only some evidence not previously covered, such as the male-to-female diviners among South African Zulu, or the transwomen who serve as shamans among the Ambo people in southern Angola, or the female-to-male Inuits who serve White Whale Woman, a deity who herself was described as having transformed into a man or woman-man.[80]

In China, pre-Buddhist and pre-Confucian spiritual traditions were shamanic and either polytheistic or pantheistic; they are often called simply "Chinese traditional religion."[81] Although most of the chief shamans were women, transgendered or castrated and/or homosexual men also became shamans. One of them was Qu Yuan, China's first major poet, who wore skirts with floral designs to indicate his gender-variance and probable homosexuality.[82]

In Japan, Shinto is the outgrowth of shamanism, retaining an extremely life-affirming view of the world that avoids moral condemnation. Shinto's chief deity is the sun goddess Amaterasu Omi Kami, who is reported to have cross-dressed as a shamanistic warrior and therefore has been described as hermaphroditic. Currently,

---

79. Feinberg, *Transgender Warriors*, 43.

80. Harriet Ngubane, *Body and Mind in Zulu Medicine* (London: Academic Press, 1977); Carlos Estermann, *The Ethnology of Southwestern Angola* (New York: African Publishing, 1976); and Franz Boas, *The Eskimo of Baffin Land and Hudson Bay* (New York: The Museum of Natural History, 1901), as cited in Feinberg, *Transgender Warriors*, 45.

81. "Yu," *Cassell's Encyclopedia*, 354.

82. "Qu Yuan," *Cassell's Encyclopedia*, 275–76.

the Japanese penal code reflects Shinto liberalism by omitting any mention of transgenderism. [83]

In Polynesia, the *mahu* perform an alternative gender role that is both transgendered and homoerotic. Villages in Tahiti often have only one mahu, but every village does have one—a male who takes on the occupations, activities, and clothing of a woman, performs female household roles, and says he wishes he had a female body. Although he fellates men, he is usually not considered homosexual. He is considered a normal man substituting for a woman and therefore engaged in standard heterosexual practices. In Hawaii, the same term, mahu, refers to spiritual functionaries associated with healing who are transgendered and usually homosexual. Beauty contests for mahus are still well attended in Hawaii.[84]

In Melanesia, the phenomenon of ritual intergenerational homosexuality is practiced among the Sambia and other peoples. The practice is widespread, standard, and even mandatory on certain occasions as young males come of age.[85]

In Korea, the *mudang* was a shaman or sorceress who frequently was a transgendered male. Pauline Park, a Korean American historian, remarks that as in many of the other shamanic traditions, mudang combined male and female. Why? Because combining genders connected a person to the spiritual realm that transcends all sexes and genders.[86]

In Mesoamerica and South America, many homosexual and/or bisexual and transgendered priests and shamans served in the villages and temples of the Aztecs, Chimu, Lacke, Lubacas, Manta, Mayas, Mbaya, Moche, Tupenambas, and others. For instance, although the Mayas of Mexico and Guatemala were hostile to homoeroticism in their earliest years, by the time of the Spanish conquest, parents were acquiring male lovers for their sons, feeling that the

---

83. Sandra A. Wawrytko, "Homosexuality and Chinese and Japanese Religions," *Homosexuality and World Religions*, 199–230; "Shinto," 31, and "Amaterasu Omi Kami," 52, *Cassell's Encyclopedia*.

84. Nanda, *Neither Man Nor Woman*, 135–36; "Mahu," *Cassell's Encyclopedia*, 224.

85. I. C. Jarvie, "Religion as a Social Category," *Que(e)rying Religion*, 311–22.

86. As quoted in Feinberg, *Transgender Warriors*, 44–45.

Mayan deity Chin, god of nurturance, magic, and divination, had sanctified this practice. In 1569, Thomas Lopez Medel described the transgendered and homosexual priests/priestesses who were serving in the Mayan temples of Guatemala and the Yucatan Peninsula.[87]

Since the sixteenth century, cross-dressing shamans have been reported among the Araucanians, a tribe native to South Chile and parts of Argentina. They are still respected and feared because of their supernatural powers. Tribes in northwest Venezuela and northern Colombia also have male cross-dressing shamans.[88]

Obviously, the social fabric of these societies was never destroyed by the gender variance in their midst. Families flourished and children developed in their own sweet way as children do. I am not implying that homosexuality as practiced in these various cultures is perfectly aligned with that within the United States today, or that the transsexual and other transgender behaviors in these cultures would mesh perfectly with those within our society. Further, it must be kept in mind that this brief survey is far from exhaustive— many, many instances of gender diversity have existed cross-culturally that have not even been mentioned. I will conclude this survey with a brief description of some of the gender blending and gender bending within Native American tribal life.

Native Americans

Paula Gunn Allen begins her book *The Sacred Hoop: Recovering the Feminine in American Indian Traditions* (Boston: Beacon Press, 1986) with several principles that are important to the descriptions to follow: Traditional tribal lifestyles are usually gynocratic and never patriarchal; women-centered social systems tend to be relaxed about sexuality and personal styles; such female-centered systems tend to produce nurturing, pacifist, "passive" males and self-defining, asser-

---

87. "Mayas," 229, "Chin," 110, and "Mesoamerican and South American," 24, *Cassell's Encyclopedia*. See also Greenberg, *The Construction of Homosexuality*, 163–68.

88. Greenberg, *The Construction of Homosexuality*, 56–57.

tive, decisive females; and "the physical and cultural genocide of American Indian tribes is and was mostly about patriarchal fear of gynocracy." (Although white racism would appear to me to be the most basic motive of that genocide, the racism itself may have been exacerbated by the fear of gynocracy in Native American life.)

Allen also comments that the sacred, ritual ways of Native Americans are similar to those of other sacred cultures, with tribal lives incorporating many features similar to those of tribal people in Southeast Asia, Melanesia, Micronesia, Polynesia, and Africa. In other words, traditional Native Americans share in a worldwide culture that predates Western "civilization" and was viciously attacked and nearly dismantled by that "civilization" (2–6).

Because domestic violence and even teenage and childhood violence have become epidemic in our society, we desperately need women who are decisive and (especially) men who are nurturing and pacifist. So it seems important to pay close attention to what tribal societies were doing to produce such positive results.

The traditional Navajos, for instance, were sophisticated enough to emphasize the independence of sexual orientation from gender identity and presentation, a distinction some people in twenty-first century America still find difficult to make. Accordingly, while the Navajos recognized three sexes (males, females, and hermaphrodites or *nadle*), gender assignments included not only these three, but also those who were "nadle pretenders" or "pseudo-*nádlech*," who were anatomically normal and might today be called psychological androgynes or non-operative transsexuals.[89] The nadle are referred to as "Two-Spirit," a term that implies transgenderism, same-sex intimacy, and divine calling; they are respected, considered sacred, and thought to ensure wealth. They serve in either a shamanic or artistic capacity, and have special chants for curing sickness and insanity and aiding childbirth.[90]

89. Jerrold E. Levy, *In the Beginning: The Navajo Genesis* (Berkeley: University of California Press, 1998), 214. See also W.W. Hill, "The Status of the Hermaphrodite and Transvestite in Navajo Culture," *American Anthropologist* 37 (1935), as cited in Bullough and Bullough, *Cross-Dressing, Sex, and Gender*, 5.

90. "Nadle," *Cassell's Encyclopedia*, 246; Levy, *In the Beginning*, 214.

But Navajo tribespeople are not eager to describe nadle to white anthropologists, who are too often insensitive to the whole context in which nadle lives have been lived.[91] Consequently, when asked if "gays" exist in their culture, they have answered with a resounding no—not in order to be devious, but because the term *gay* would distort the meaning of the shamanistic ceremonial functions of nadle—and also of *hwame, alyha, miati, winkte,* and *berdache* in general.

Throughout his study of sexual diversity in American Indian culture, Walter L. Williams utilizes the term *berdache* to designate a morphological male who has a nonmasculine or androgynous character, being either asexual or the "passive" partner in sex with a man, distinct from either male or female and honored for his ceremonial, spiritual, and artistic contribution.[92] Williams explains that traditional Native thought does not fall into the binary trap of thinking that a person's sex is always certain and that gender identity and sex role inevitably follow upon morphological sex. Because American Indian worldviews could accommodate life's ambiguities, the gender variance of the berdache was accepted calmly in many tribes.

Will Roscoe also makes use of the term berdache to mean those whose lifestyles bridged men's and women's social roles. Although berdaches formed sexual relationships with members of their own sex, they were defined in terms of gender-mixing rather than sexuality.[93]

Mark Thompson also uses the term berdache in a positive way, citing the Gay American Indians database that finds berdaches in over 130 American Indian societies.[94]

But Paula Gunn Allen, a Laguna Pueblo/Sioux Indian, says that the term berdache is misapplied to both lesbians and gay males, since the original Arabic word referred to a sex-slave male child: Hence, berdache "has no relevance to American Indian men and

---

91. Walter L. Williams, *The Spirit and the Flesh: Sexual Diversity in American Indian Culture* (Boston: Beacon Press, 1992), 35, 184–85, 191.

92. Ibid., 1–5.

93. Roscoe, "Wewha and Klah: The American Indian Berdache as Artist and Priest," *Que(e)rying Religion*, 89.

94. Mark Thompson, *Gay Spirit: Myth and Meaning* (New York: St. Martin's Press, 1987), 73.

women."[95] And Leslie Feinberg explains that berdache was a deroga-
tory term used by European colonizers to label any Native person
who did not seem to fit binary notions of male or female. The blan-
ket term disregarded distinctions of self-expression, social interac-
tion, and complex economic and political realities.[96] Native people
today ask that "Two-Spirit" be used instead of berdache, which perhaps is the reason why the very comprehensive *Cassell's Encyclopedia* offers no listing for berdache. I have defined and discussed the
term here only because it is key to many academic papers and anthropological studies of sex/gender-fluid thinking among traditional
Native Americans.

Among the Mohave in the American Southwest, Two-Spirit or
third gender female shamans were called *hwame*. They usually took
other women as their lovers, were believed not to menstruate, and
had a gender status distinctly different from men, women, or *alyha*,
their male counterparts in Mohave society.[97]

Among the Hedatsa people, two-spirit male shamans were called
miati. They were instructed by a deity named Village Old Woman
to leave behind their masculine clothes and behaviors and to take
on women's roles. Once they had been claimed by this Holy Woman,
they could not resist. They might be pitied for the spiritual responsibility they had been forced to shoulder, but they were respected as
benevolent, mysterious, and holy.[98]

Within the Lakota tribe, the two-spirit shamans are called *winktes*.
They are felt to be "born that way": beautiful, effeminate, and homosexual,[99] made half-man, half-woman by the Great Spirit. As
one Lakota shaman, Lame Deer, explained, "To us a man is what
nature, or his dreams, make him. We accept him for what he wants
to be. That's up to him."[100]

---

95. Allen, *The Sacred Hoop*, 31.
96. Feinberg, *Transgender Warriors*, 21.
97. Williams, *The Spirit and the Flesh*, 239–42.
98. Ibid., 29–30.
99. Ibid., 49.
100. John Free and Richard Erdoes, *Lame Deer, Seeker of Visions* (New York:
Simon & Schuster, 1972), as quoted in Williams, *The Spirit and the Flesh*, 25.

After sixteenth century European explorers were impressed by women in Brazil who followed men's pursuits and married other women, the Amazon River was named after the similar women warriors celebrated in ancient Greece. Anthropologist Evelyn Blackwood found mention of such gender blending of females in thirty-three North American groups, mostly in California, the Southwest, the Northwest, and the Great Basin.[101] Walter Williams describes these manlike women under the name Amazons, and Paula Gunn Allen has assured him that today there are Amazon women who are recognized as such in a number of tribes.[102]

Clearly, the existence of centuries of gender fluidity has not meant an end to heterosexual marriages and reproductive activities among Native American tribes, nor among any of the other groups examined in this chapter's overview.

Our Cultural Fear of Gender Variance

Kathy Rudy, who teaches women's studies and ethics at Duke University, has published a lengthy analysis of the Christian Right in her book *Sex and the Church: Gender, Homosexuality, and the Transformation of Christian Ethics* (Boston: Beacon Press, 1997). She argues that the Christian Right offers a salvation that dictates Christians must be either male or female, heterosexual, and living within an identifiably "traditional family," in which women stand for submissiveness, passivity, and lack of economic productiveness, but also for spiritual connectedness to God. According to this "gendered theology," Rudy argues, male-male sex puts one partner in the role of "woman" and thus disrupts the gender hierarchy (64). The revocation of abortion rights is necessary here in order to insist that women fulfill their "essential nature" and "highest vocation": motherhood (58).

---

101. Evelyn Blackwood, "Sexuality and Gender in Certain Native American Tribes: The Case of Cross-Gender Females," *Signs* 10 (autumn 1984): 27–42, as cited in Williams, *The Spirit and the Flesh*, 233.

102. Williams, *The Spirit and the Flesh*, 251.

Indeed, a "gendered theology" of masculine-feminine complementarity has surfaced where one might least have suspected it: in the turn-of-the-millennium lesbian subculture. This theology is documented in a 1999 video directed and produced by independent filmmaker Karen Everett: *My Femme Divine*.[103] The film depicts butches as adult tomboys who project their denied femininity onto femmes whom they then regard with worshipful adoration. The femmes claim to use lipstick, net stockings, and the like in order to prove that "femininity" is not exclusive to heterosexuals. Repeatedly, the image of Michelangelo's Pieta flashes on-screen, with commentary implying that the butch lies in the arms of the Divine Femme, having at last found the "Mommy" who will deny her nothing. Although Karen Everett says she eventually found divine wholeness within herself instead of projecting it onto a partner, there is no filmic exploration of how she as a complete person would relate to a similarly complete person. Throughout, the butch-femme culture is depicted as an "opposition" in which each needs the other for completion. From whence are these complementarity concepts derived? From combining Carl Jung's animus/anima with the Book of Mormon, which says that without opposition there can be no creativity, no growth. So although Everett claims to be an *ex-*Mormon, she has built a theology on Mormonism that (except for its lesbianism) fits hand-in-glove with the "gendered theology" of the Christian Right.

Returning now to Rudy's book *Sex and the Church*: I question Rudy's repeated references to working *for* one's salvation (56 and 59, for instance), because in my thirty-five years in fundamentalism I learned one thing for sure: Works are the *result* of salvation, never its *cause*, faith in the redemptive death of Jesus being the only means of salvation. Nevertheless, I recognize that Rudy is correct in her insight that centering theology on gender leads to a system "in which all social and theological roles are connected to one's genitals" (44). Although Rudy does not say so, this is the reason intersexual babies

---

103. For purchase information, fax Karen Everett at 415-641-7841.

must be surgically altered as soon as possible, in order that they might know their proper place within the system.

Rudy claims that anybody who does not "fit the paradigm of their biological sex" (including working women, "sensitive" men, disabled men, and homosexuals) is "excluded from the church" (44). Again, this is an overstatement in that acceptance of Jesus as personal Savior would make room for any one of those categories—even homosexuals, as long as they were willing not to "practice." But that does not negate Rudy's correctness about the centricity of gender in the Christian Right. She asks that the church become the Christian's primary community, as opposed to centering oneself in nuclear family values.

My own sense of community ranges beyond Christian baptism, which is the boundary Rudy suggests (80)—for instance, I admire Simone Weil's hesitation to be baptized because that would divide her from the Jewish people and other members of humankind. I want the planet and all the creatures in it to be my ultimate community. But inasmuch as the limitations of human energy in time and space force us to take up smaller communities, Rudy's remarks about the local congregation as primary community take on a meaningful urgency. And she is surely right that gay people have recently "become experts at impersonating straight nuclear families"—except, of course, for the fact that one partner is the wrong gender (75). She argues, I think persuasively, that the pertinent question is not whether we are living monogamously or in communities where loving support exists in a different pattern, but whether our acts unite us into one body and whether our contexts enable our lives to transcend meaninglessness (83).

My chief reason for interacting with Kathy Rudy at this point is that she so clearly defines what it is that contemporary Christians fear about gender diversity and fluidity. Members of the Evangelical Right are familiar with books like James Robison's *Attack on the Family* and Tim LaHaye's *The Battle for the Family*, books that regard gender blending or bending as nothing short of the Antichrist's own work (9). The Family Protection Act introduced into Congress in 1979, and reintroduced in various versions every few years since, would use tax incentives to encourage women to stay at home and increase parental power over girls by denying access to birth control without parental consent. Even without passage, this Act has served to keep the "traditional family" (and the binary gender construct) front and center in American politics (53–54).

That the "family values" so dear to the Christian Right are for heterosexual nuclear families only is clarified by attempts to exclude from sex education curricula even the most passing reference to same-sex families (63). Meanwhile, books like Jerry Arterburn's *How Will I Tell My Mother?* urge parents of boys to "discourage girlish behaviors" and to get counseling for any son who has been labeled a sissy. Should a boy "seek out a lifestyle of sodomy," family members should refuse to speak to him until he pledges to "go straight" (96).

Next to these refusals to allow young people to become fully whoever they were meant to be, the cross-cultural gender fluidities I have been describing seem far more biblical. If God truly is "above all, through all, and in all" (Eph. 4:6), how can we truncate human growth in order to protect the rules society has made to guard its own abstractions? To expand on one of Kathy Rudy's statements, "When sex acts [or identities or even performances], whether gay or straight [or otherwise], monogamous or communal, function in a way that leads us to God, they ought to be considered moral. The family does not guarantee such moral status, and indeed sometimes prevents us from fully participating in the community . . . "(84).

From another perspective, as we have seen, transgenderists (including homosexuals) have brought and still offer valuable talents to any society that will embrace their presence. As Apache transman Gary Bowen puts it, "Spirit gives each of us Visions of who we are which we must manifest in the material world to the best of our ability. Transgender people, combining elements of male and female, are at the interstice of the material and spiritual worlds, and are thus able to act as mediators for the benefit of our communities."[104] What a gift!

---

104. Gary Bowen, "An Entire Rainbow of Possibilities," *Trans Liberation*, 63–66.

CHAPTER SEVEN

≋ Imagining and Constructing an Omnigendered Society

Some thirty-five years ago at Nyack College (New York), one of my prize literature students was David Sten Herrstrom, who understood that it was more important to take notes on the questions raised than on the answers generated. I was not surprised, but very pleased, when he earned his doctorate with a dissertation on the mystical poet and artist William Blake. Through the years, David has honored me by sending along copies of his newest poems and essays, the most recent being a 1999 monograph about Jesus as depicted by John the Apostle. Entitled *The Book of Unknowing: Ranging the Langscape*, the monograph tosses off insights that apply not only to Jesus and John and the Christian gospel but also to this "omnigender" book that David, at the time, did not even know I was writing.[1]

For instance, Herrstrom writes that "Don Quixote finds the world to be an enchanted place where giants are changed to windmills; Jesus makes the world a magical place where he changes water to wine, reads [the human] mind (John 2:25) and wakes the dead. For both, enchantment serves to preserve desire intact against the world's most corrosive agents. Its strategy is simple. Breaking down conventional categories and rendering reality uncertain—bread can be body and death life—makes possible the construction of a new reality" (44).

This book has been about a different sort of "enchantment": the breaking down of conventional gender categories and thus render-

---

1. For information about how to obtain this as-yet-unpublished monograph, write Dr. Herrstrom at P.O. Box 219, Roosevelt NJ 08555.

ing uncertain the binary gender construct. But this deconstruction of gender polarity can also "make possible the construction of a new reality": a society in which men, women, and all people in between are respected as being made in the image of a God who is neither male nor female and yet is inclusive of every degree of "masculinity" or "femininity."

The forerunners of this society, its prophets and its martyrs, have been certain transsexuals, intersexuals, transvestites, liberated male and female heterosexuals, drag artists, transgenderists, bisexuals, gay men, and lesbian women. By their lives and deaths, they have helped make society more aware of the injustices perpetrated by the binary gender construct and its accompanying heterosexism. Herrstrom writes concerning Jesus and Quixote that "to defend huge desires in any age appears to those without desire to be madness" (44). Similarly, people like Hesse's Siddhartha, who have thirsted and hungered simply to be themselves, have seemed to conformists to be creating only madness and mayhem. But I predict that eventually those with the "huge desires" to be authentic will emerge as the sanest people in a world that has become obsessed with gender conformity.

Herrstrom writes that "while boundaries are blurred change can occur. Jesus inhabits a shape-shifting universe, where above and below merge, the human and the natural world flow into each other, worlds without limits where any transformation is possible" (83). Concerning Jesus' first miracle at the wedding in Cana, Herrstrom invokes the transgendered Dionysus: "guests [at the wedding] would remember legends of Dionysus, a miracle-worker who also called himself God and took as his own the world of water and blood" (84). He comments on the importance of crossing boundaries: The Israelites must cross the Red Sea, Joshua must cross the Jordan River, Jesus must separate from his mother and cross over into society, each of us must cross the birth waters and emerge from womb to world, and eventually each must cross the threshold between the present world and the world to come.

And "to cross a boundary is to erase it" (84). That's the frightening part. To date, transgender politics has consisted mainly of deconstruction, revealing the irrationalities and injustices of attempting to force everybody into a mold of either "masculine male" or "feminine female." To many observers, the trans-ing of gender seems like a wanton removal of all the old landmarks. If crossing gender boundaries erases those boundaries, how will social order be maintained? That is the point of this final chapter: to try to envision a differently constructed social order that respects the biodiversity of the human condition without destroying all coherence, to imagine some of the steps that might take us there, and to suggest a religious and/or spiritual vision that could provide the stamina to achieve such a transformation.

What Might an Omnigendered Society Look Like?

Not being clairvoyant or even much of a futurist, I must rely on several people who have thought more deeply than I about what a truly gender-fluid society might look like. As we saw in chapter 6, many cultures have been (or still are) vastly more relaxed about gender than our own. Native American traditional cultures perhaps come as close to omnigender as any recent society ever has. But because of white racist persecutions and the resulting and understandable reluctance of Native Americans to reveal what their traditions were in all their fullness, we cannot use them as role models as much as some of us would like. So I will rely on some of the leaders of the transgender movement, particularly Martine Rothblatt and her book *The Apartheid of Sex* (New York: Crown, 1995), for this peek into an omingendered future.

Rothblatt, an attorney and a launcher of global satellite communication systems, has served as vice-chair of the Bioethics Subcommittee of the International Bar Association and has participated in global legal discussions of the Human Genome Project. Having spent most of her life as a man, Rothblatt is the father of four children, all of whom still call her Dad now that she is living as a woman. Not only is Rothblatt transgendered, her business is transnational and her family is transracial. When one of her children's friends asked her why she wore women's clothes, yet was a dad, her answer was direct: "Because I am part man and part woman." The youngster's response was "Oh, that's cool," as she returned to her computer games. All of which goes to prove Rothblatt's thesis: "X and Y chromosomes mean as much or as little as we allow; biology is not destiny. I believe the best way to end the oppression of women is to end the apartheid of sex" (160).

Rothblatt cites Gordon Allport's suggestion in *The Nature of Prejudice* that we should imagine everyone in the world lined up from the darkest to the lightest person. Could we possibly tell where "black" begins? Where "white" ends? No, because races exist only in our minds, which tend to simplify reality by grouping things together, skin tones signifying races and sets of characteristics becoming racial stereotypes. Although Rothblatt does not ask us to do so, it teases and boggles the mind to imagine the same exercise with maleness and femaleness, starting with the most "masculine" of heterosexual men on one end and running through to the most "feminine" of heterosexual women at the other. With the myriad gradations of biological and psychological transgenderists standing in between, where would maleness end? Where would femaleness begin? It is hard to fault Rothblatt's logic: "The legal division of people into males and females is as wrong as the legal division of people into black and white races" (xiii).

Here are some of the characteristics of a society that encourages freedom of gender, as Rothblatt describes them. Everybody would have their own unique sexuality, falling in love with another person because of their emotional response to the person's entire being, not the person's genitals (140). Since people would not be categorized as exclusively male or female, nobody would be categorized as inherently homosexual, heterosexual, or bisexual either. People would be considered unisexual in that they could choose to identify themselves and their lover anywhere within the whole spectrum of sexual continuity (141). Children would be brought up as males, or females, or simply as persons, according to the option of their parents—at least until the child is old enough to decide and express their own gender identity (89). Just as parents currently have the option to bring up their children as black, as white, or simply as human, parents in an omnigendered society would be free to proclaim simply that "it's a *baby*!" if they so desired. In such a society, intersexual babies could comfortably be brought up that way until they could express their own preference about sex assignment, hormones, and surgery.

There would be no sex/gender typing on governmental records such as birth, marriage, or death certificates, passports, and motor vehicle licenses (90–91). Just as in 1975 the question about race was stricken from marriage application forms by order of the United States Supreme Court, in a nondiscriminatory society the issue of sexual dimorphism would disappear from marriage applications, which would simply require that the two people are of legal age and not already married (83). Already our society does not require people to marry within their ancestors' nationality or religious tradition or (recently) race; "the same watershed will come to sex" (85).

In this omnigendered society, the International Bill of Gender Rights would be observed, either in the original form approved at the Second International Conference on Transgender Law and Employment Policy (August 1993) and reproduced in *The Apartheid of Sex* (167–70), or in some acceptably modified form. This bill would assure the individual's right to define and express their own gender identity without being "circumscribed by what [any given society may deem] to be masculine or feminine behavior." It would include the right to control and change one's own body "cosmetically, chemically, or surgically, so as to express self-defined gender identity" and to be free from unwanted psychiatric diagnosis or treatment. It would assure the right to competent medical and professional care, to consensual sexual expression, to form committed and loving relationships and/or mutual contracts, to conceive and/or adopt children, to nurture and have custody of children, and to exercise parental rights.

Bathrooms in a gender-fluid society would be unisexual. Inside, they would look like women's restrooms today: no urinals, only sit-down toilets enclosed in privacy stalls. (As I write, a marine troop carrier, the USS *San Antonio*, is being built without urinals in any of the heads,[2] a precursor of the society to come.) Children would be taught to sit down to urinate, regardless of their genitals. To dis-

---

2. "Shipshape, Gender-Wise," *Time*, 27 March 2000, 34.

courage sexual predators, public lavatory space would be under automatic video surveillance; but simply the fact that any person of any gender, age, strength, and sexuality might enter the rest room at any time should in itself be an important deterrent to rape or other unwanted attentions (92–95).

Since schoolchildren could no longer be lined up and/or segregated according to their genitals, more intrinsic factors would have to be utilized. For instance, lines could be formed according to proximity to either side of the classroom, and learning groups could be formed according to level of ability in the specific subject area. (I am not thinking about grouping all the "brightest" together, either, but about making a mix in which the less able in any area can be stimulated by the more able, and people can help one another learn. That's not at all impossible. I formed such groups for years in my own classrooms.) And starting in grade school, hopefully, society would reward genuine merit instead of practicing "discrimination based on innate body size, shape, or reproductive function" (122).

Language, too, would shift away from binary pronouns (his/her) toward gender-inclusive wording. I doubt that Rothblatt's suggestions for new pronouns will ever take hold: *hers* to replace his/her; *heesh* to replace he/she; *hirm* to replace him/her (127). Although language modulates constantly, individual proposals are usually not the way change occurs. I suspect we may eventually use the plural forms *they*, *them*, and *their* to replace binary singulars, as I have been doing here and there in this book. That was sometimes done in early modern English (Shakespeare's English), and the tendency has constantly reasserted itself ("everybody should turn in their papers now"), even though deemed incorrect by prescriptive grammarians. But it would be truly a major step to say, concerning an individual known to be male, that "Charles left their book on their desk" and perhaps ultimately too confusing. Wherever possible, switching to the plural is preferable: "Charles and others left their books on their desks." But clearly, pronouns are something we'll have to work out as we go along.

As for *sir* or *ma'am*, they will probably be dropped and replaced by a respectful glance. Mr., Mrs., and Ms. will probably be dropped also, as they frequently are today, simply using a person's full name to signify respect ("Dear Martine Rothblatt" rather than "Dear Ms. Rothblatt").

Sex-segregated prisons would also become relics of the past. As Rothblatt comments, "The solution to sex and prison is strict supervision, solitary confinement for sexual assault, and education. . . . A multisexed prison environment may, in fact, be more rehabilitative in that it better resembles the real world" (62).

In athletics, there would be no need for sex testing because there would be no sex-segregated competition. Instead, individual competitions would be organized around weight, height, or other relevant categories rather than genital configuration. Just as the boxing world came up with weight categories to make competition as fair as possible, other sports could devise categories more relevant to the sport than the genitalia of the competitors. In the Olympics, for instance, countries with populations of lower average height or weight than those of other countries would have a fair chance of winning medals within their own height or weight category. Since separate is never equal, athletes with vaginas would at last have equal access to sports arenas, practice times and areas, top athletic scholarships and salaries, and first-rate coaching (73–74). And people of atypical chromosomal makeup would no longer be humiliated by exclusion from competition.

All of this may sound either somewhat outlandish or impossibly idealistic, particularly as it challenges the hugely lucrative parallel businesses of men's and women's collegiate and professional sports. As a longtime fan of Yankees baseball, I feel the pain. On the other hand, there is really no reason why first-rate women players could not be incorporated into currently male professional teams. Even football is attractive to some women and transgenderists; and if they are good enough and courageous enough, why not? Just as Jackie Robinson broke major league baseball's color barrier, someday a gifted person will break through the sexual apartheid of professional sports.

It is impossible to deny Rothblatt's observation that separate is not equal. As long as society is organized dimorphically, women will always be "not quite equal" to their male counterparts and will be held to appearance and behavioral standards impossible for most women to meet. And as long as the numerical frequency of heterosexuality is held to prove that it is the ideal for everyone, well-meaning attempts to be inclusive of gay men and lesbian women will always leave same-sex unions not quite equal to heterosexual marriage. Similarly, as long as athletic competition is organized according to genitals, women golfers will continue to receive inferior tee times, athletic women will continue to get lower pay and poorer perks, and on and on and on and on. . . .

I recognize that it's hard to get excited about a future in which so much is unknown. So let's try the experiment of taking something familiar that's halfway there and imagining it in an environment of gender freedom.

Consider the New York Marathon. It currently permits men and women to compete in the same race, but it lists the times and winners according to the genitals of the runners. Let's suppose that runners were categorized according to age instead of sex, age being exceedingly relevant to the speed and stamina required for running a marathon. There could be winners in the 20s, 30s, 40s, 50s, 60s, and 70+ categories, giving more people the chance to win. If we assume that men will always be able to defeat women because the average woman has only eighty-five percent of a size-matched man's upper body strength and ninety-three percent of his lower body strength (75), we are forgetting that these statistics were gathered in a sex-segregated society where women have had much less opportunity and incentive to develop physical strength and endurance. And we are also forgetting that athletes are not average people. The average African American male is 7/10 of an inch shorter than his European American counterpart, but that has not stopped African American male athletes from excelling in basketball, where height counts for a lot. As Rothblatt comments, "Fortunately race segregation in athletics is over. Sex segregation should follow that course" (75).

Ultimately, society must move toward omnigender because it is literally a matter of life and death when we look at the world as a whole. Rothblatt points out that "By the end of the 1990s"—by now and then some—"an estimated thirty million to fifty million embryos will have been aborted simply because they have a very obvious marker—a vagina" (137). The *New York Times* reported on

July 21, 1993 that in China, twelve percent of all female fetuses were either aborted or not accounted for—a total of 1.7 million missing girls every year! United Nations figures for India, Pakistan, Bangladesh, and Korea total an additional 1.5 million aborted girls each year. "At the rate the abortions have been increasing since around 1990, and with the continued spread of ultrasound technology, the gynocide rate will certainly climb to over five million fetuses per year from the current 3.2 conservative estimate" (138).

A study of 6,000 aborted fetuses in one Bombay clinic revealed that only one fetus was a boy (138). It cannot continue. Understanding sex and gender as a continuum will emphasize the unique contribution of each person and the oneness of the whole human family and thus discourage gynocide.

Other Advantages of a Gender-Fluid Society

Holly Devor, in *Gender Blending: Confronting the Limits of Duality* (Bloomington: Indiana University Press, 1989), sees gender blending as a way of teaching society to value "adaptability and flexibility rather than obedience to gender roles, so that the most respected and socially valued personality types would be those which were able to make use of any behaviors which served their purposes in any situation" (153–54). An omnigendered society would recognize that sex identity, sex attribution, gender identity, gender attribution, and gender roles can be combined together in any configuration. Specific genders would be social statuses available to anybody according to personal disposition and exhibited behaviors.

As Devor sees it, in this future society "masculine" men and "feminine" women would be viewed as embodying relatively immature stages of gender development. The goal of mature personal development would be a balance and a blending of gender characteristics (154). But I would hope and trust that in an omnigender culture, "masculine" men and "feminine" women would not necessarily be judged as immature but would be as acceptable as anyone else as long as they were truly comfortable and fulfilled by that gendering. Our goal is not to produce a different gender underclass, but to do away with gender hierarchies altogether.

As masculinity, femininity, and everything in between are redefined, many men will be encouraged to overcome their arrested sexual development, male violence against women will hopefully lose its steam, and knowledge will come to be understood as a communal activity, a result of mature interdependence. Joanne Carlson Brown and Carole R. Bohn have defined the adult sexual behavior of many American males as an impulsive, uncontrolled, and adolescent idealizing of sex as power and autonomy that disregards the subjective experience of the female as Other.[3] They also comment that the Western tendency to grant primacy to the thoughts of a few "genius" males such as Freud or Einstein has caused us to forget the contributions of the women, children, servants, neighbors, and friends to the discoveries of these "great men." Brown and Bohn see the solution to these problems mainly in terms of modifying the binary through greater male-female give-and-take. But a blending of "masculine" and "feminine" in many people would quickly defuse many of these problems by granting everyone more opportunity to feel, enact, and appreciate gender roles and presentations formerly considered foreign to oneself.

Marjorie Garber in *Vested Interests* wonders whether "the very real power" of cross-dressing is *not* that of being "an exotic other," but rather consists of being "a reminder of the repressed that always returns" (321). She mentions Islam's double standards regarding cross-dressing, the "peekaboo quality of both/and, male *and* female" which seems to European observers to be "part of the fascination" (322). In turn, Garber causes me to wonder whether in America of the '30s, '40s, and '50s as I was growing up, gays and lesbians were required to be relatively closeted as stimulants to the imaginations of the majority. Until a person is able to enjoy genuine intimacy, straightforward frankness can breed boredom. Perhaps for the same reason, gays and lesbians cooperated, consciously or unconsciously enjoying the stimulus of being masked and mysterious. If any of this is true, Garber's ruminations (and my own) suggest a further benefit of a society in which people are encouraged to dress however they like freely and

---

3. Joanne Carlson Brown and Carole R. Bohn, *Christianity, Patriarchy, and Abuse: A Feminist Critique* (Cleveland: The Pilgrim Press, 1989), 131.

openly, with nobody being classified as "otherwise": Life, being considerably less conflicted and more ordinary, would push all of us toward learning how to relate to one another without artificial stimuli such as pornography and peekaboo and game-playing hierarchies.

Garber also suggests that crossing the boundaries of gender stirs fear of the possibility of crossing racial barriers, and vice versa (274). Our society has such a "powerful cultural desire to binarize" (265) that to threaten any one boundary is to threaten them all. And my own experience bears Garber out. More than once I have noticed people fixing me in what T. S. Eliot might call "a formulated phrase"—and the phrase would be, "Is it male or female?" The Chevalier d'Eon, the "most famous transvestite in Western history" (259) wrote concerning his/her sexual indeterminacy that s/he was mortified "at being what nature has made me"—yet, as Garber comments, "it was his observers who were most profoundly unnerved, who wished most ardently and passionately for a resolution to this enigma, an end to undecidability, the fixing of gender identity once and for all" (264).

Since I do not believe in racial boundaries or any other boundaries that separate and antagonize, I am contented to be a person who sometimes causes people to feel a confusion they cannot instantly settle. Like the English Romantic poet John Keats, I consider "negative capability"—the ability to live with uncertainty—to be a valuable trait.

In an omnigender society, we would often meet people who looked either/or, neither/nor, and would have to relate to them simply as human beings. Consider: Why do we want to know the sex of a baby before we begin to relate to that baby? Why isn't it enough to relate to that baby as an individual, letting its responses signal to us what sorts of behaviors are preferred? In the 16th and 17th centuries, and until quite recently, boys and girls were dressed identically until age seven, when boys were "breeched"—put into pants (85). I have a family photo of my mother and her siblings and parents in which my uncle, who was born in 1909, is in a pretty dress just like his older sisters. Perhaps we ought to return to the practice of dressing young children alike—and in an omnigender society we probably would, though the clothing would probably be overalls to protect crawling knees rather than dresses that can be "crawled up." Adults would be forced to relate to children and one another not as a sex or gender category, but as the embodied souls and spirits we are, utterly unique and complex on the level of body and personality, but very similar and sublimely simple on the level of the inner being.

Scientific and Educational Steps for Getting There

Kate Bornstein estimates that the transgender revolution will take one thousand years to complete.[4] I hope it won't take that long. But however long it takes, every journey begins with the first few steps. In the case of sex/gender, the very first steps have already been taken. Using radio and TV talk shows, films, music, theater, and dance, transgenderists have been deconstructing binary gender by cross-dressing and gender-blending. Transsexuals have literally put their lives on the line; so have many gay, lesbian, bisexual, and otherwise transgendered people. But in books like Rothblatt's, Bornstein's, Feinberg's, Devor's, and in this book as well, the work of education has begun.

But there is a very long way to go. Dr. Anne Fausto-Sterling is one of the pioneers along this gender pathway. Professor of biology and women's studies at Brown University, Fausto-Sterling has shown that the concept of scientific objectivity is an illusion. Science is not too pure and lofty to get involved in messy social and political controversies—far from it. In fact, social and political debates have always dictated the course of scientific research, starting with the questions scientists ask and continuing with the methods they employ and the surgical and chemical technologies as well. Writes Fausto-Sterling, "We will, I am sure, continue to fight our politics through arguments about biology. I want us never, in the process, to lose sight of the fact that our debates about the body's biology are always simultaneously moral, ethical, and political debates about social and political equality and the possibilities for change."[5]

---

4. Private conversation, 12 March 2000.

5. Anne Fausto-Sterling, *Sexing the Body: Gender Politics and the Construction of Sexuality* (New York: Basic Books, 2000), 255.

Simultaneous turns out to be a key concept in Fausto-Sterling's new book, *Sexing the Body*, as she suggests some steps we might take toward a more equitable gender system. The book is simultaneously a narrative accessible to general readers and a scholarly academic work, documented with 192 pages of notes and bibliography in order to show that even her most passing claims "have substantial backing in the academic literature" (x). And repeatedly the claims themselves have to do with simultaneity: From fertilization to old age, we human beings are simultaneously natural and unnatural—products of biology, environment, culture, and history, so that a single behavior may have many underlying causes (25–27).

For instance, behind the humanitarian wish to "correct" the genitals of intersexual babies so that they can live "normal" lives there are three "unexamined assumptions: that there should be only two sexes, that only heterosexuality is normal, and that particular gender roles define psychologically healthy men and women" (44). The humanitarian motive and the damaging assumptions are simultaneously interlocked and difficult to sort out.

But if over a period of time we chose to let mixed-gender bodies and altered patterns of gender-related behavior become visible, through that process we will have "chosen to change the rules of cultural intelligibility" (76). Instead of continuing to assume that because completely male or female bodies are the most *frequent* body types, therefore they are not only *natural* but *normal* and *socially ideal*, our increased awareness of biological variation would enable us to "conceptualize the less frequent middle spaces as natural [even though they are] statistically unusual" (76). And as the separation of church and state becomes more of a reality, "the last laws regulating consensual bedroom behavior will become unconstitutional" (113). Thereafter, people with unusual genitals might even come to be viewed as "the most desirable of all possible mates, able to pleasure their partners in a variety of ways" (113).

Fausto-Sterling describes the tremendous amount of brain research that attempts to find a definitive gender difference in the corpus callosum, concluding that "the real excitement of studies on the corpus callosum lies in what we can learn about the vastness of human variation and the way in which the brain develops as part of a social system" (145). She also describes the debate that developed from importing the idea of sex antagonism into the area of hormone biology, showing that "reading gender into and from bodies is a more complex matter than merely allowing the body to speak the truth" (169). Hence, after describing the chemicalization of gender through the so-called "sex hormones," Fausto-Sterling asks that we call them *steroid* hormones instead, because they are in fact "powerful growth hormones affecting most, if not all, of the body's organ systems" (193).

Fausto-Sterling spends a chapter describing research on the sex life of rats, research that reveals a complex relationship between nature and nurture in which "sexual distinctions were far from clearcut" (224). For instance, during the 1970s, biochemists learned that testosterone could influence rodent brain development only after it had been transformed into estrogen! And male rodents that exhibited lordosis (female receptive behavior) also mount vigorously and father offspring, while females that mount also mate and bear young (225).

At the same time that I was reading Fausto-Sterling concerning rodent sexuality, I was interested to notice a brief article in *Audubon* magazine announcing that near California's Kesterson Reservoir, during recent routine wildlife monitoring of the same area where toxic agricultural runoff had poisoned thousands of birds in the 1980s, one-third of the mice and voles appeared to have both male and female reproductive organs. So there are not only "bisexual" but also "intersexual" mice and voles. Anyone who is distressed by intersexuality should develop a keen interest in toxic waste cleanup, since the U. S. Bureau of Reclamation implies a connection and reminds us that mice and voles are "mammals—not so much different from you and me."[6] Although I do not find otherwise healthy intersexuality distressing, I am happy for anybody's willingness to join in the ecology movement!

Fausto-Sterling concludes her book with a chapter working toward a new theory of human sexuality based on three principles: that

---

6. "Of Mice and Men, and Women," *Audubon* (March–April, 2000): 14.

nature/nurture is indivisible; that organisms are active processes (moving targets); and that no single academic or clinical discipline can provide us with the truest or best way to comprehend our topic (235). As many as eight thousand genes can be expressed in a developmentally stimulated cell, and genetic function can be understood only within the context of the cell (236–37). Furthermore, because "Brains and nervous systems are plastic . . . anatomical change often results when the body's nervous system responds to, and incorporates, external messages and experiences" (239). For instance, when a woman trains for long-distance running and her constitution falls below a certain ratio of fat-to-protein, her menstrual cycle shuts down—proof that gonadal function responds to exercise and nutrition levels (242). For another instance, biological motherhood is not always the same experience. It differs emotionally and physiologically depending on a woman's age, health, finances, and social location (single? married? lesbian?) (243).

Studies of how children "do gender" show that gender relations are not fixed, but vary according to contexts such as race, class, and ethnicity (248–49). Fausto-Sterling suggests the metaphor of Russian nesting dolls to help us envision the various simultaneous components of human sexuality. The outermost doll would be the social and comparative history of sex; the second largest would be the current culture as seen by analysts, literary critics, anthropologists, and sociologists; the third largest doll would be individual relationships and development; the fourth, the mind or psyche; the fifth, the location or activity that links events outside the body to those inside the organism; and the innermost doll, the cells. Only the complete assembly makes full sense. The metaphor breaks down because, unlike the dolls, the human components change shape with time. Nevertheless, the metaphor helps us visualize the fact that since all layers are interlinked, change at any one level requires change in the entire system (253–54).

What Dr. Fausto-Sterling's work suggests as the most important step toward a more complete, "less false" knowledge about human sexuality is Developmental Systems Theory as the scaffolding for thought and experiment. Developmental Systems Theory (DST) sees nature and nurture as one indivisible, dynamic system. The effect of switching to DST is like the change when a person puts on 3-D glasses (228). Although DST is not really new, it is vitally important to put it into practice, since all societies have had a tendency to oppose culture (nurture, experience) to nature. Paul Halsall of Fordham University made a remark on his Internet site that illustrates the need for DST: He writes that to many historians of the past twenty years, "*Gender* is the cultural meaning given to the rather limited *facts* of biology."[7] Halsall describes the kind of splitting that DST defuses and Fausto-Sterling decries.

Scholars working together in multidisciplinary teams could best understand the limits of working from within a single discipline while simultaneously respecting and utilizing the contributions of their own and the other disciplines. When we have studied gender from the perspectives of history, language, literature, the arts, education, the media, politics, psychology, religion, medicine and science, society, law, and the workplace, we will be in a better position to understand the body as "a biosociocultural system" (376). And a better informed society could surely come closer to awarding jobs, status, income, and social roles on the basis of individual differences of physique, intellect, and inclination (115), instead of relying on gender stereotypes and hierarchies.

Martine Rothblatt in *The Apartheid of Sex* refers to the fact that almost forty years ago, science historian Thomas Kuhn wrote that "virtually all science is not a pure search for truth, but an effort to further confirm some preexisting, generally accepted model or framework, which he called a 'paradigm.' . . . In short, science looked not for truth *per se* but for truth within the confines of accepted theories" (97–98). Rothblatt calls the old gender paradigm *sexual dimorphism* (I have called it the *binary gender construct*); and as we have seen, this old paradigm "has been used to enforce the superiority of one apparent sex over the other and as a framework for research to prove one sex has a different nature from the other" (102). The new gender paradigm Rothblatt calls *sexual continuism* (I have called it *omnigender*). Just as the Copernican paradigm changed the face of astronomy, the

---

7. <http://www.fordham.edu//halsall/pwh/index-old.html>. Accessed 11 March 2000. Emphasis is his.

Darwinian paradigm changed the face of anthropology, and the Freudian paradigm changed the face of psychology, the new gender paradigm will change the face of human interrelationships.

Rothblatt predicts that when the human genome is understood more fully, sexual identity will not be found in the part of the chromosome that directs semen and ova production, but elsewhere. At that point, "All that will be left of a male or female difference will be reproductive systems that social choice and biotechnology can make available to any person, regardless of anatomical birthright" (123). Therefore, in an omnigendered society, sex would be more a matter of human creativity than of genitally-driven destiny.

Political Steps for Getting There

No doubt, if and when more scientists utilize Developmental Systems Theory and work in multidisciplinary teams open to the possibility of a new gender paradigm, their findings will gradually shift attitudes in society as a whole. But in a democratic society where the majority rules, change can take a long time even after attitudes have begun to shift. For instance, although most Americans would give at least lip service to the concept that men and women are equal citizens deserving of equal opportunity, "at current rates of change, it still would take more than three centuries to achieve equality between the sexes in political representation."[8]

And, of course, merely electing equal numbers of males and females is not the same as electing people with a firm commitment to human equality. Yet a transformative vision of gender equity is necessary in order to transcend, convince, and overcome the opposition of moneyed, seniority-oriented "old boy" networks. As law professor Deborah L. Rhode, in *Speaking of Sex*, comments, "we are unlikely to establish gender equality as a political priority without substantial changes in the electoral process" (247). Although Rhode is talking chiefly about dimorphic male-female equality, what she says is just as true in the context of achieving omnigender equity.

How then to bring about change a little more rapidly than three centuries (Rhode's estimate) or a thousand years (Bornstein's esti-

---

8. Deborah L. Rhode, *Speaking of Sex: The Denial of Gender Inequality* (Cambridge: Harvard University Press, 1997), 245.

mate)? Deborah Rhode offers some suggestions born of her several decades at Stanford Law School: Those who care must agitate for campaign finance reform so that the system is "less hostage to financial influence"; must try to increase voter knowledge; and must seek public recognition of gender pioneers. Only five percent of national historic landmarks are currently dedicated to women (249). Imagine the percentage of publicly displayed paintings, statues, and plaques honoring transsexual leaders or gay or lesbian leaders! Even retrieving our history is a major project, let alone achieving public recognition. I remember gazing in awe at the bust of lesbian novelist Willa Cather in the state capitol in Lincoln, Nebraska. Even though she was being honored for her local-color artistry, not for her transgender leadership, it was a *first* for me, and a great moment.

Rhode also suggests the old standbys: writing letters, organizing fund-raisers, building networks among colleagues and friends, sending checks to organizations with gender-related concerns. "Overall," Rhode writes, "America's foundations target less than five percent of their funding to the specific needs of women and girls. Some sixty women's funds are now struggling to fill the gap, but their endowments remain quite modest" (249).

The need for funding is even more desperate, of course, in those organizations that are working to expand society beyond binary gender definitions. In my own charitable giving, increasingly I am trying to give larger percentages to those organizations least likely to attract widespread funding because of their cutting-edge commitment to justice for people of all sexes and/or genders. I hope others will do the same as the following principles become better known: that male-female gender differences have been overemphasized because of unquestioning acceptance of the binary gender construct; that everybody suffers because that construct does not meet the needs of society as well as an omnigender construct promises to do; and that the objective of an omnigendered society is "to provide equal, nondiscriminatory opportunity for personal fulfillment to all persons."[9]

---

9. Martine Aliana Rothblatt, *The Apartheid of Sex: A Manifesto on the Freedom of Gender* (New York: Crown, 1995), 103.

As much as I support Deborah Rhode's suggestions, however, I am still left pondering her statement that if we are ever to make gender equity a priority in American politics, we need "substantial changes in the electoral process." Lani Guinier is someone who has given considerable thought to those "substantial changes." Although Guinier's focus is primarily racial equity, Yale law professor Stephen L. Carter is certainly correct that "whenever there are consistent winners and losers, her analysis applies."[10] In my opinion, Guinier is a person to take very seriously because of her honorable career as a civil rights litigator with, as Carter comments, "a deep firsthand knowledge of both the theory and practice of her art."[11]

President Clinton has admitted that withdrawing his nomination of Guinier to head the Civil Rights Division of the Justice Department was the low moment of his first year in the White House. And since the transgender political movement is also a Civil Rights movement, we do well to consider Guinier's suggestions about how to break through what she has made the title of her 1994 book, *The Tyranny of the Majority*.

Guinier's point is that "In an ideal democracy, the people would rule, but the minorities would also be protected against the power of majorities" (4). To achieve that, "we may need an alternative to winner-take-all majoritarianism . . . the 'principle of taking turns'" (5). But "giving the minority a turn does not mean the minority gets to rule; what it does mean," Guinier explains, "is that the minority gets to influence decision-making and [therefore] the majority rules more legitimately" (5). When minorities perceive that the system is fair enough to respond to their concerns, political stability is enhanced: "losers continue to work within the system rather than seeking to overthrow it" (9).

For decades I have been involved in the effort to achieve equal representation and opportunity for women in the Christian ministries and local and national religious decision-making bodies. And

---

10. Stephen L. Carter, foreword to Lani Guinier, *The Tyranny of the Majority: Fundamental Fairness in Representative Democracy* (New York: The Free Press, 1994), xv.

11. Ibid., xx.

for almost as long, I have been active in the effort to achieve justice for Christian gay, lesbian, bisexual, and transgender (GLBT) people. Repeatedly, these causes have been frustrated by the tyranny of the majority. For instance, although "only" 46 percent of the American general public still believes that homosexuality is sinful,[12] those churchgoers who are elected as delegates to denominational general conventions tilt in the other direction, with roughly 46–48 percent supportive of equality for their gay, lesbian, bisexual, and transgender members, and about 52–54 percent denying that equality on the basis of the "sinful lifestyle." Yet that slim majority continues to block access to church rituals or union ceremonies for those GLBT members who request them. (I would prefer to say simply *transgender* on the basis of the definitions in chapter three, but am using the older terms for the sake of clarity in a transitional time.)

And although 83 percent of the general public says that homosexuals should have equal rights in employment, within most Christian denominations that 52–54 percent majority continues to block the ordination of openly GLBT ministers or priests. In many local congregations where a large minority wants to proclaim the congregation a welcoming and safe space for GLBT people, that move is similarly blocked by the tyranny of a small majority.

It is in these and similar situations that Guinier's suggestions could make a difference. One suggestion is to give minorities a voice in the decision-making process by the use of *cumulative voting*. Each voter is given multiple votes which they can distribute as they see fit. For instance, a church voting on five new policies could give each member ten votes, which they could distribute according to the intensity of their preference. Some voters might put all ten of their votes for or against a policy that would forcefully impact their lives. Other voters, feeling less strongly impacted, might put two votes for or against each policy. "Like-minded voters can vote as a

---

12. John Leland, "Shades of Gay," reporting on two new *Newsweek* polls in *Newsweek*, 20 March 2000, 49. Recent Gallup research indicates that despite the official Vatican position, 47 percent of American Catholics believe "homosexuals can be good Catholics." See Charles Austin, "Christians Grappling with Sin's Shifting Face," *The Record*, 8 March 2000, A1 and 14.

solid bloc or, instead, form strategic cross-racial [and/or cross-interest] coalitions to gain mutual benefits. This system . . . allows voters to organize themselves on whatever basis they wish." Therefore, "any self-identified minority can plump or cumulate all its votes for one candidate [or one policy]" (15).

Guinier does not pretend that cumulative voting is a radical new idea; rather, she points out that in Clinton County, Alabama, which uses cumulative voting to elect both the school board and the county commission, the system has elected three white Republicans and four Democrats (three white and one black), whereas previously only white Democrats had been able to achieve election (15–16). And in some Western European democracies that use similar cumulative voting systems, national legislatures have "as many as 37 percent female members compared to little more than 5 percent in our Congress" (16).

Guinier is more cautious about her second remedial voting tool, *supermajority voting*, which requires that "more than a bare majority of voters must approve or concur before action is taken" (16). Again, this voting system is nothing new: Guinier points out that it was used to give small-population states equal representation in the U.S. Senate. And the Reagan administration approved the use of supermajority rule in Mobile, Alabama, where "the special five-out-of-seven supermajority threshold is still in place today and is credited with increasing racial harmony in that community" (17). The advantage of supermajority voting is, of course, that it gives "bargaining power to all numerically inferior or less powerful groups, be they black, female, or Republican" (17)—or, I might add, Democrat, people of any non-normative race or ethnicity, and people of any non-normative gender or sexuality.

I am in full agreement with Guinier's basic thesis that "democracy in a heterogeneous society is incompatible with rule by a racial monopoly of any color" (19). And I extend that thesis to say that democracy in a heterogeneous society is incompatible with rule by a gender monopoly of any one inflexible configuration. Those who agree with me will want to take steps to move society toward an omnigender construct.

Without Spiritual Vision, Movements Languish

According to the Hebrew Scriptures, "Where there is no vision, the people perish" (Prov. 29:18, KJV). In my time, I have seen various social activists fall by the wayside for lack of a coherent source of spiritual renewal, a vision of God and humankind that could sustain them when their cause suffered setbacks and postponement, and hope deferred made their hearts sick. The *New Revised Standard Version* of the Bible gives a less individualistic, more community-oriented flavor in its translation of the same passage: "Where there is no prophecy, the people cast off restraint." The book of Proverbs was edited in the 6th century B.C.E. by counselors and educators in court circles; so this advice originally referred to knowing and obeying the laws of Israel's post-exilic community.[13] What might it mean in the context of transgender politics and the whole gender-equity movement?

The vision I would suggest is rooted in the Hebrew and Christian Scriptures and is upheld by the sacred texts of the world's other major religions as well. (I believe in lifting up the liberating strands within sacred texts, rather than trashing the entire text because of the divisive and oppressive uses made of those texts by certain interpretive communities.) One truly liberating insight within the Hebrew and Christian Scriptures is that all human beings have their being within God's being (Ps. 139:3–10; Acts 17:24-28) and that God also lives within all people and other creatures (Jer. 23:24; Eph. 1:23; 1 Cor. 12:6). And this is, I believe, the vision without which transgender activists will become exhausted, and at the same time the prophecy without which the omnigender movement will "cast off restraint" by becoming splintered, fragmented, and divided against itself.

A human ego that identifies exclusively with the body it inhabits is inherently divisive because bodies look different and act differently from one another. Trusting the appearance that each body is separate from every other body leads to intense individualism and

---

13. Carol R. Fontaine, "Proverbs," *Women's Bible Commentary*, 153.

unrestrained "grabbyness": What you lose, I gain. But recognizing that the body is not solid and separate as it appears to be—breath mingling with other breath, molecules interwhirling in a constant exchange of energy—opens human beings to community, to an inter-indebtedness that is both mortal and immortal. By mortal inter-indebtedness I mean that because in this world our bodies are mortal and in a constant state of flux, we owe one another compassion and an insistence on justice for every body. (Such justice involves considerable restraint of the ego's "me first" attitude.) But because there is Spirit in each of us that was not born with our bodies and will not die with them, we also owe one another the awed respect due to one manifestation of the Eternal by another manifestation of the Eternal: an immortal inter-indebtedness that pulses with spirited desire and joy.

The majority of this book has been devoted to exploring the range of differences within human embodiment. But behind every word I have written lies the conviction that from a spiritual, eternally real perspective, we are all one. The essence of us all is the Single Spiritual Source from which we came, in whom we live, and to whom we will return in a journey without any distance. Gender justice matters precisely because from an eternal perspective there *is* no gender, bodies as we know them are temporary and constantly changing, and all of us are the offspring of God Herself/Himself/Itself.

Any movement that lacks a unifying vision is doomed to burnout because of the transitory nature of individual bodies and the body-identified personalities that inhabit them. Even before the Christian Gospels were written, Christians had begun to splinter into body-identified groups: "'I belong to Paul,' or 'I belong to Apollos,' or 'I belong to Cephas,' or 'I belong to Christ'" (1 Cor. 1:12, NRSV), and Paul was forced to call the movement back toward the unifying vision without which Christianity would never have become a major world religion. So it should be no surprise that movements for sexual and gender justice should be subject to similar fragmentization.

Michelangelo Signorile has described the gay and lesbian civil rights movement of the year 2000 as fragmented into "dozens of micromovements, each exploding with activity in its own right and crossing over into other civil rights movements."[14] Among these micromovements are the push to recognize the presence of openly homosexual people in the military; the attempt to pass hate crime legislation that includes sex and gender diversity; attempts to prevent discrimination in the workplace, housing, and so forth; securing rights for non-normative parents and families; repealing sodomy laws; helping queer youth establish their place in public schools and society; seeking cures for domestic violence; reforming health care; insisting on fair representation in the media; transgender inclusion; seeking ordination for self-affirming queer people; seeking religious and state recognition of same-sex marriage; and so forth. Signorile comments that activists in many of these minimovements feel somewhat isolated, wishing for a groundswell of support around their issues but sensing that it is really not present. According to Signorile, the best that queer activists can hope for is that "we'll come together now and again for specific, brief moments that touch us all" (104), such as the demonstrations for hate crimes legislation after the murder of Matthew Shepard in 1998 or the recent protests against the homophobic remarks of talk-show host Dr. Laura Schlessinger.

Signorile may be right that a mature, intricate, and complex movement can hope for nothing better than "short but explosive moments [of unity that] will continue to occur organically" and "can't be staged by gay leaders or gay groups, no matter how large their budgets become" (104). But I am saying that what is needed to undergird a movement toward gender justice-for-all is a vision of essential spiritual oneness, a sense of common humanity that breeds mutual listening, mutual restraint from "using" one another, and mutual compassion. It is spiritual vision that will keep us working during the periods in between the exciting "short explosive moments" of political unity.

Given the limitations of human time and energy, activists inevitably must focus on their own issues and their own methods. But

---

14. Michelangelo Signorile, "Together, United?" *The Advocate: Special Commemorative Issue* (20 April 2000): 102.

that fact of life need not promote *antagonistic* splintering if there is mutual respect, listening, cooperation, and compassion.

In his book *Harvest of Rage: Why Oklahoma City Is Only the Beginning*, Joel Dyer describes going openly into armed anti-government compounds and asking militia members what they were thinking and why they were angry. He found the people more than willing to talk: "They're angry, and they want to tell someone why, but the only time a reporter ever shows up is to cover a shootout or ask stupid questions about how many guns they have. No one ever shows up to really talk [with] them, *which involves listening*."[15] Dyer explains that when a farmer is losing his farm because he hasn't been able to pay his debts, the person who commiserates and cries with that farmer is most often a John Bircher or a local militia member who then offers anti-government activism as a reason to continue living. The farmer might go in a different direction, Dyer comments, if someone with a different message were there to commiserate with what the farmer is going through.

In other words, Dyer was received humanely by militia members because he approached them with the assumption that, like himself, they were human beings with human feelings and needs—not a different, evil breed separate from himself. His approach illustrates the kind of vision I am trying to clarify. We must learn to speak—and to listen for—the divinely human eternal face that lies beneath the innumerable differences that appear to divide us from one another. Otherwise, the only harvest we can hope for is a harvest of rage.

William Mason, an African American transgenderist whose drag name is Peaches, describes a process that might help us catch the vision. With several others a few years ago, Mason founded an organization called Workfairness that fights for the human rights of people on Public Assistance. And this is what he has discovered: "Some of those same people that used to dis me now have found respect for me. People that need help don't care if you are a Drag

---

15. Dyer, as quoted in "Listening to Militia Members," *The Witness* (April 2000): 26; emphasis mine.

Queen, Trans, Bi, Lesbian, or what. If you can help them, you get respect; teach them, you get respect; fight for them, you get respect."[16]

The point here is pretty obvious: if our discriminatory attitudes vanish when we ourselves need help, that tells us we really ought to rid ourselves of discriminatory attitudes when we are not in immediate need of help. Moses recorded this principle as a commandment from God's mouth: "You shall not hate in your heart anyone of your kin . . . but you shall love your neighbor as yourself: I am the Lord" (Lev. 19:17–18, NRSV). As this scripture implies, it is because God alone is God that the rest of us are in no position to judge or look down on one another. Instead, because we all come from one Source, we are wise to recognize and receive one another as kin. Gender-rigid or gender-fluid, heterosexual, homosexual, bisexual, transsexual, intersexual, cross-dresser, drag artist, two-spirited, shape-shifter, however we might describe ourselves: The fact is, we are family.

Making a Common Cause

Perhaps more than any other transgender leader, Leslie Feinberg has taken on the prophetic role of insisting that oppressed people must make common cause with all other oppressed people, regardless of the kind of oppression they experience. For instance, in *Trans Liberation*, Feinberg explains that

> the dominant theories in any society reflect the economic interests of those who dominate the society. How can it be otherwise? Who pays an army of spin-doctors and public relations experts to try to mold popular opinion? Who determines educational curricula? Who owns and controls the monopolized television, publishing, and media? The cacophony of theorists hired to defend the status quo is meant to drown out the voices of those who are fighting for change. (115)

---

16. William Mason, "I finally got that respect," *Trans Liberation*, 129–30.

To encourage people who are demoralized by the status quo and think it is impossible for them to make a difference, Feinberg quotes an African proverb: "Until the lions come to power, the hunters write the history" (119). Urging that *if* everyone oppressed by sex or gender rules were to make common cause with everyone oppressed racially, economically, or for any other reason, then our sheer numbers would be overwhelming, Feinberg also quotes the 19th century poet-prophet Percy Bysshe Shelley: "Rise like Lions after slumber/ In unvanquishable number—/ Shake your chains to earth like dew/ which in sleep had fallen on you—/ Ye are many—they are few" (frontispiece).

And, just as we would expect from so inclusive a prophet, Feinberg insists that there is room for those comfortable in traditional gender designations as well as those who are not: "It's true that this binary system is oppressive. But what is so restrictive about it is that it tries to force all human variance into two tiny categories. It's not true that the only revolutionary position is to fight from outside that system. People who identify as women and men can wage an important defense of the right to other identities. And vice versa! . . . We all have the right to find our place on the circle of sex and gender, and still defend every other point on its circumference" (118).

Someone centuries ago defined God as a circle whose center is everywhere and whose circumference is nowhere—and by that definition, God is and must be above all, through all, and in all. In *Paracelcus* II (1835), Robert Browning defined God as "the perfect poet/ who in His person acts His own creations"—and for that reason Buddhists say that if you meet the Buddha, you should kill him. That is, any single entity claiming to be "the Whole Enchilada" commits blasphemy against a Creator and creation that cannot be limited in that fashion. God is either everywhere, or nowhere—and either way, we owe one another the respect due to that which says "I am." So while it is not politically necessary to agree about a precise definition of that "personified incomprehensibility"[17] we refer to as God, I think it is vitally important to honor the Presence within

---

17. G. C. Lichtenberg, *Reflections* (1799) as it appears in H. L. Mencken, *A New Dictionary of Quotations* (New York: Knopf, 1962), 465.

us that stirs and inspires us toward compassionate action. The terminology is not as important as the experience of that glowing inner warmth that recognizes "no high, no low, no great, no small;/ [But] fills, [and] bounds, connects, and equals all."[18] This is the ultimate reason to love ourselves, and to love our neighbor (anyone who needs us) as we love ourselves: because that unquenchable desire to connect is within us. (People who have submerged that desire need compassionate confrontation and rehabilitation, not brutal punishment.) And for those of us who believe God is indeed fully present in every person, place, and time (as the Bible says), the motive for living lovingly is very powerful indeed: "those who do not love a brother or sister whom they have seen, *cannot* love God whom they have not seen" (1 John 4:20, NRSV; emphasis mine).

The religious leaders of Jesus' day were ready to stone him to death because "You, although only a human being, are making yourself God" (John 10:33). Not only to save his life at that moment but also to make clear the meaning of all of our lives, Jesus responded to their charges by saying, "Is it not written in your law, I said, you are gods?" (John 10:34).[19] Jesus was using the words of Psalm 82:6 in a way that was new to the Pharisees and so utterly radical that even many Christians to this day still cannot believe it. Jesus was not only claiming his own divinity; he was sharing it with the rest of humankind.

Jesus argued, "If those to whom the word of God came were called 'gods'—and the scripture cannot be annulled—can you say that the one whom the Father has sanctified and sent into the world is blaspheming because I said 'I am God's Son'?" (John 10:35–36). In other words, Jesus defended his own divinity by basing it on the divinity of all those to whom God's word was given. Did Jesus, a Jew, mean only Jews? No. Jews, of course, consider Torah to be the word of God, and a Jewish Midrash concerning Exodus 19:2 states that "if

---

18. My paraphrase of Alexander Pope's words about God in his 1732 poem, *An Essay on Man*, I. 279–280. See *The Norton Anthology of English Literature*, vol. 1, 5th. ed., ed. M. H. Abrams et al. (New York: W. W. Norton, 1986), 2270.

19. Although he and I interpret this exchange somewhat differently, I thank Dr. Herrstrom for pointing out its significance to me in *The Book of Unknowing*, 74.

the Torah had been given in the land of Israel, Israel might have said to the nations of the world, 'You have no share in it.' Therefore the Torah was given in the wilderness, i.e., in public for all to see; and everyone who wishes to receive it, let [them] come and receive it."[20]

Accordingly, both Jesus and his opponents understood that he was interpreting Psalm 82:6 to mean that not only Jews but all human beings are divine and that he had been sanctified and sent into the world to teach exactly that. Hence Jesus prayed that "the world may know that you have sent me and have loved them even as you have loved me" (John 17:23). Unlike various cult leaders, Jesus did not exalt himself above other people, but rather taught that all of us are the beloved children of the One God, still one with our Source, as children remain interconnected with their parents regardless of how they may feel about their parents. Because we are members of one global divine/human family, the only ethic that makes sense is kindness, compassion, and mutually respectful justice.

No wonder, then, that John's Gospel depicts Jesus' demonstrating that "truth cannot exist apart from a relationship" in which the truth frees a person to act and follow the One who transcends divisiveness. "John insists with Jesus that the act frees 'you' into more life in this world, breaking down the walls between tribes, genders, and classes; and in the next as well, erasing the threshold between life and death."[21] It is this category-transcending, passionate, and compassionate vision of the human face divine that will stimulate and sustain our attempts to achieve omnigender justice. For as Galatians 3:28 puts it, "in Christ Jesus"—that is, in a humanity that respects ourselves as beloved siblings stemming from one Divine Spirit[22]—"there is no longer Jew or Greek, there is no longer slave or free, there is no longer male and female, for all of you are one."

---

20. *Mekhilta*, as quoted in *The Bible Reader: An Interfaith Interpretation*, ed. Walter M. Abbott, S. J., Rabbi Arthur Gilbert, et al. (New York: Bruce Books, 1969), 93.

21. Herrstrom, *The Book of Unknowing*, 72.

22. This phrase is not an expression of heresy, but of Christian Humanism. See "Humanism, Milton and Christian," *A Milton Encyclopedia*, vol. 4, ed. William B. Hunter Jr. (Lewisburg: Bucknell University Press, 1978), 31–44; and Virginia Mollenkott, *Adamant and Stone Chips: A Christian Humanist Approach to Knowledge* (Waco, Tex.: Word Books, 1967).

≋ Index